Berklee

GUITAR CHORDS 101

Rick Peckham

To access audio, visit:
www.halleonard.com/mylibrary

Enter Code
5640-2704-0770-7846

Edited by Susan Gedutis

BERKLEE PRESS
Editor in Chief: Jonathan Feist

Senior Vice President Pre-College, Online, and Professional Programs/
CEO and Cofounder of Berklee Online: Debbie Cavalier

RECORDING
Guitar: Rick Peckham
Bass: Fernando Huergo
Drums: Gen Yoshimura
Engineer: Peter Kontrimas
Recorded at PBS Studio in Westwood, MA

ISBN: 978-0-87639-227-0

1140 Boylston Street • MS-855BP
Boston, MA 02215-3693 USA

Visit Berklee Press Online at
www.berkleepress.com

Study music online at
online.berklee.edu

Distributed By

7777 W. Bluemound Road • P.O. Box 13819
Milwaukee, Wisconsin 53213

Visit Hal Leonard Online
www.halleonard.com

Berklee Press, a publishing activity of Berklee College of Music, is a not-for-profit educational publisher.
Available proceeds from the sales of our products are contributed to the scholarship funds of the college.

CONTENTS

Audio tracks are included on the website referenced on the title page of this book.

ACKNOWLEDGMENTS

It's been an honor to work in the Performance Division at Berklee College of Music for the past forty years. Berklee's faculty, resources, and opportunities have more than lived up to their worldwide reputation.

Thanks to the thousands of students all over the world who have taken the guitar courses I've authored at Berklee Online. I've learned so much about the art of teaching and guitar playing in this challenging environment. Evaluating recorded submissions assignments and engaging in conversation during office hour/chat sessions have been inspiring and enlightening. Thanks to faculty members Bruce Saunders, Norm Zocher, Bruce Bartlett, Amanda Monaco, Tim Miller, Kevin Belz, Scotty Johnson, and others who have facilitated sections of *Berklee Guitar Chords 101*.

Regarding the *Berklee Guitar Chords 101* book project, thanks to Sue Gedutis Lindsay for her positive spirit and her editing skills and to Jonathan Feist for his contributions as well. Thanks to Jack Petersen, the first Guitar Department chair at Berklee for providing me with my understanding of harmony and chord construction on the guitar. Thanks to William Leavitt for bringing the Berklee Guitar Department to attention of the world. Chair Emeritus Larry Baione and Professor Jim Kelly have been a continuing source of musical and educational inspiration. Thanks to Chair Kim Perlak and Assistant Chair Sheryl Bailey for their continuing support. Thanks to Debbie Cavalier, Boriana Alexiev, Heath Nisbett, and Dan McFadden at Berklee Online.

The recorded examples will make practicing and learning this material much more pleasurable for all. Thanks to Peter Kontrimas for recording/mixing/mastering the performances and to bassist Fernando Huergo and drummer Gen Yoshimura.

Thanks to Anne Peckham, my wife and Berklee's Voice Department chair.

I have benefitted so much from the Berklee experience. The best part of it all has been the opportunity to work with the vastly diverse universe of students who learn and create here. Welcome to the club!

INTRODUCTION

If you want to take your guitar playing beyond the standard C-A-D-E-G open-position chords, this book is for you. Through step-by-step lessons you can do on your own or with a teacher, you will develop both the technical *and* the theoretical tools you need to understand and play all chords, in all inversions, in all positions of the fretboard. Move through the lessons steadily and consistently, and by the end, you'll have developed a solid command of the entire fretboard, as well as harmonic knowledge, tone, time feel, facility, and technical endurance.

The *Berklee Guitar Chords 101* approach:

- Learn-by-doing. First you play it, then you learn the theory, and then you can adapt it to a variety of other settings or styles.
- Play with good tone with an accurate, grooving time feel—intonation is a given (tuners, please).
- Develop a functioning toolbox of chordal vocabulary, including triads, four-part chords, and guide-tone shells.
- Use the circle of fourths, inversions, and substitutions in etudes, drills, and examples in blues, jazz, and pop styles to gain fluency.

ABOUT THE AUDIO

To access the accompanying audio, go to www.halleonard.com/mylibrary and enter the code found on the first page of this book. This will grant you instant access to every example. Examples with accompanying audio are marked with an audio icon.

REGARDING NOTATION

Note that the circled letters ⑥ ⑤ ④ ③ ② ① in the traditional notation staff refer to the strings, from lowest pitched ⑥ to highest ①. The numbers above the notes are fretting fingers 1 (index), 2 (middle), 3 (ring), and 4 (pinky).

The six-lined tablature staff (TAB) is also standard format, with the bottom line representing ⑥ and the lines above indicating ⑤④③②①. The numbers on the TAB lines refer to fret numbers.

Chord Diagram Notation

Standard chord diagrams represent the shape of the chord on a right-handed guitar fretboard, with the lower pitched strings on the left. Fret numbers are found to the right of the chord diagram. An × on the chord block represents a muted or omitted string. As we'll find, the × strings—the ones you don't play—are as important to a pure chord sound as the fretted fingers. The numbers found at the bottom of each chord block represent the fingers of the fretting hand. When it comes to the × on a chord block, silence is golden! Play the following example to hear the difference between a correctly played triad voicing and a version with improperly muted strings.

1

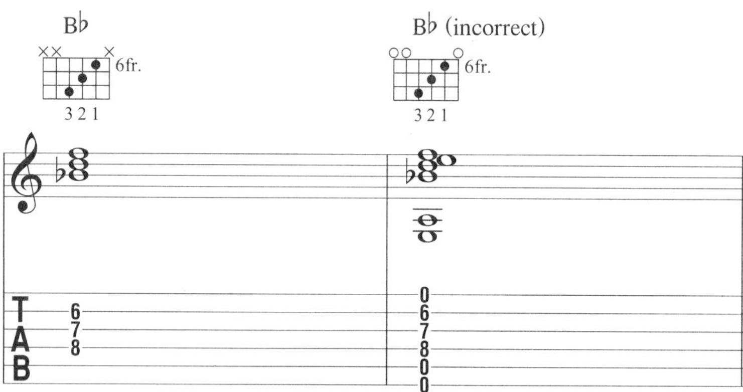

FIG. I.1. Proper and Improper Muting. × indicates strings that should not sound.

"High" vs. "Low" Strings

When discussing "higher" or "lower" strings, we are referring to the pitch of the string, not the location on the guitar as it relates to the floor or the ceiling. "Higher" strings refer to strings ③②①, and "lower" strings are ⑥⑤④. Although it's closest to the floor when we hold the guitar, the highest string is ①. The lowest string, even though it's closest to the ceiling, is ⑥. If the pitch of the string is higher, it's a higher string!

LESSON 1

Triads

A "triad" is a three-note chord. The triad is the heart of chordal harmony. Building from the triad before moving on to more complex chord structures will provide an essential foundation for thorough control of the instrument.

HOW TO BUILD A TRIAD

Triads may be built by stacking thirds upward from any scale degree. When we only use notes from that scale, we call the resulting set of chords "diatonic triads" or (more generally) "diatonic chords." ("Diatonic" means "of the scale.")

Chords are commonly referenced using Roman numerals that correspond to each scale degree. For example, a "I chord" is the chord that has scale degree 1 as its root. The II chord has scale degree 2 as its root. The V chord has scale degree 5 as its root, and so on.

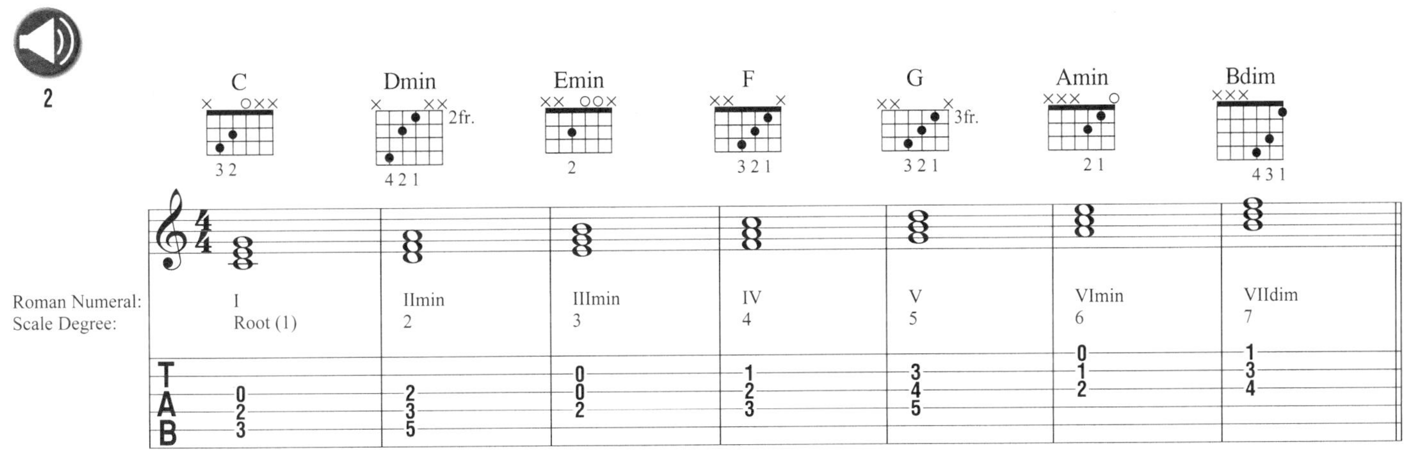

FIG. 1.1. Diatonic Triads in the Key of C Major

In the diatonic major scale, there are three types of triads: major, minor, and diminished. In figure 1.1, the VIIdim chord is played down in first position, allowing for performance by those playing guitars without a cutaway.

Although we'll discuss all triad qualities, we will start with major triads.

In any major diatonic scale, major triads appear on the first (I), fourth (IV), and fifth (V) degrees.

We can *arpeggiate* the triads by playing the chord tones one at a time, or we can play the chord tones all at once, by plucking the strings or by use of a brisk strum, parallel to the strings, with a pick (plectrum) or thumb/fingers.

Triads are built upwards in intervals of thirds from a fundamental note, called a "root," which is like the tonic of a scale. The first major chord found in the diatonic major scale includes the tonic, third, and fifth of the major scale.

Each of these notes is described by a number corresponding to its scale degree (or interval) away from the root: 1, 3, 5. These numbers correspond to *their relationship to the root*, as in "E is the third of a C major triad."

Play the C major scale, triad, and arpeggio.

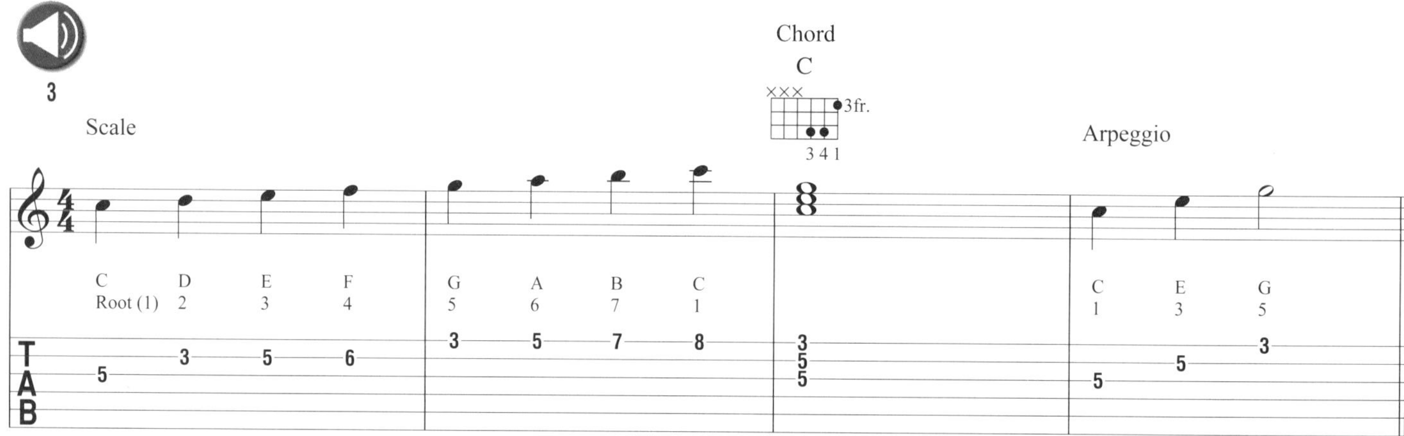

FIG. 1.2. C Major Scale, Triad, and Arpeggio

The C major triad is spelled C E G. In the key of C, notes 1, 3, and 5 of the C major scale provide you with the notes of the C major triad. Another way to think of triads is in terms of intervals. From the root, the major triad has a major third and a perfect fifth. It can also be seen as a major third (C to E) between the lower tones with a minor third (E to G) between the top two tones.

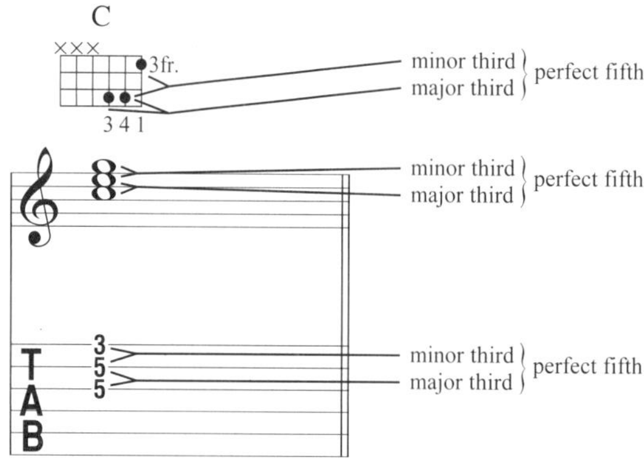

FIG. 1.3. Intervals in a C Major Triad

As a matter of convention, if a chord symbol consists of a single letter and no suffix, the quality major should be assumed. C = C major.

Exercises: Major Triads on ③②①

As you work on each exercise, always practice with solid time feel and a full tone, playing through the twelve keys in major triads on strings ③②①, moving up the fretboard in half steps, or *chromatically*. Moving up one fret at a time on the guitar neck is one of the easiest ways to accustom yourself to a voicing shape.

As a performance note, guitars with a cutaway allow easier access to higher fret positions; many steel-string acoustics and nylon strings have no cutaway. If you find that your instrument makes it difficult to go above the twelfth fret in bar 11 (the B♭ major), shift down to first position on the same string set to allow you to play each triad more easily.

In the chord diagrams, the × marks above the strings indicate that the strings should not be strummed or sounded. Muting the unwanted strings is a challenge for many, and it takes time and experience to play a clean, focused sound. Guitarists solve this problem by directing the strum of the pick to the "fingered" strings, avoiding the lower strings. Mute (or deaden) ④ using the tip of your third finger on your fretting hand to avoid extra string noise from this borderline string. For now, do your best, playing with the recording.

Exercise 1.1. Root Position Major Triads on ③②①

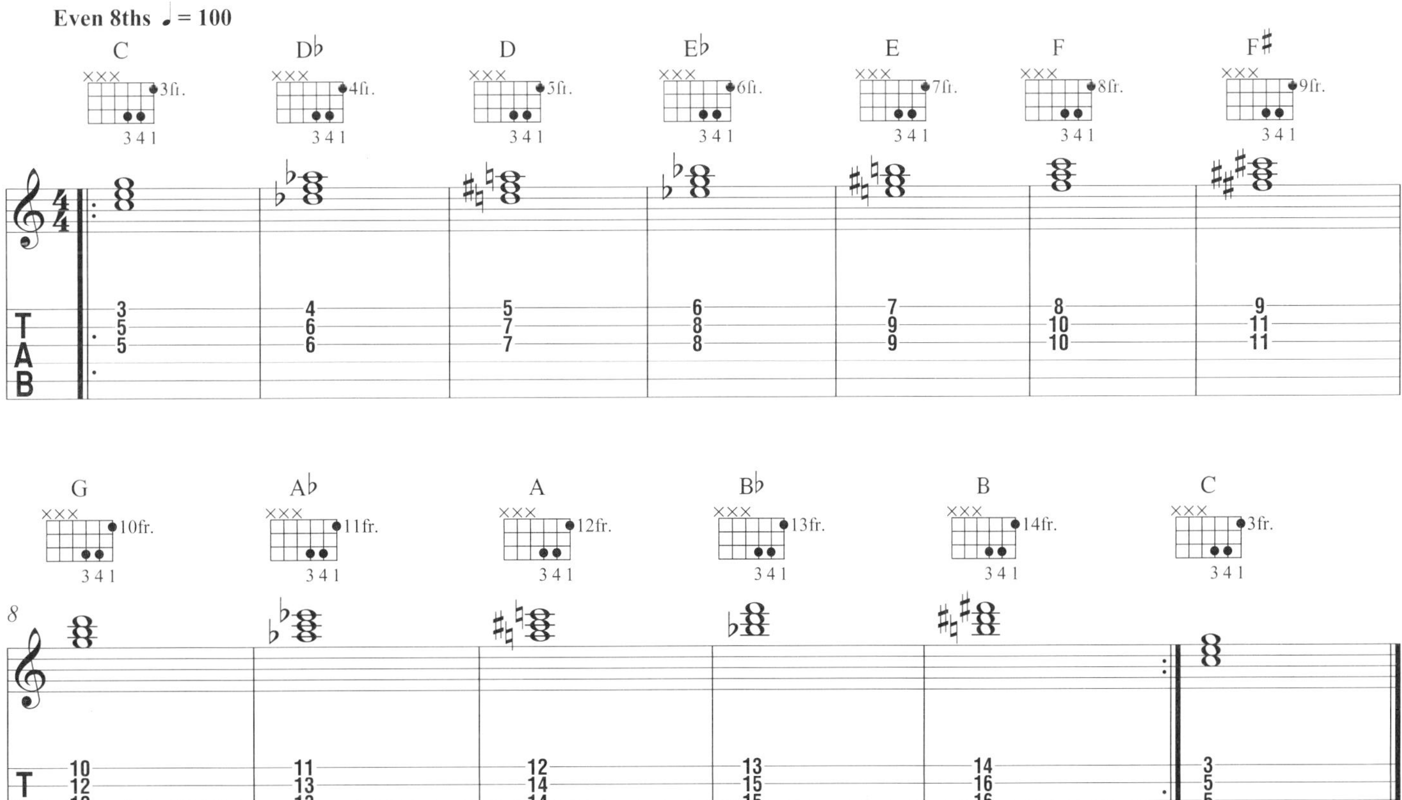

FIG. 1.4. Exercise 1.1. Root Position Major Triads on ③②①

Exercise 1.2. Root Position Major Triads on ③②①: Mixed Rhythms

Let's get used to the mechanics, sound, feel, and flow regarding a single major triad shape. We'll continue practicing with the same shape, moving up the fretboard, one fret at a time, on the top string set ③②①.

This exercise starts in whole notes to help you get used to each position, then "speeds up" at rehearsal letter B, where the rhythmic duration is reduced to half notes. This gets you moving through the twelve keys twice as fast, without having to change the tempo.

SOLID TAKE: TONE, TASTE, FEEL

Great guitar playing involves *tone*, *taste*, and *feel*.

- **Tone:** The character of a note's attack, the warmth at the center of the note, the clarity of the sound, the beauty of the overtones produced, as well as the note's finish, are all elements of a guitarist's tone. The attack, sustain, decay, and release of every note are involved. When using an electric guitar, the pick (fingernail or finger), strings, pickup, effects, and amplifier are all central to the tone.
  Clear, ringing tone can only best be achieved by placement of the fretting finger right next to the intended fret, without being on top of it. If a finger is too much on top of the fret, the note will be slightly muffled and short. If a finger is in the fret's area but too far below it, a buzzing sound is likely to occur.
- **Taste:** "Taste" refers to choices regarding amount of musical content and the volume you play it at. It can take years of experience to know how to play just the right amount of musical material with a group in a performance: not too much and not too little. Volume level of the guitar should be appropriate to the player's role at every given moment—not too loud and not too soft.
  Strive to play with the right level of activity at the right volume. If you are too loud, you are taking up too much space, but if you're too soft, that can be even worse! Accompaniment that monopolizes the balance of the group's sound is inappropriate, but it needs to be heard to "exist." Accompaniment volume and level of activity should support the group. Solo volume should lead the group. Listening to recordings of your performances and rehearsals can be a productive way of objectively measuring your progress. As a rule, the more players in the group, the fewer notes needed from the guitarist.
- **Feel:** Sounding a full chordal attack at the precise point of chord change is massively important. It's a big challenge to play a new voicing with spot-on accuracy right on beat 1, but that's a responsibility that we all need to honor. A smooth, quick transition from one chord shape to the next is often difficult. Play with good time feel, but think ahead to the next chordal shape. It's often necessary to leave a chord voicing a bit before the upcoming chord change, to allow an on-time arrival. As the saying goes, "Early is on time. On time is late. And late is unacceptable!" Working to plant the fingers in place a bit early for a cleaner, fuller sound at the point of chord change is the way it's done. It's perfectly acceptable to leave one chord a little early to make sure you arrive at the next one exactly on time.

FIG. 1.5. Exercise 1.2. Root Position Major Triads on ③②①: Mixed Rhythms

LESSON 2

Major Triads on ④③②

On the second set of three strings, ④③②, both the major third interval between ④③ and the minor third between ③② have the same visual spacing. The structure involving major third/minor third remains consistent; the shape "looks different" than the triad on ③②①, but the sound is the same. The root of the chord is found in the lowest voice.

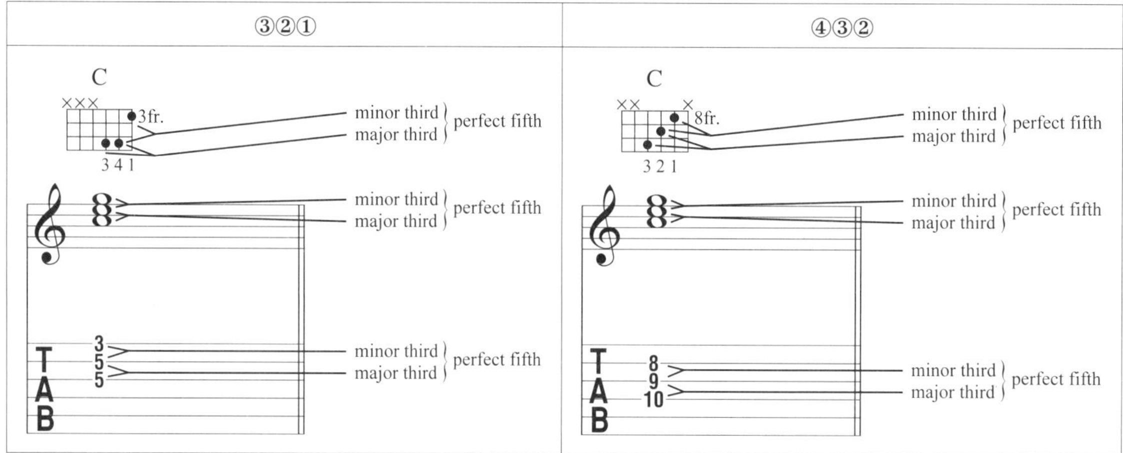

FIG. 2.1. Intervals in a C Major Triad on ③②① and ④③②

Exercise 2.1. Root Position Major Triads on ④③②

Play through the major triads on the ④③② string set, starting from G, starting in the third position (first finger positioned at the third fret). Again, in bar 11, at the F chord, jump down to first position to allow you to play through all twelve keys. The challenge here is to sound the chord tones on the desired three strings, while not allowing the other three strings to get in the way of a pure voicing. On the chord blocks, the × marks are nearly as important as the fingered strings. Strings ① and ⑤ are on the borderline, and it's necessary to use the side of the first finger to mute ① and the side of the third finger to mute ⑤. Your strum should avoid ⑥.

Go for a pure chordal sound with three notes (and only three notes) consistently sounding on each voicing. Guitars with cutaways can follow the voicing all the way up the fretboard. Shift down twelve frets if it is difficult for you to play in the higher range. Play each triad for one bar each.

Focus on accuracy with sounding the tones on the second string set ④③②. At rehearsal letter B, the chords ascend in half the time. Remember to pay attention to the muted strings as well—no extra points for extra strings sounded!

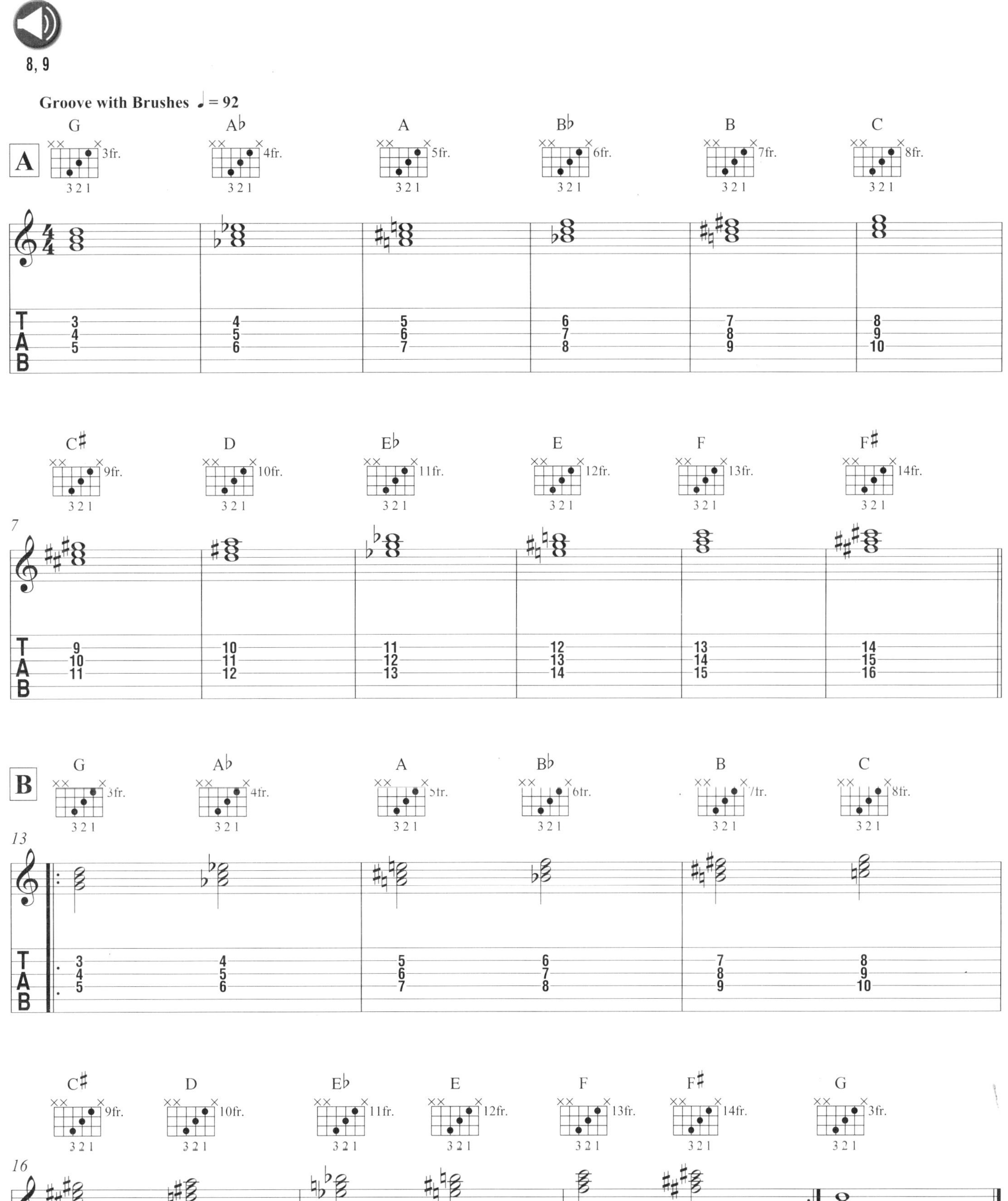

FIG. 2.2. Exercise 2.1. Root Position Major Triads on ④③②

LESSON 3

Using the Circle of Fourths with Triads

It's relatively easy to move chord shapes up and down the neck in half steps, fret by fret. But chords frequently move in intervals of a perfect fourth up (or a perfect fifth down).

If we move from chord to chord by fourths, we arrive at what is called the "circle of fourths," also often known as "cycle IV," shown in figure 3.1. A *cycle* is a series of events that recur regularly and usually leads back to the starting point. If you start at any note and continue around the wheel to the note that is up by a fourth, you will eventually end up back at the same note. In so doing, you will have covered all twelve notes in the chromatic scale, without repetition.

Clockwise, the diagram is called a circle of fourths; counter-clockwise it is a circle of fifths. (I prefer circle of fourths, but both ways of referencing it are common. "Cycle" refers to the pattern; "circle" refers to the diagram.)

Whatever technical component (chord, scale, melodic phrase, etc.) you are working on, if you can transpose it around the cycle of fourths, you have much better control of it as it would most likely appear in the "real world" of music.

Where did the circle of fourths come from? Related keys share many notes in their major scales and key signatures. The more notes in common, the more related the keys are. C major shares six notes with its adjacent neighbors on the circle, G major and F major, so the keys are seen as closely related. Each is a fourth away from C, in either direction.

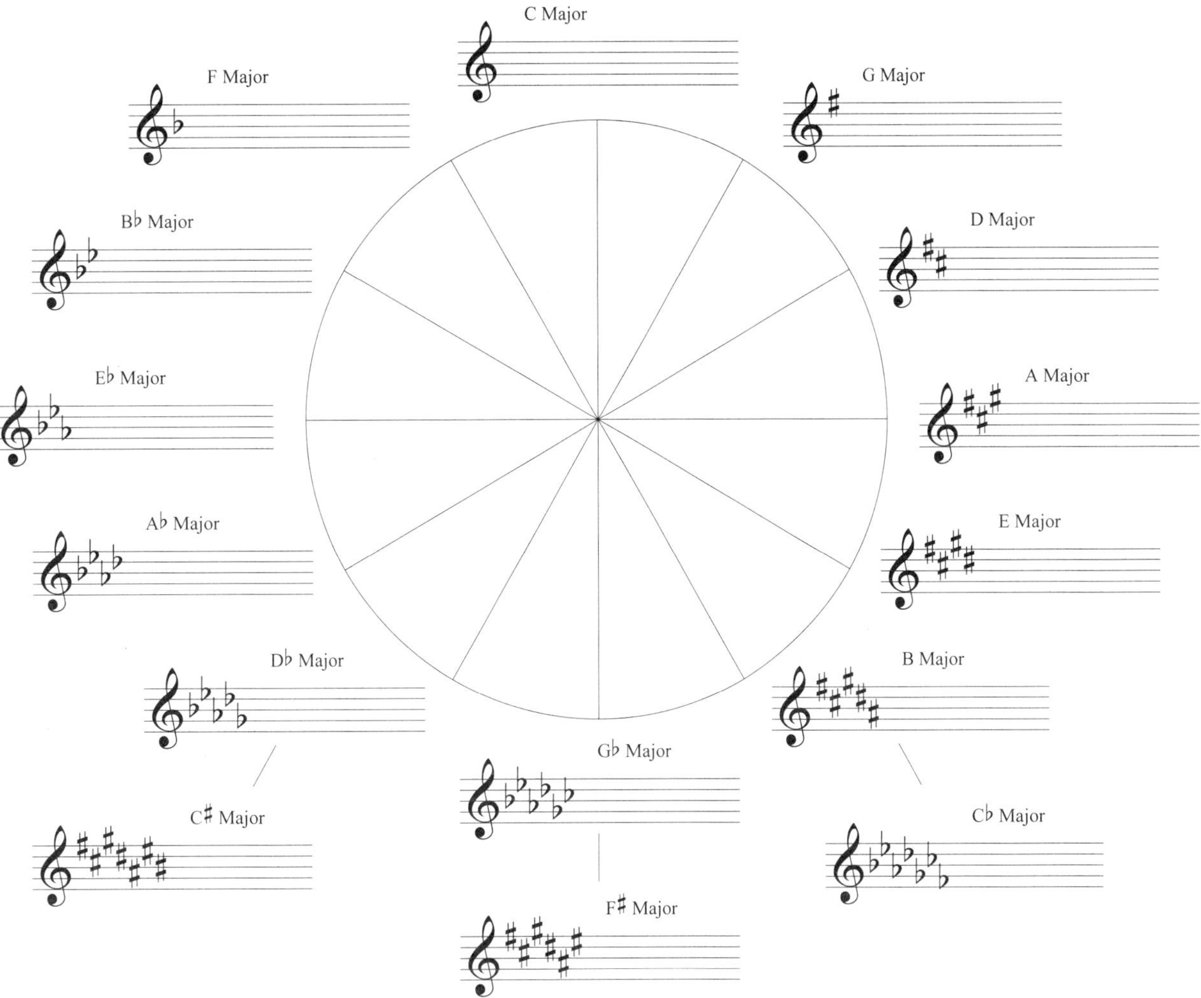

FIG. 3.1. Circle of Fourths

Root motion often locks into the sequence of roots found in the circle of fourths. In chord progressions, root motion that moves up a perfect fourth (same as down a perfect fifth) is the strongest and most common. In basic chord sequences, such as I VI II V, after the tonic chord sounds, VI II V I follows the up-a-fourth sequence. In the common III VI II V I sequence, the up-a-fourth sequence reveals the root motion all the way through.

Play through the following example, using commonly known chord shapes in the key of C.

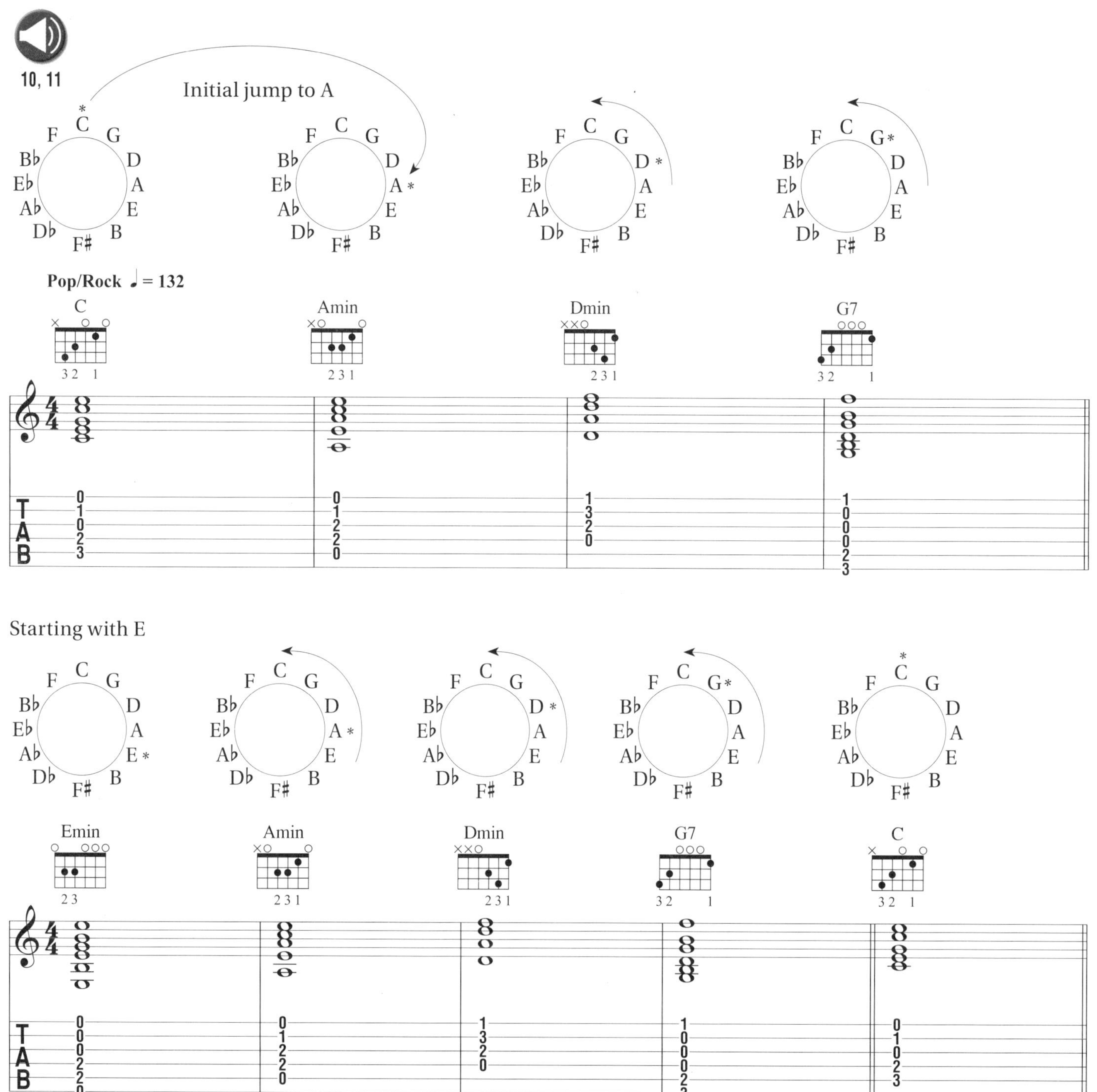

FIG. 3.2. Common Chords Using Circle of Fourths Root Motion

One way to memorize the circle of fourths is to recite or sing each note name while playing on the ⑥ and ⑤ strings. It's also helpful to sing the circle of fourths while away from the guitar to reinforce and more deeply ingrain this essential concept. It is true that there are, in fact, fifteen key signatures, but twelve keys shown here. You can think of the key of D♭ as C♯, F♯ as G♭, C♭ as B, but these are not as commonly used so they are not included in this diagram.

Using the most common keys will take you a long way towards thinking and playing through twelve keys. Play and sing the following while playing the notes on the guitar. Use the circle of fourths, notation, TAB, or fretboard diagram to assist your performance.

Sing and play!

12, 13

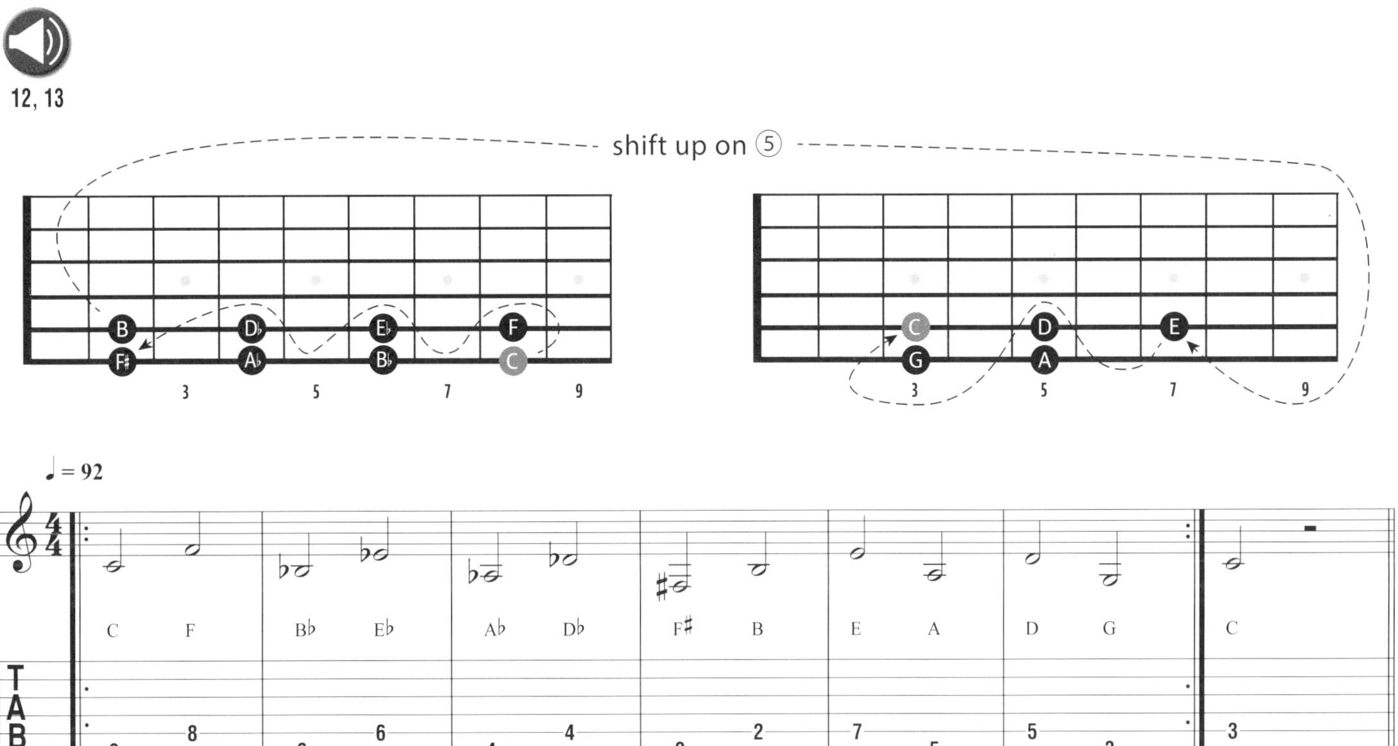

FIG. 3.3. Root Motion in Fourths on ⑥ and ⑤

The ability to think of this root motion will help you with practice as well as application. Functional chord progressions most frequently resolve up a perfect fourth.

Another means of learning and memorizing the circle of fourths is to practice writing the notes on a piece of paper very quickly. Sing the notes as you write them down, in counterclockwise order.

Practice writing the circle of fourths on the given circles on a blank piece of paper. It's helpful to think of a clock face, with C at 12 o'clock and F♯ at 6 o'clock. E♭ is at 9 o'clock, and A is at 3 o'clock. As a practice drill, I ask students to write out the circle of fourths as many times as they can in 90 seconds. Sing the notes as you write them.

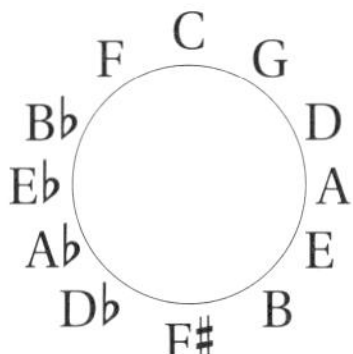

14, 15

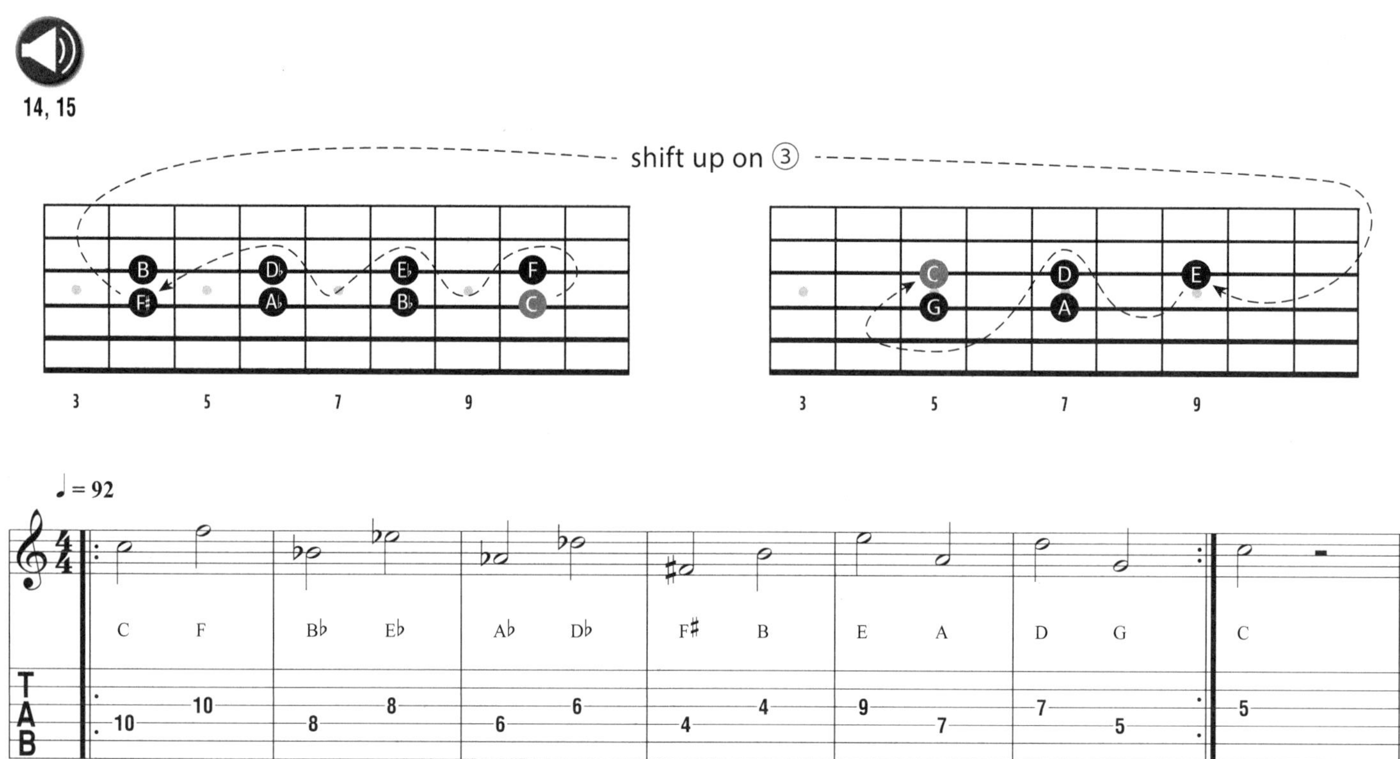

FIG. 3.4. Root Motion in Fourths on ④ and ③

SOLID TAKE: SWITCHING CHORDS

Switching chord shapes around in the circle of fourths involves some position shifts. There are several slick moves that I try to use, such as lightly lifting and muting the strings so that you cannot hear a note sound—then shifting to the intended fret, thinking of the next shape, letting go, and letting fingers float on top of strings but not dragging along them and then moving up to the intended fret. Use the fretting fingers as a guide to get you up to the other position.

The key is to play the current shape while envisioning the next chord shape in your mind. Work to plant the fingers in place a bit early for a cleaner, fuller sound at the point of chord change. It's always best to reduce the duration of the current chord to get a guaranteed on-time delivery of the next chord.

Exercise 3.1. Root Position Triads through Circle of Fourths on ④③② and ③②①

In this exercise, we will work to gain fluency with major triads through the circle of fourths. Play through major triads with chord roots moving in perfect fourths, alternating the second set of three strings ④③② with the top string set ③②①.

FIG. 3.5. Exercise 3.1. Root Position Triads through Circle of Fourths on ④③② and ③②①

LESSON 4

Using the Circle of Fourths with Arpeggios

The term "arpeggio" refers to playing the tones of a chord in succession, as opposed to playing all tones simultaneously. Being able to arpeggiate chords provides an expressive way to play through the notes of a chord and also helps you really hear the chord tones.

Play each chord tone individually, seamlessly extending into the next, while not allowing the notes to ring haphazardly together. Playing one note at a time is more challenging than it might seem. To make a cleanly arpeggiated sound, mute the string with the same finger as you leave each chord tone by lightly lifting that finger. Another way to avoid string noise is to use the palm of your picking hand. The goal is a smooth and flowing legato type of articulation, without breaks between the chord tones.

When playing a chord, go for a simultaneous sounding of the chord tones. When playing an arpeggio, go for a golden thread of continuity from one note to the next.

FIG. 4.1. C Major Arpeggio

CHORD SPELLING BASICS: MEMORIZING AND RECITING NOTES SEPARATED BY THIRDS

If you were asked to spell the notes of an A major triad, might you say:

(a) "A D♭ E"

(b) "A C♯ E"

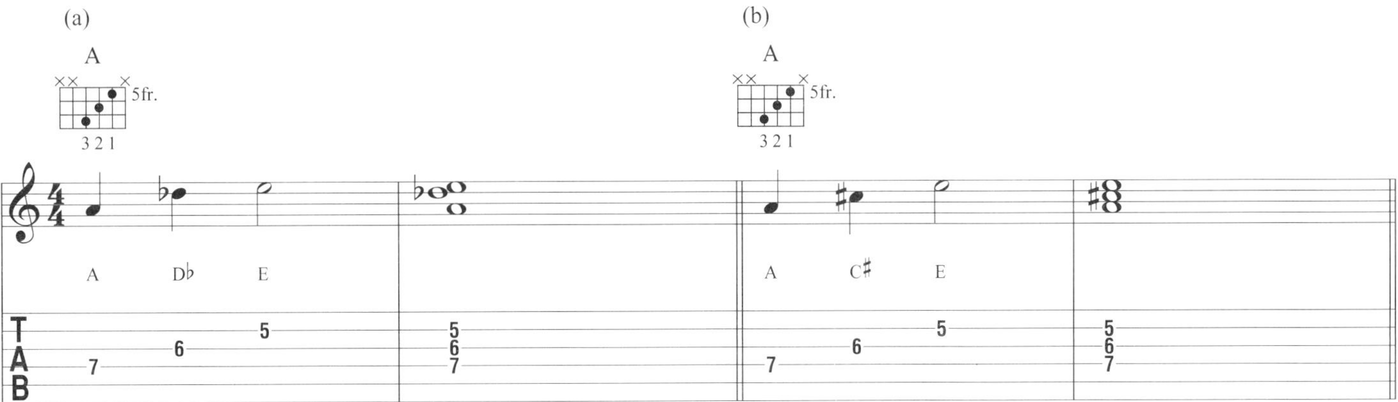

FIG. 4.2. Correct Spelling of A Major

The correct answer is "A C♯ E." The notes C♯ and D♭ feel and sound the same on the fretboard, but since root position triads are built in thirds, practicing recitation of thirds might help you to get the correct answer more quickly.

Spelling chords is much easier when you can recite note names in thirds. If you are clear with the idea of thirds, it's much easier to know when to go with flats or sharps when spelling chords.

The easiest way to get this going is to practice in the key of C, a great theoretical gateway. Following the pattern of diatonic thirds in the key of C, starting from C:

C E G B D F A C (back to original root)

Here's an outstanding way to enhance your ability to spell chords correctly. Memorize and recite diatonic notes in thirds.

Leaving out sharps and flats, since we're in the key of C, here's what you should recite (sing the note names at pitch, if you wish):

19

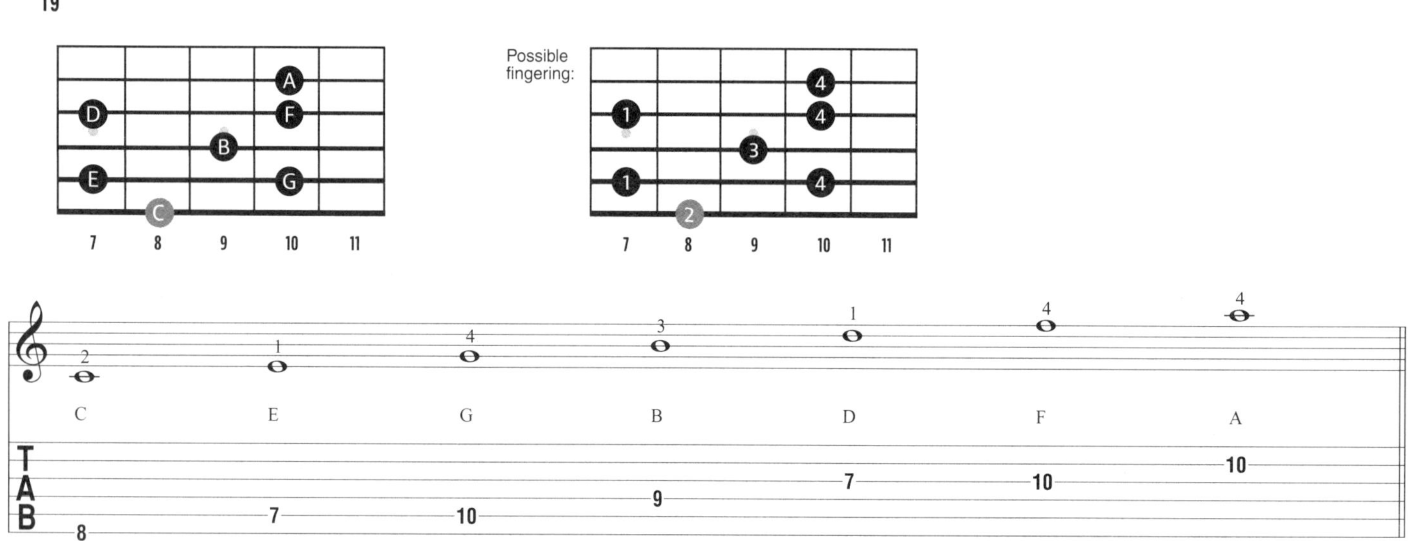

FIG. 4.3. Diatonic Notes in C

It is a bit of a tongue twister at first, but just like the circle of fourths recitation, repetition is our not-so-secret weapon in our quest for fluency. Practicing this exercise will help you recognize and understand patterns in sight-reading examples. Melodic leaps of a diatonic third are frequently missed by guitarists, and you're much more likely to play what you already know.

Although practicing the figure 4.3 example may be enough, and starting from every note may be too much, it's worthwhile to do the same exercise, utilizing the key of C from F to F. Choose either octave or both for study and practice.

20

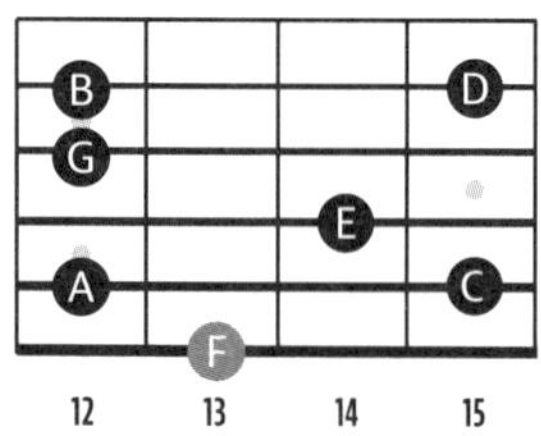

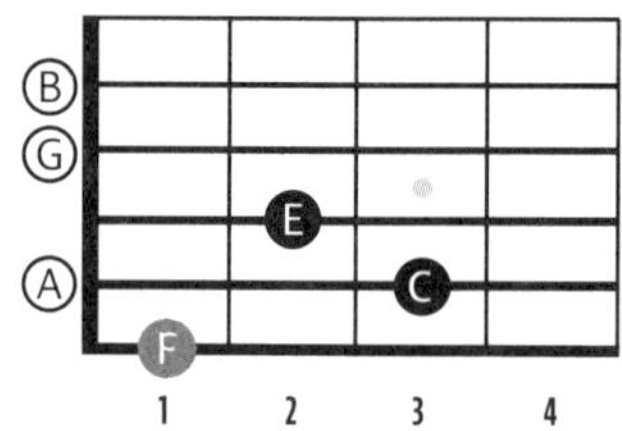

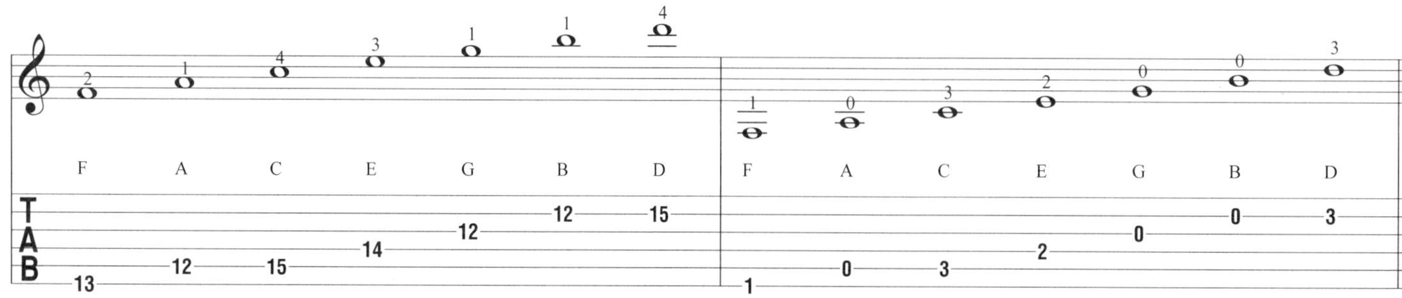

FIG. 4.4. Spelling Practice: Thirds Starting from F in Two Octaves

C Major Diatonic Note Names in Thirds, Starting from C and F

Practice reciting or singing the C major diatonic note names in thirds, starting from C and F.

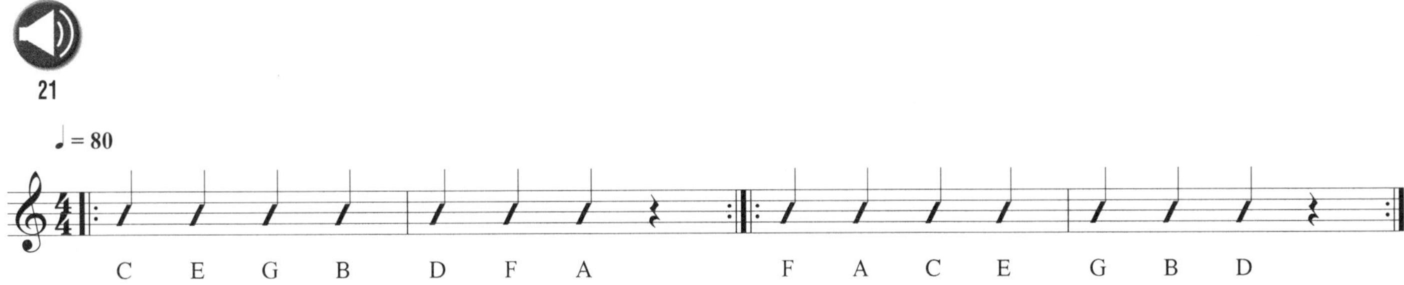

FIG. 4.5. C Major Diatonic Note Names in Thirds, Starting from C and F

With time and practice, you can start from any of the seven notes, reciting the cycle-3 pattern. Some students have benefitted from using a metronome set to quarter note = 60 bpm and reciting the pattern starting from every note.

SOLID TAKE: FRETTING FINGER PLACEMENT IS THE KEY TO *TONE.*

Regardless of the style you're playing, tone production is "job 1." It is a challenge to get all the notes of a chord to "sound" properly. When I'm playing on the fret, I'm not just playing somewhere in the fret region. I am playing with my fretting fingertip placed right up next to the intended fret without being on top of it. This "sweet spot" is right where all of our heroes, the greatest guitarists feel well at home. For example, Charlie Christian, Django Reinhardt, Grant Green, Jimi Hendrix, Wes Montgomery, Sharon Isbin—all our favorite heroes who have achieved a great tone—are able to get that sound in this way.

USING CIRCLE OF FOURTHS WITH ARPEGGIOS DRILL AND PRACTICE

Using the notated example, practice spelling the note names of the chords aloud. Then arpeggiate them and play them as chords. The recorded performance is in two versions: one with the answers provided and another one where you are able to answer the questions on your own.

Exercise 4.1. Major Triads through Circle of Fourths: Spell and Play

22, 23

Groove ♩= 72

Chord:	Spell:	C (3fr., 341)	C (3fr., 341)	Chord:	Spell:	F (8fr., 341)	F (8fr., 341)
C	C E G	TAB: 5 5 3	TAB: 3/5/5	F	F A C	TAB: 10 10 8	TAB: 8/10/10

9

Chord:	Spell:	B♭ (6fr., 321)	B♭ (6fr., 321)	Chord:	Spell:	E♭ (6fr., 341)	E♭ (6fr., 341)
B♭	B♭ D F	TAB: 8 7 6	TAB: 6/7/8	E♭	E♭ G B♭	TAB: 8 8 6	TAB: 6/8/8

17

Chord:	Spell:	A♭ (4fr., 321)	A♭ (4fr., 321)	Chord:	Spell:	D♭ (4fr., 341)	D♭ (4fr., 341)
A♭	A♭ C E♭	TAB: 6 5 4	TAB: 4/5/6	D♭	D♭ F A♭	TAB: 6 6 4	TAB: 4/6/6

FIG. 4.6. Exercise 4.1. Major Triads through Circle of Fourths: Spell and Play

Exercise 4.2. Major Triads on ④③② and ③②①

24, 25

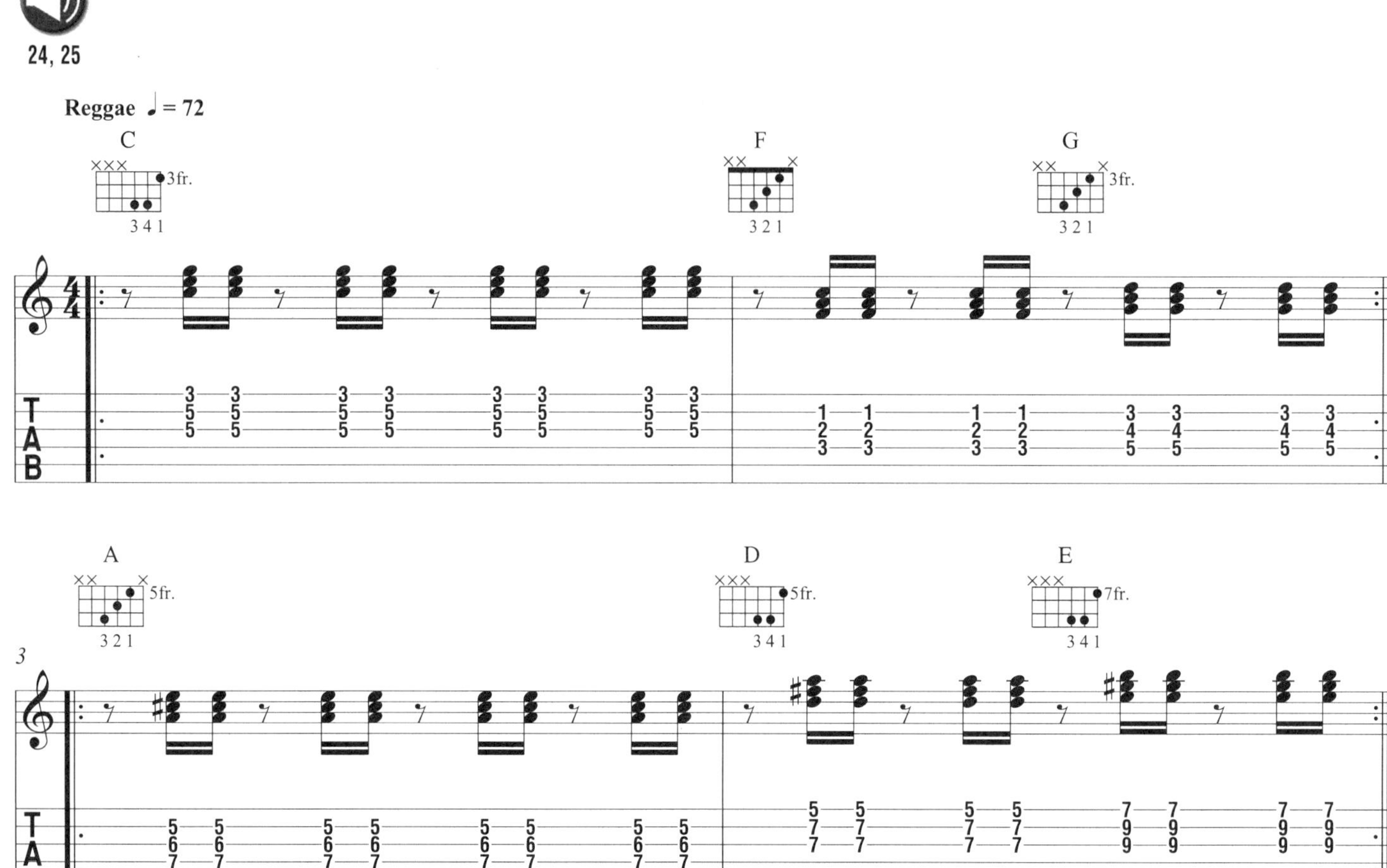

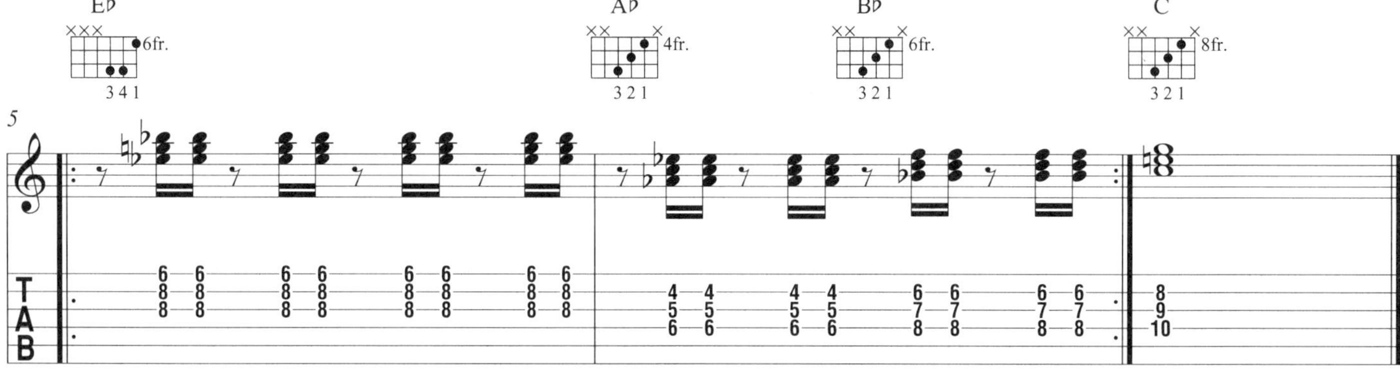

FIG. 4.7. Exercise 4.2. Major Triads on ④③② and ③②①

LESSON 5

Minor Triads

Let's expand our vocabulary to include minor triads. Root position major and minor triads contain perfect fifth intervals. Minor triads contain a minor third above the root, as opposed to the major third above the root found in major triads.

C minor is spelled C E♭ G. The interval between C and E♭ is a minor third, and the interval between E♭ and G is a major third.

For minor triads on the top three strings ③②①, the minor third between ③② has the upper-pitched note one fret below the lower note. The major third between has the upper note one fret below the lower note. The interval between C and G is a perfect fifth.

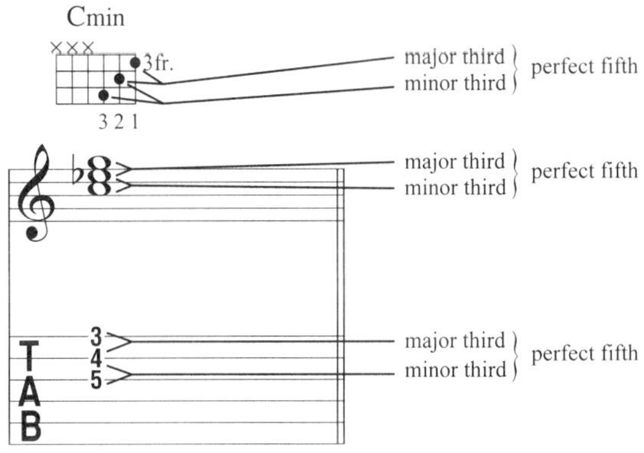

FIG. 5.1. C Minor Triad Intervals on ③②①

On strings ④③②, the minor third on ④③ has the upper note two frets below and the major third on ②③ is straight across on the same fret.

Here is the C minor triad in eighth position:

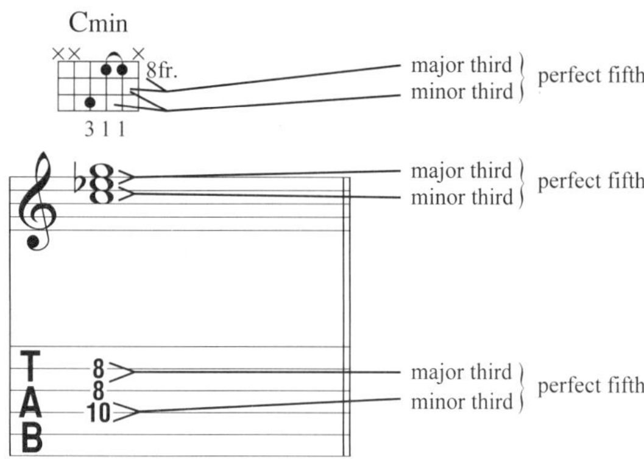

FIG. 5.2. C Minor Triad Intervals on ④③②

MODIFY MAJOR TRIAD SHAPES INTO MINOR

If you can play major triads, adjusting the major third to minor is all that needs to be done to get a minor triad. For string set ③②①, the third of a root position triad is found on ②. For string set ④③②, the third is on ③. Both chord qualities contain the same root and perfect fifth.

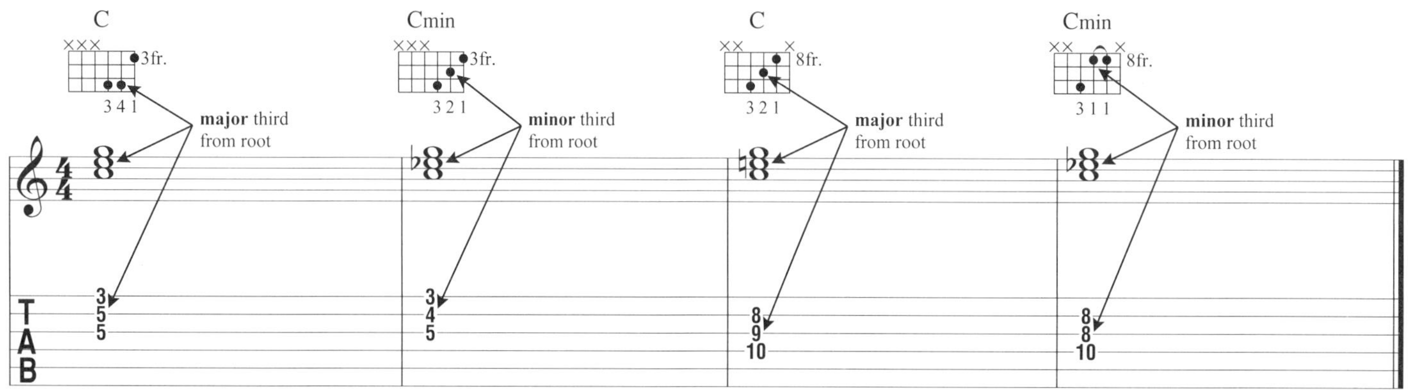

FIG. 5.3. Using C Major to Find C Minor

SOLID TAKE: NO EXTRA POINTS GIVEN FOR EXTRA STRINGS SOUNDED!

Remember to consider the many muted notes on most of the chord blocks, expressed through the × marks on the strings that are not to be included in the sound. In order to get a consistent sound in your chordal playing, it's important to avoid sounding extra strings. In addition to fretting the given notes, our fretting hand needs mute the strings adjacent so that they don't result in an extra note or two.

On the ④③② string grouping, students often sound ④③②①. Even though the unintended note produced may not always be dissonant, the intention here is to have control of three-note triads to allow you to build from a consistent foundation.

If you are using a pick with your strumming hand, ensure that your strums are focused on the prescribed strings. A slight angling of any barred fingers can help you to mute the extra strings on the higher strings. It takes some time and practice to gain control of the subtle bends in your fretting fingers—not only finding the chord tones, but muting the uninvited next-door neighbor strings! The ends of your fretting fingers can provide a helpful way to mute an extra string on the lower string adjacent to the chord shape.

Exercise 5.1. Spell and Play Minor Triads through Circle of Fourths

In the same way that you practiced major triads, work through the circle of fourths with minor arpeggios. Using the notated example, practice spelling the note names of the chords aloud. Then arpeggiate them and play them as chords. The recorded performance is in two versions: one with the answers provided and another one where you are able to answer the questions on your own.

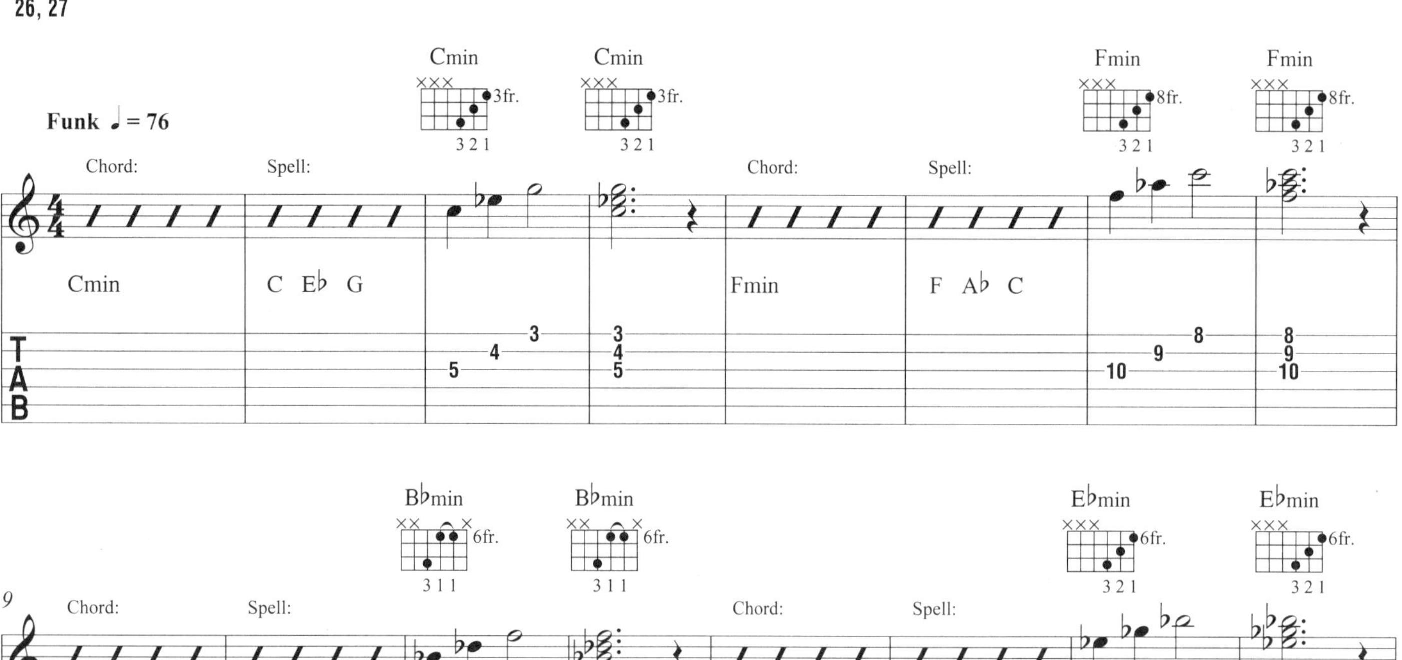

FIG. 5.4. Exercise 5.1. Spell and Play Minor Triads through the Circle of Fourths

Exercise 5.2. Minor Triads on Strings ④③② and ③②①, Moving in Perfect Fourths

28, 29

Play through the following exercise, switching the focus to minor triads. Once again, root motion utilizes the circle of fourths. Now play minor triads through cycle IV, alternating string set ④③② with string set ③②①.

Bossa Nova ♩ = 82

Cmin (8fr., 3 1 1) | Fmin (8fr., 3 2 1) | B♭min (6fr., 3 1 1) | E♭min (6fr., 3 2 1) | A♭min (4fr., 3 1 1) | D♭min (4fr., 3 2 1)

7

F♯min (2fr., 3 1 1) | Bmin (2fr., 3 2 1) | Emin (7fr., 3 2 1) | Amin (5fr., 3 1 1) | Dmin (5fr., 3 2 1) | Gmin (3fr., 3 1 1)

13

Cmin (3fr., 3 2 1) | Cmin (8fr., 3 1 1) | Cmin (8fr., 3 1 1) Fmin (8fr., 3 2 1) | B♭min (6fr., 3 1 1) E♭min (6fr., 3 2 1) | A♭min (4fr., 3 1 1) D♭min (4fr., 3 2 1)

18

F♯min (2fr., 3 1 1) Bmin (2fr., 3 2 1) | Emin (7fr., 3 2 1) Dmin (5fr., 3 2 1) | Amin (5fr., 3 1 1) Gmin (3fr., 3 1 1) | Cmin (3fr., 3 2 1) Cmin (8fr., 3 1 1) | Cmin (8fr., 3 1 1)

FIG. 5.5. Exercise 5.2. Minor Triads on Strings ④③② and ③②①, Moving in Perfect Fourths

LESSON 6

Spread Triad Voicings

It's been helpful for my *Chords 101* students to visualize everyday playing cards as a way to gain an understanding of chord voicings. Let's allow the ace of hearts card represent the root—a "heart" card to reflect its importance. The 5 of spades represents the fifth of the chord and the 3 of spades can be the third. We're about to shuffle chord tones around, so using playing cards can help us visualize.

Major Triad Chord Tones	Playing Cards
5	5♠
3	3♠
Root	A♥

FIG. 6.1. Triadic Chord Tones as Playing Cards

We are going to be working through the world of triad inversions, but first, let's look at an amazing variation of root position triads. The term "spread triad," often called "open triad," refers to voicings that are spread out more than an octave. Found in virtually every musical style, open triads serve the purpose of making the mighty triad sound even bigger! Although they are relatively easy to play, many guitarists have yet to use this versatile approach to the Mighty Triad.

The term "spread" is used in contrast to the term "close." Close-position triads are configured to have the chord tones as close as possible, all found within a single octave. We've been working with close-position triads with the root in the bass.

To build a C major as a spread triad, simply take the middle chord tone (tone 2) of a close-position triad and raise it up an octave. Let's move the middle card up to the right. For this spread triad, the middle chord tone change octaves. The sound difference is huge! It's easier to demonstrate this on string set ⑤④②.

30

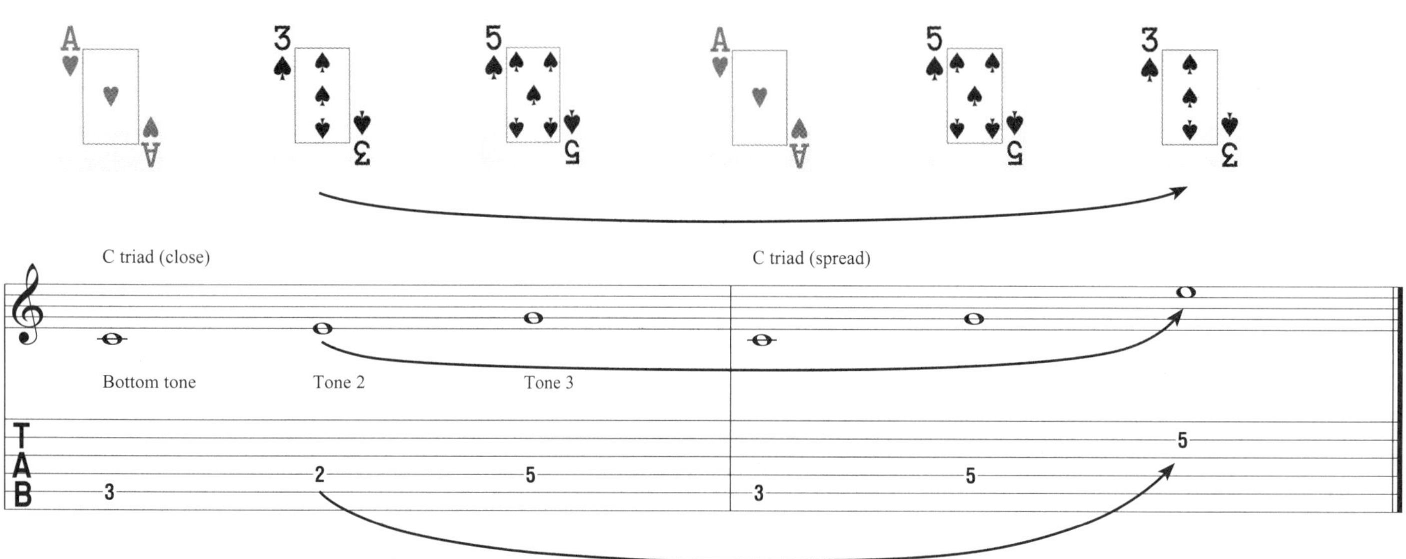

FIG. 6.2. Using Cards to Understand "Spread" Triads

Figure 6.3 is an example of a close position and a spread triad shape for C major. To allow easier playing, the open ③ is changed to fifth fret of ④ for the spread triad.

31

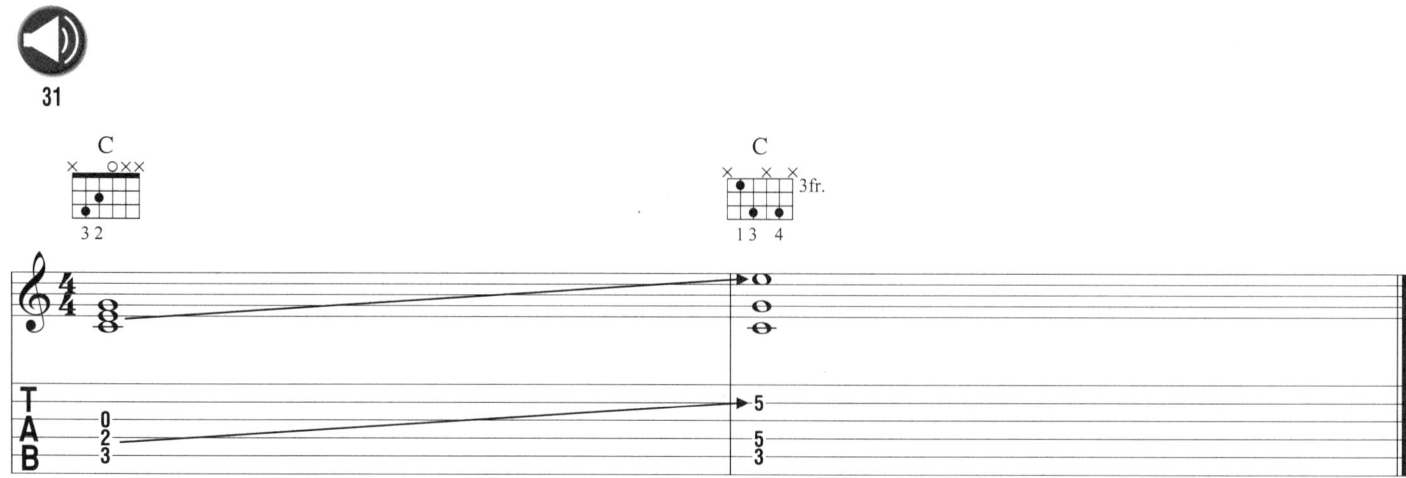

FIG. 6.3. Raising the Second Tone from the Bottom to Build a Spread Triad

RAISE 2: A BRIDGE FROM ARPEGGIOS TO VOICINGS

Here is a great way to combine arpeggios with chord voicing construction. We'll be using this approach for four-part chords in upcoming chapters, so it's good to start with it now.

1. Arpeggiate the triad.
2. Move the second voice (tone 2) from the bottom up one octave.
3. Play the resultant shape.

32

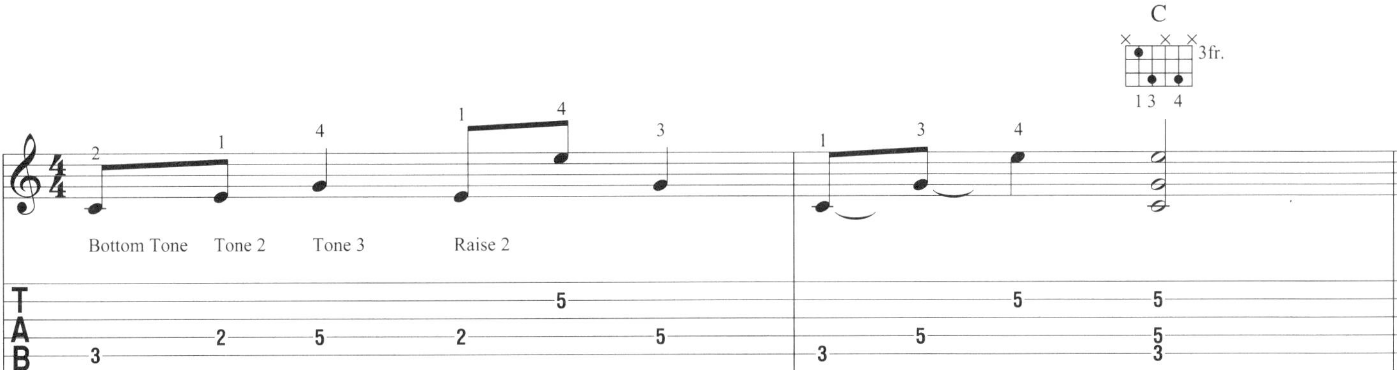

FIG. 6.4. Modifying a Close Triad to a Spread Triad

Let's do the same thing with C minor.

1. Arpeggiate the triad.
2. Move the second voice (tone 2) from the bottom up one octave.
3. Play the resultant shape.

33

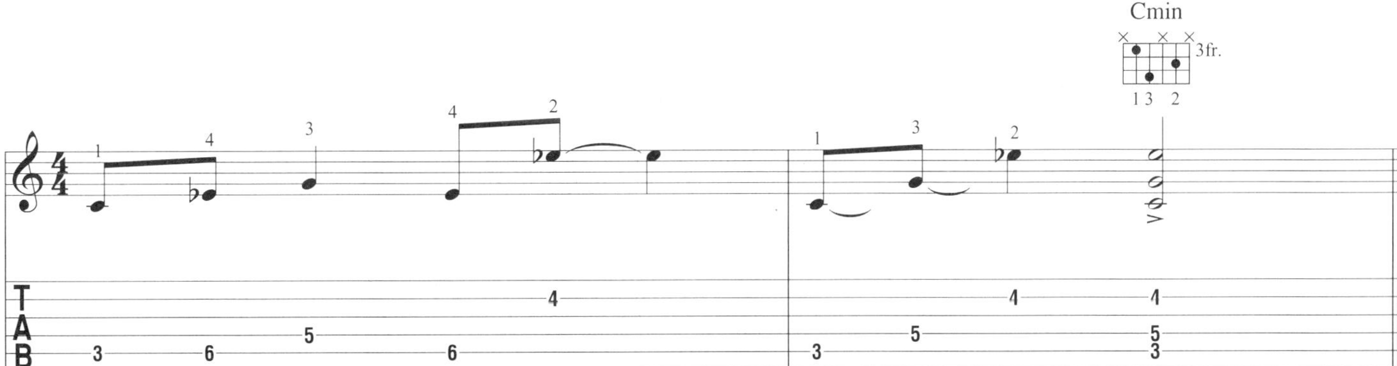

FIG. 6.5. Modifying a Close Minor Triad to a Spread Triad

Exercise 6.1. Pop/Rock Spread Triads through Circle of Fourths

Play with the accompaniment track, paying special attention to the pure sound of the chord tones, while muting the "unwanted strings." Play with a sustained legato, arpeggiating the chord tones; then attack the full chord, giving each chord its fullest rhythmic value.

34, 35

A

Pop/Rock ♩ = 60

C 3fr. | F 8fr. | B♭ 8fr. | E♭ 6fr. | A♭ 6fr.

6 D♭ 4fr. | F♯ 4fr. | B 2fr. | E 2fr. | A 7fr.

11 D 5fr. | G 5fr. | C 3fr. | C 3fr.

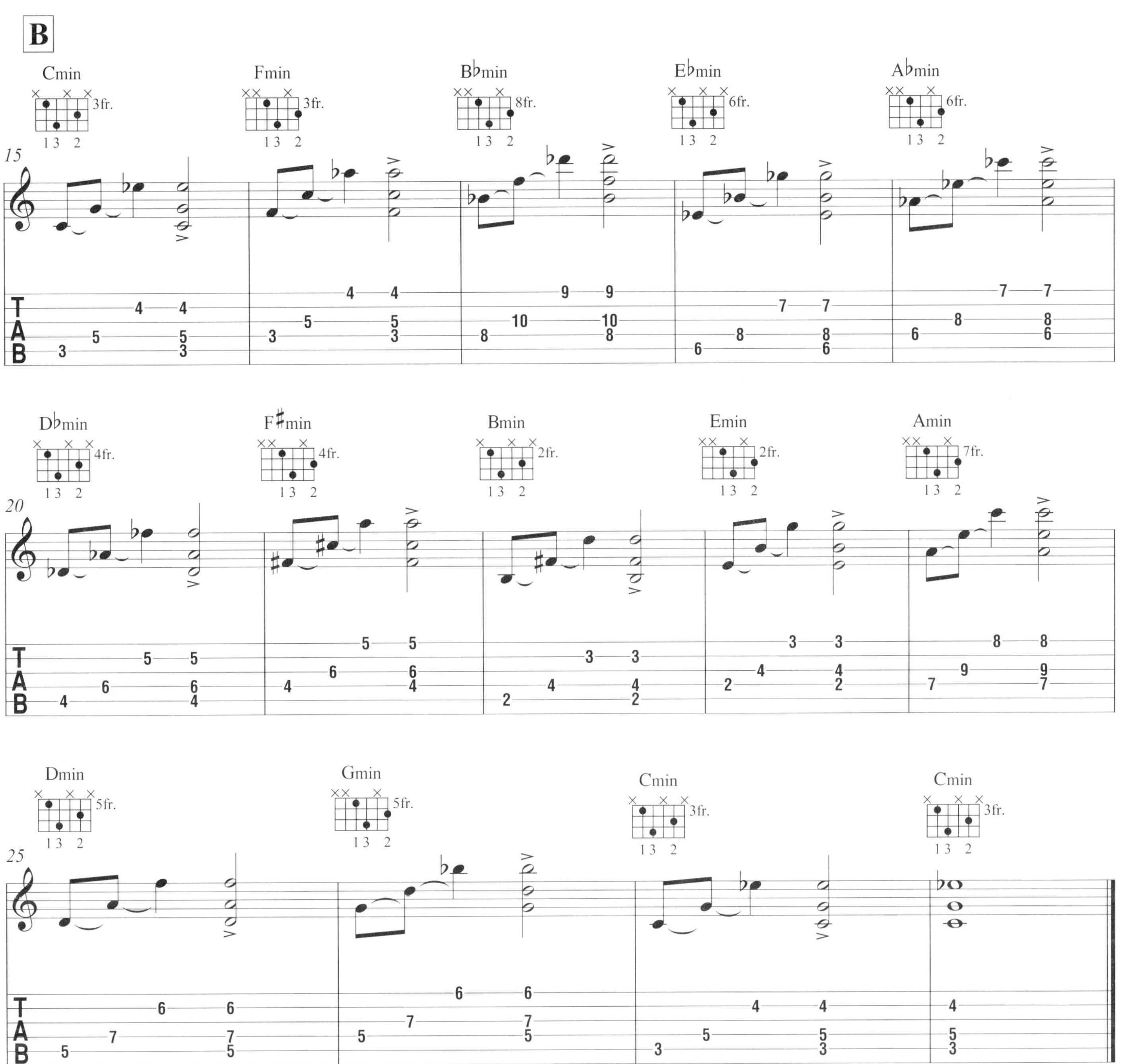

FIG. 6.6. Exercise 6.1. Pop/Rock Spread Triad through the Circle of Fourths

Exercise 6.2. Mixing Major and Minor Spread Triads

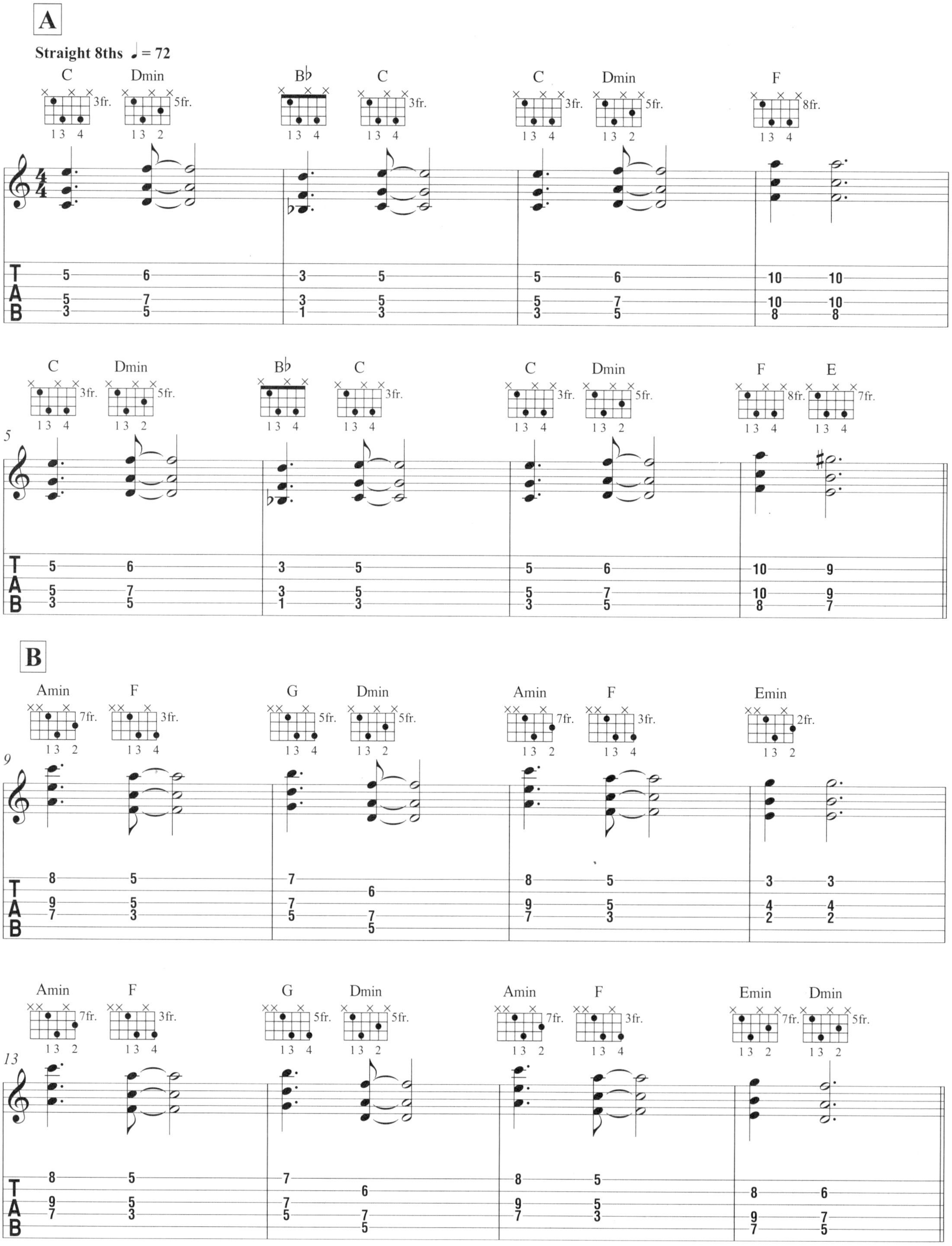

A

Straight 8ths ♩ = 72

C Dmin | B♭ C | C Dmin | F

5 C Dmin | B♭ C | C Dmin | F E

B

9 Amin F | G Dmin | Amin F | Emin

13 Amin F | G Dmin | Amin F | Emin Dmin

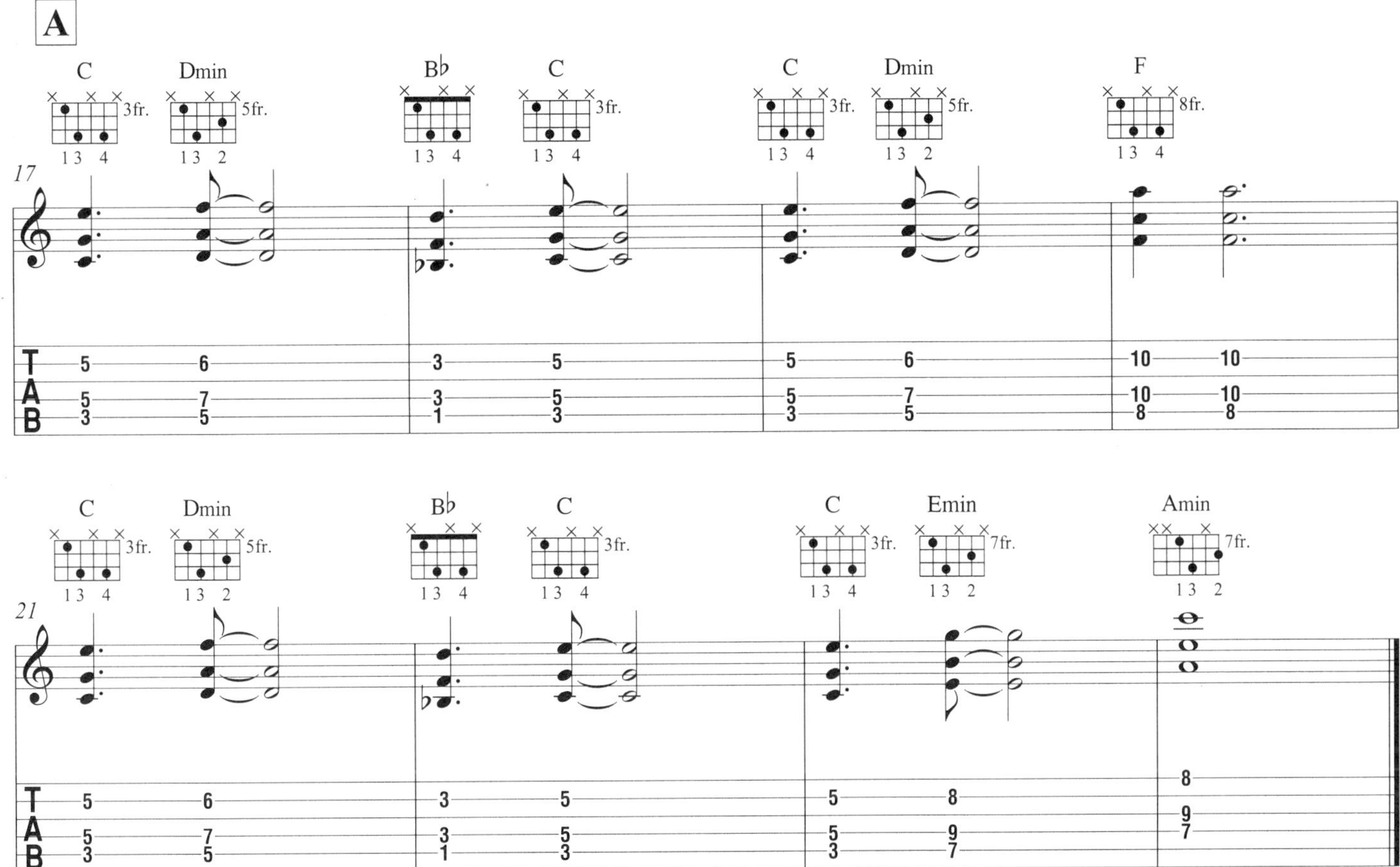

FIG. 6.7. Exercise 6.2. Mixing Major and Minor Spread Triads

SOLID TAKE: SPREAD TRIADS IN MAJOR AND MINOR

There are three major challenges with playing open triads:

1. Choosing a triad configuration on the fretboard that fits under your fingers. There will often be several variations available with different string sets and fingerings. Make the best choice.
2. Making the open triads ring with clarity—no extraneous notes or muffled chord tones!
3. Muting the unused strings to make the chord tones shine. Guitarists can strum these shapes with a pick, combine a pick with fingers, or pluck with fingers. Fingerstyle performers often have an easier time getting a clear sound on these voicings, although a hybrid approach (pick and fingers) can work well too.

It Is a challenge to mute the unwanted strings when playing spread triads, but again, careful focus of the strum and use of the sides of fretting fingers are the secret to getting it done. Similar to a magician's sleight of hand, we need to do what it takes to achieve a musical sound. It takes time, effort, and patience. Listen for a clear sound and work with your hands to put things on course to make it all happen.

LESSON 7

Inversions

The root of a chord you're playing doesn't have to be the lowest note in the voicing. With triads, the 3 or 5 can also be the lowest note of the chord performed, and the root can appear in the middle or top as well. Such voicings are called "inversions."

Chord inversions help to smooth out motion from chord to chord, harmonize melodies, and allow smooth bass motion. On the guitar, inversions allow you play some form of a given chord virtually anywhere on the neck. Inversions are your friend!

Inversions can be difficult to conceptualize on the guitar due to the fact that you can play the same pitch in numerous places on the instrument. Middle C can be played in five places: ② first fret, ⑤ fifth fret, ④ tenth fret, ⑤ fifteenth fret, ⑥ twentieth fret. Couple that with different approaches to guitar technique and stylistic vocabulary, and you've got a whole lot of choices available for any single chord. We'll be working to develop clear choices from a solid foundation.

The more you know about chords on the guitar, the larger the number of options you'll have. We're going to work with inverting triads from the high strings to the low strings and from the lower range of the neck up to the higher frets.

Inverted chords are notated with a slash (/) in the chord symbol, followed by a letter indicating the chord's bass note. C/E means a C triad with E in the bass—first inversion of a C major triad. A guitarist might decide to play an inversion anytime, though, even if an alternate bass note is not indicated in the chord symbol, especially when playing in a band with a bass player.

38

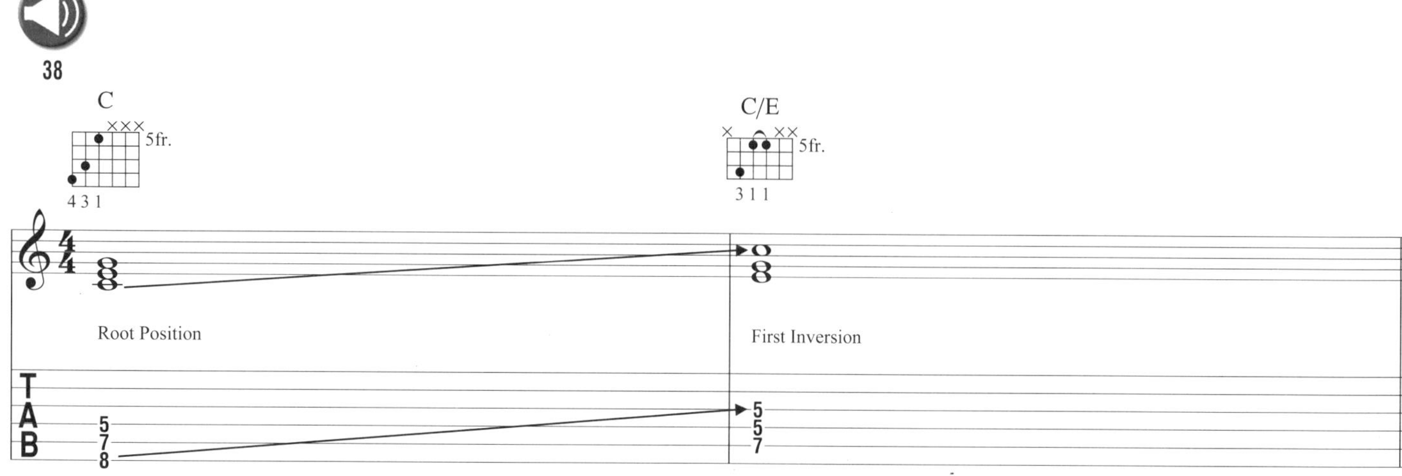

FIG. 7.1. C Major in Root Position and First Inversion

To complete the set of options, we move the 3 up an octave, leaving the 5 in the bass position.

Chord Voicings (Low to High)	C Major Triad Root Position (C)	C Major Triad First Inversion (C/E)	C Major Triad Second Inversion (C/G)
	5 G	A C	3 E
	3 E	5 G	A C
	A C	3 E	5 G

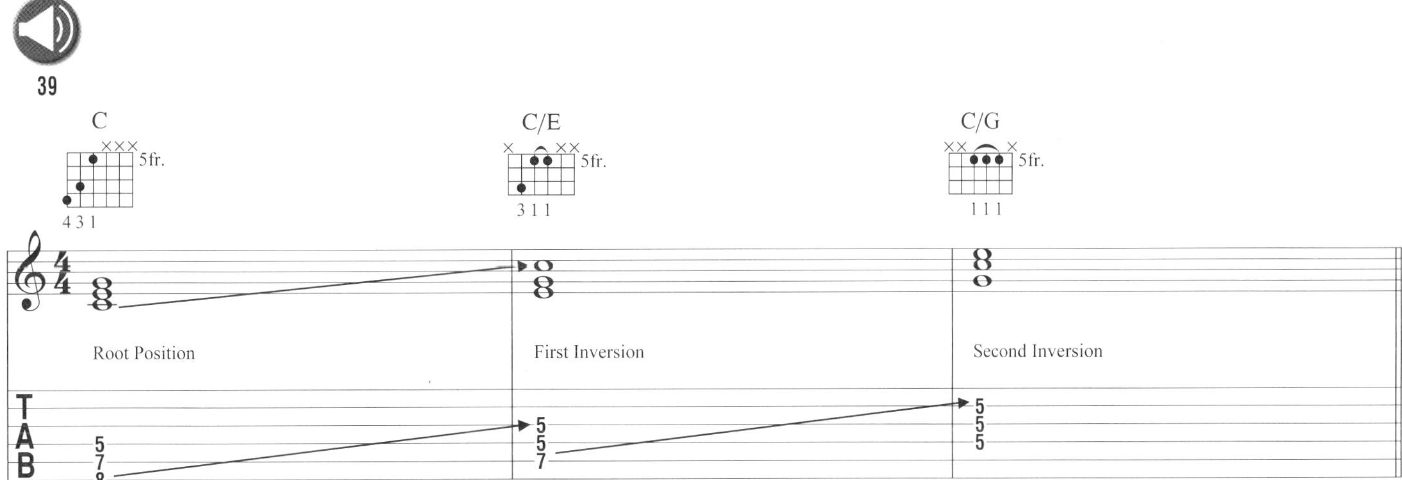

FIG. 7.2. C Major in Root Position, First Inversion, and Second Inversion

THE CHORD INVERSION GENERATOR: A WAY TO UNDERSTAND AND BUILD INVERSIONS

The concept of chord inversions is central to attain fluency with chordal shapes. Some people learn best with standard notation, right on the fretboard, or even through use of playing cards! Many of the online students have benefited from the use of inversion generator tables.

Inversion generator tables are a handy way to write out the inversions of any chord shape.

1. Place the voicing you'd like to see in all inversions in the first column.
2. Put the chord tones in close position (alphabetical/scalar) order on the bottom line.
3. Fill in the upper rows, referring to the first tone and filling in the remaining lines.
4. Play through the voicings described in the table's columns.

Let's start with a C triad in root position. The chord voicing is arranged from lowest pitch to highest.

Step 1: Place the chord you'd like to see in all inversions into the first column.

Chord Voicings Chord Tones (Low to High)	Root Position (Root in Bottom)	First Inversion (3 in Bottom)	Second Inversion (5 in Bottom)	
	G			Lead
	E			
	C			Bottom Note
	Chord Tones in Close Position Order (Alphabetical/Scalar Order)			

FIG. 7.3. Inversion Generator Step 1: Chord Tones in Left Column (Root Position, Close Voicing)

Step 2: Put the chord tones in close position (alphabetical/scalar) order on the bottom line.

Chord Voicings (Low to High)	C MAJOR			
	Root Position	First Inversion	Second Inversion	
	G			Lead
	E			
	C	E	G	Bottom Note
	Chord Tones in Close Position Order			

FIG. 7.4. Inversion Generator Step 2: Chord Tones on Bottom Line (Root Position/Close Voicing)

Step 3: Fill in the upper rows, referring to the first tone and filling in the remaining lines.

Chord Voicings (Low to High)	C MAJOR			
	Root Position	First Inversion	Second Inversion	
	G	C	E	Lead
	E	G	C	
	C	E	G	Bottom Note
	Chord Tones in Close Position Order			

FIG. 7.5. Inversion Generator Step 3: Filling in the Remaining Cells

In the second row from the bottom, E is followed by G and then C. In the top row, G is followed by C and E.

Step 4: Play through the voicings presented in the table's columns.

40

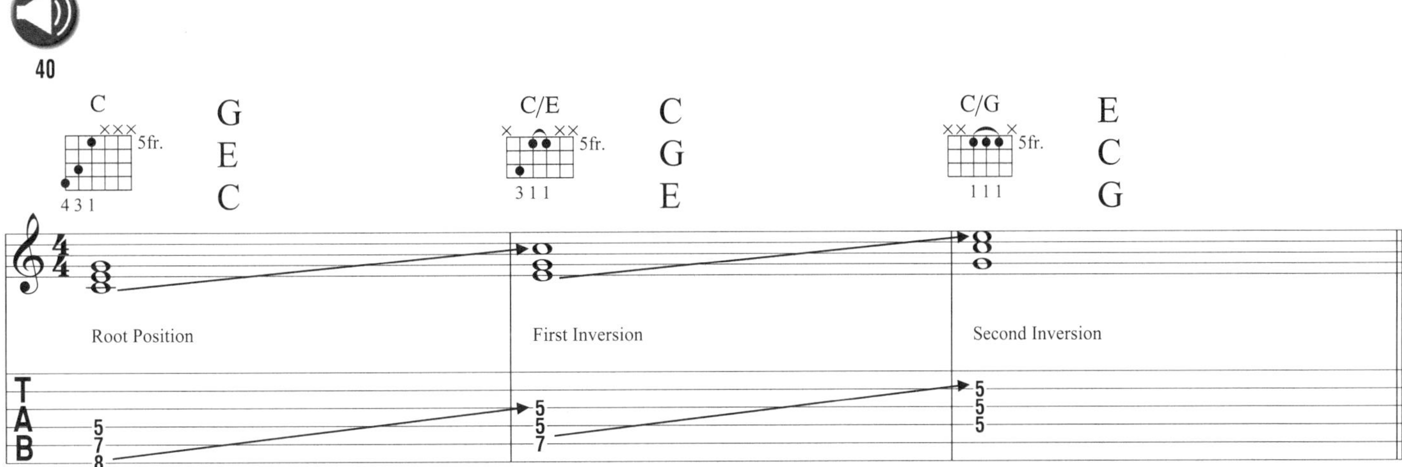

FIG. 7.6. C Major Triad Inversions

SOLID TAKE: ROOT POSITION DOES *NOT EQUAL* FIRST INVERSION.

Q: *What is the difference between a triad's* ***bass note*** *and the* ***root*** *of a triad?*

A: The bass note is the bottom-most note of a voicing, and it can be any chord tone (the root, 3, or 5). The root of the chord is the tone that identifies the chord's foundation when the chord is built from the root. The root can be the lowest tone in a chord voicing, but the root can also appear in the middle or top of a voicing. In a root position chord, the root and the bass note are the same.

Q: *Why isn't the root position chord called the "first inversion" of a chord?*

A: *Chords 101* online students have often assumed that the root position chord, since we spell that one first, should be called the "first inversion." Not so!

- Root position: Root is in the bottom voice of the triad
- First inversion: 3 is in the bottom voice of the triad
- Second inversion: 5 is in the bottom voice of the triad

Let's follow through the same process, using a D minor triad.

1. Place the voicing you'd like to see in all inversions in the first column.
2. Put the chord tones in close position (alphabetical/scalar) order on the bottom line.
3. Fill in the upper rows, referring to the first column and filling in the remaining lines.
4. Play through the voicings described in the table's columns.

Steps 1 and 2 for D minor.

Chord Voicings (Low to High)

D MINOR			
Root Position	**First Inversion**	**Second Inversion**	
A			Lead
F			
D	F	A	Bottom Note

Chord Tones in Close Position Order

Step 3 for D minor.

Chord Voicings (Low to High)

D MINOR			
Root Position	**First Inversion**	**Second Inversion**	
A	D	F	Lead
F	A	D	
D	F	A	Bottom Note

Chord Tones in Close Position Order

Step 4 for D minor.

41

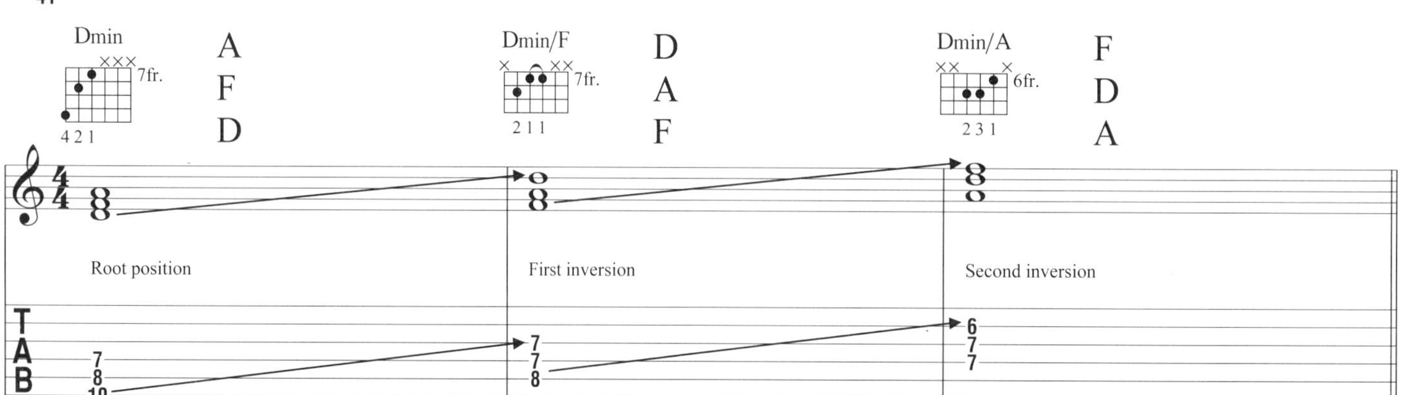

FIG. 7.7. D Minor Triad Inversions

Exercise 7.1. Inversion Generators

Without changing the given notes, fill in the blanks with the correct notes. Solve the puzzle by completing the missing chord tones. Find the voicings on your fretboard.

Chord Voicings (Low to High)

F MAJOR			
Root Position	**First Inversion**	**Second Inversion**	
C			Lead
A			
F	A	C	Bottom Note

Chord Tones in Close Position Order

Chord Voicings (Low to High)

G MINOR			
Root Position	**First Inversion**	**Second Inversion**	
			Lead
Bb			
G		D	Bottom Note

Chord Tones in Close Position Order

Chord Voicings (Low to High)

E♭ MAJOR			
Root Position	**First Inversion**	**Second Inversion**	
	E♭		Lead
E♭		B♭	Bottom Note

Chord Tones in Close Position Order

Chord Voicings (Low to High)

A MINOR			
Root Position	**First Inversion**	**Second Inversion**	
			Lead
	E	A	
A			Bottom Note

Chord Tones in Close Position Order

Chord Voicings (Low to High)

F♯ MAJOR			
Root Position	**First Inversion**	**Second Inversion**	
C♯			Lead
		F♯	
	A♯		Bottom Note

Chord Tones in Close Position Order

Exercise 7.2. Triad Inversion Blues

Pay special attention to a precise delivery of the entire chord sound, right at the point of chord change. Perform with the demo and backing tracks, working to get a solid rhythmic lock with the rhythm section.

42, 43

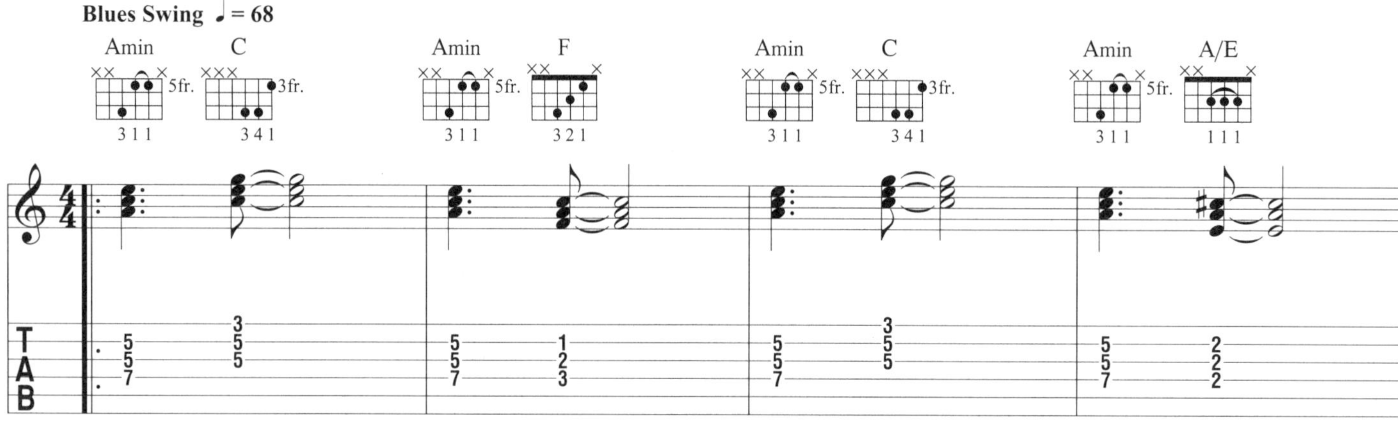

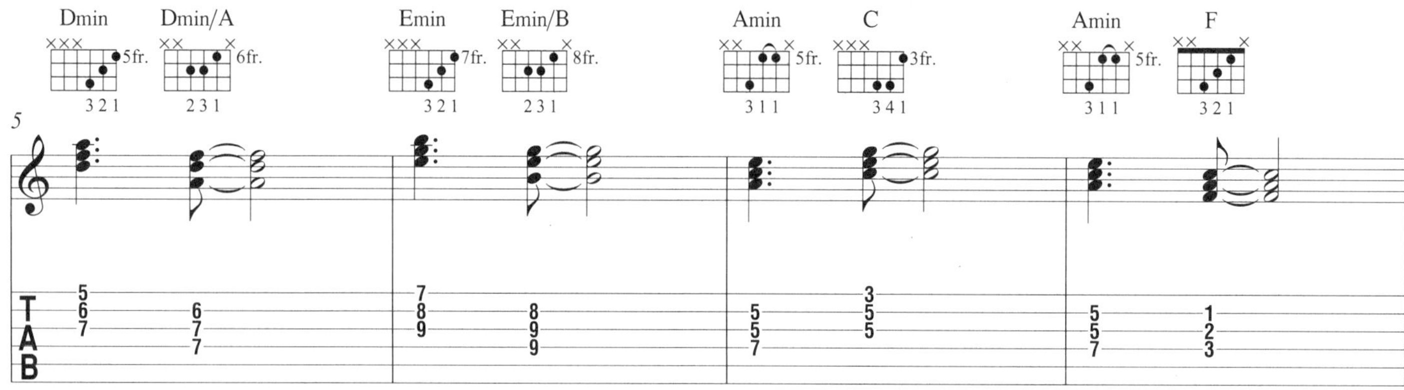

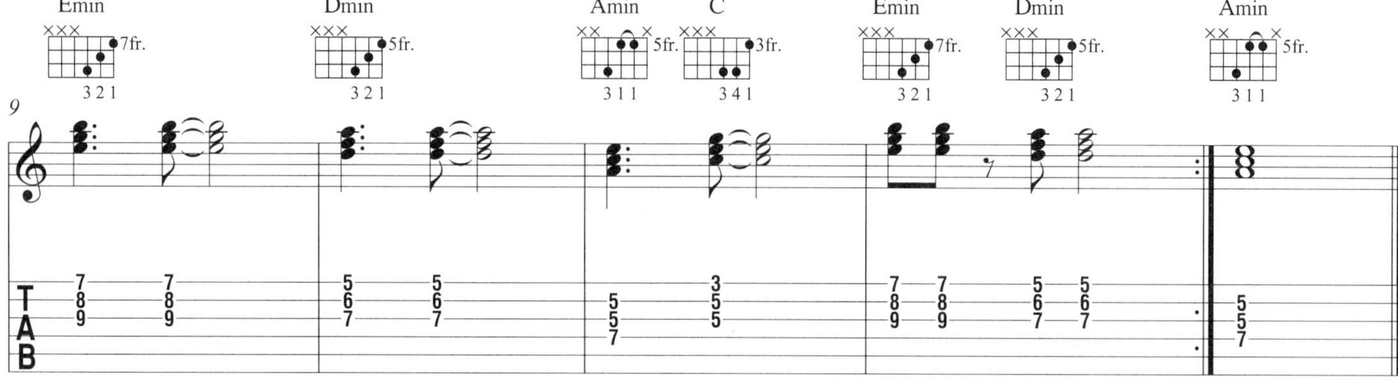

FIG. 7.11. Exercise 7.2. Triad Inversion Blues

Solid Take: Chord Changes

The term "chord change" is not exactly synonymous with "chord symbol." In fact, the term "chord change" refers to the point when one chord's duration has run out and it's time for a new chord. When players refer to "playing changes," the voicing is important, but the most important skill to have involves full delivery of the new sound, right at the point of chord change. The listener needs to hear the whole chord sound, right on time! Any effort that you expend to make a new chord sound right at the point of chord change is worth it.

Beginning guitarists are often more concerned with sustaining the current chord, often arriving late to the new chord. It is *better to leave the current chord early* than to arrive late at the new voicing. It's one of those things that sounds so natural when you hear it done, but when you try to do it yourself, you see what a challenge it really is.

Full, on-time delivery, please! The most challenging part of playing chord changes is the point at which the chord changes.

LESSON 8

Gospel Triads

A powerful way to use major and minor triad pairs is found in the concept of gospel triads. Combining a major triad with its nearby upstairs neighbor, found two frets or one major second above, yields an amazingly beautiful set of sounds for use in song sections with extended periods of a single major chord.

In the same way, combining a minor triad with its nearby *downstairs* neighbor, found two frets *below*, gives us a similar option for an extended period of minor tonality.

Time to get this concept under your fingers so that you can start using these options in your playing today. Let's start by reviewing the root position, first inversion, and second inversion of the C triad on the string set ③②①.

44

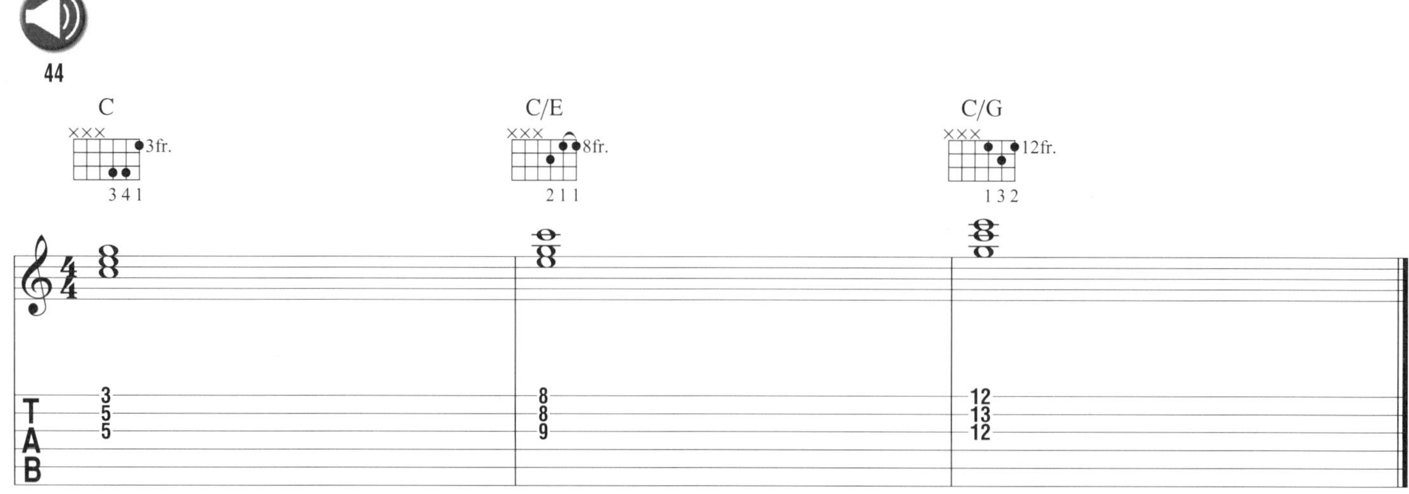

FIG. 8.1. C Major Triad Inversions on String Set ③②①

Next, let's run through the inversions of a D minor triad on ③②①. D minor is the upper-neighbor triad of C major.

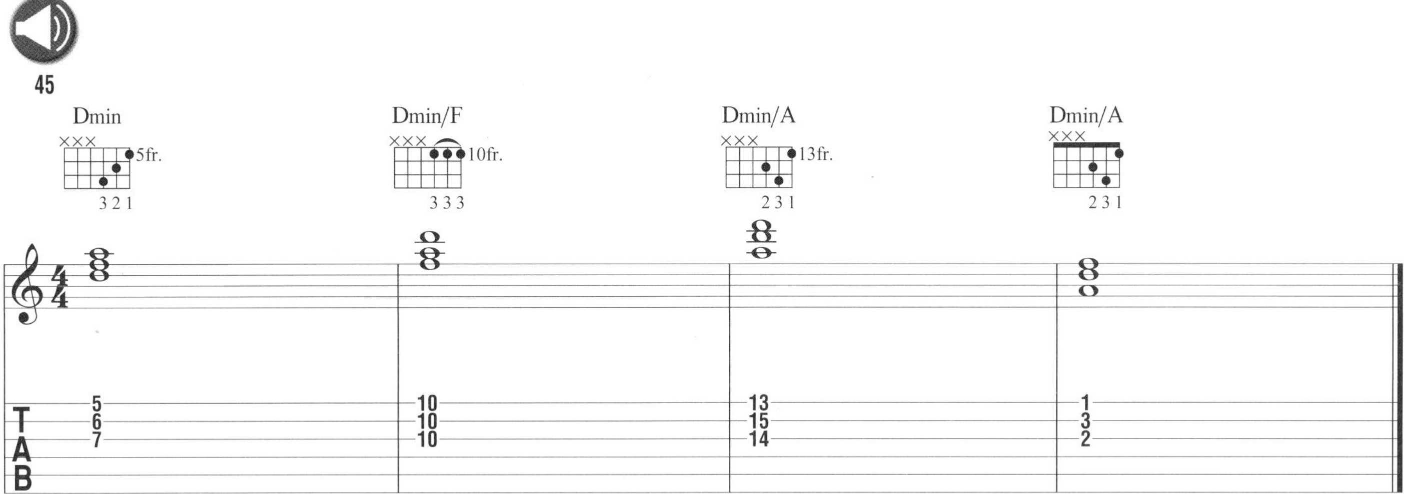

FIG. 8.2. D Minor Triad on ③②①

If your guitar has a cutaway, you may wish to play the second inversion Dmin/A in the thirteenth position, as depicted here. Steel-string acoustic and nylon string guitarists might prefer the first position Dmin/A for ease of playing. Try to learn both.

The following examples will be using this higher position of Dmin/A for demonstration. Please adapt as needed.

Performance of the two triads, in various inversions, produces a beautiful resultant harmonic texture.

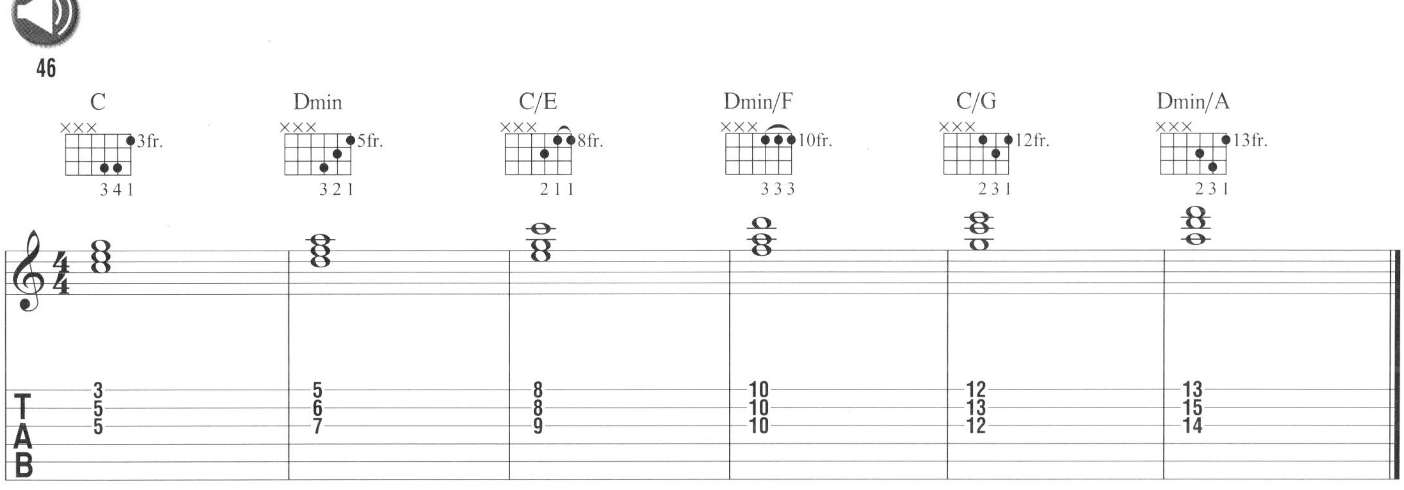

FIG. 8.3. Gospel Triads: C Major and D Minor Triad on ③②①

This set of voicings works very well when a guitarist is looking to have harmonic motion over a static section of a piece. The gospel C/Dmin triad pair works well when there's an extended period of C major tonality *or* an extended period of D minor tonality.

Exercise 8.1. C Major/D Minor Vamp Emphasizing Major

Using the backing track, experiment with the use of the C major and D minor triads over the bass line provided. One suggestion: When beginning or ending of your phrases, emphasize one of the C major triad inversions. It can be helpful to think of C as "home" and D minor as "away from home."

Here's the bass line, in case you want to play along or if you'd like to record the bass line in sequencing software or a looper.

47, 48

FIG. 8.4. Exercise 8.1. C Major/D Minor Vamp Emphasizing Major

Use the same voicings, but this time, emphasize the Dmin member of the triad pair at the beginning and end of phrases. This time, Dmin can be thought of as home, and C is away from home.

Exercise 8.2. C Major/D Minor Vamp Emphasizing Minor

49, 50

FIG. 8.5. Exercise 8.2. C Major/D Minor Vamp Emphasizing Minor

GOSPEL SCALE

Another use of the gospel triads pair is to arrange the chord tones to build a resultant scale. C major and D minor have no common tones, so this six-note, or *hexatonic*, scale can be useful for improvisation or melodic fills when accompanying others. In figure 8.6, filled-in noteheads correspond to the D minor triad tones and the hollow noteheads are from the C triad.

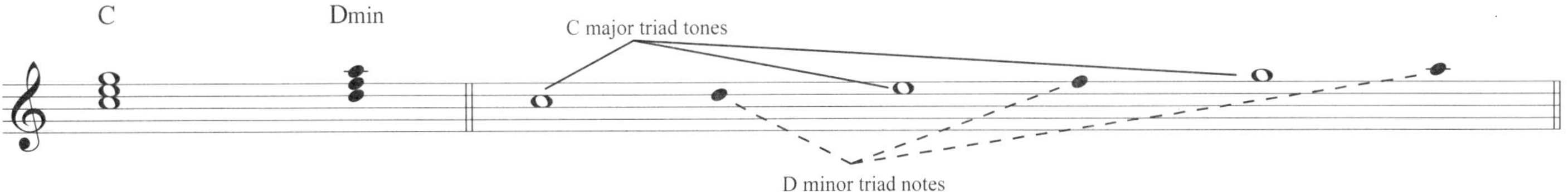

FIG. 8.6. Combining Notes of C Major and D Minor

Here is a possible fingering strategy for the C/Dmin gospel scale starting from C. The resultant scale is identical to a C major pentatonic scale with an additional note, the fourth.

51

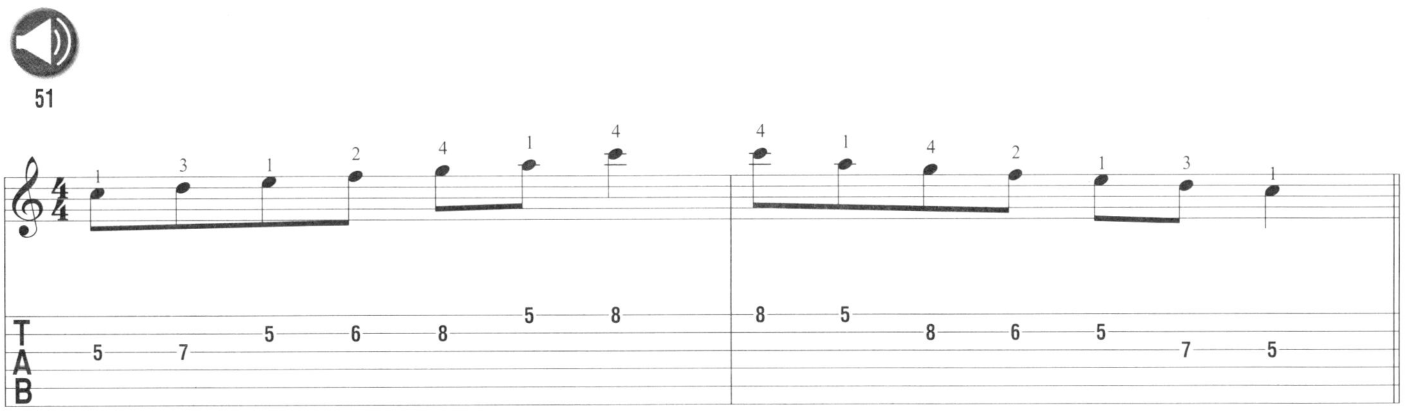

FIG. 8.7. C Gospel Scale

Is this scale:

1. C major pentatonic with an added fourth degree?
2. C major scale with a missing seventh degree?
3. Both of the above?

The answer is (3) Both of the above.

Due to the use of this set of sounds in so many different styles, this scale is known by many names, including the following: gospel scale/hexatonic scale/bluegrass scale/Celtic scale/Grateful Dead scale/Allman Brothers scale

Running the same scale, but starting from A to A, you may find that this fingering is an easier adaptation of the scale commonly known as A minor pentatonic with an added note, again the F.

IMPROVISATION WITH THE GOSPEL SCALE

Exercise 8.3. A Minor Seventh Pentatonic with ♭6 Added

The same gospel scale can be played from any of its notes. Seeing A as the root, a minor seventh pentatonic with a ♭6 added is another way to see the six notes we've been working with. Using the scale from A or the scale from C, practice improvising over the preceding C major and D minor exercises. Attempt to play a melodic phrase with some harmonic punctuations. Work to show the world that improvisation involves both melodic and harmonic options!

52

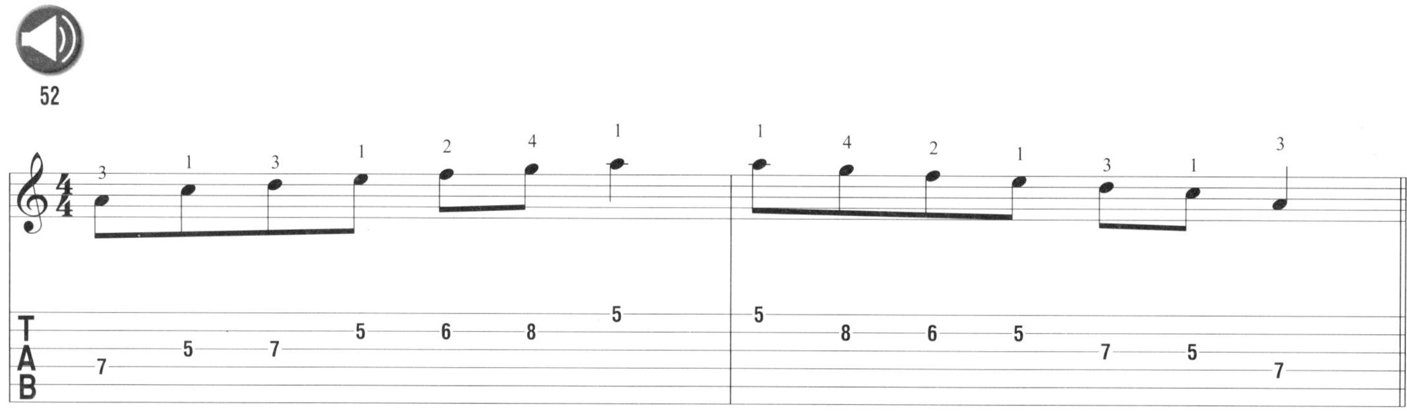

FIG. 8.8. Exercise 8.3. C Gospel Scale from A

Exercise 8.4. Gospel Triads

In this exercise, the G major tonality is our target for chords and improvisation.

53, 54

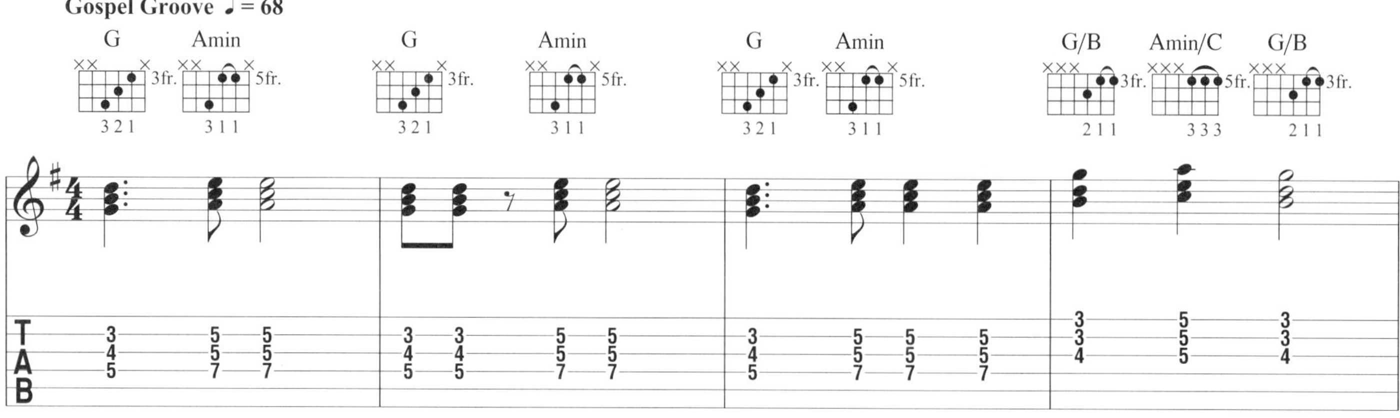

FIG. 8.9. Exercise 8.4. Gospel Triads

LESSON 9

Suspended 4 Triads (4 Replaces 3)

Another common type of triad is the sus4, or *suspended fourth* triad. Standard practice among writers and arrangers when manipulating chords is to use the rule of "4 replaces 3." The resulting triadic shape contains the same root and 5 as major or minor triads, but with the fourth degree instead of a major or minor 3 in the middle. Neither major nor minor, sus triads offer an interestingly vague color, providing a tension that is easily resolved by bringing the suspended 4 down to the 3.

55

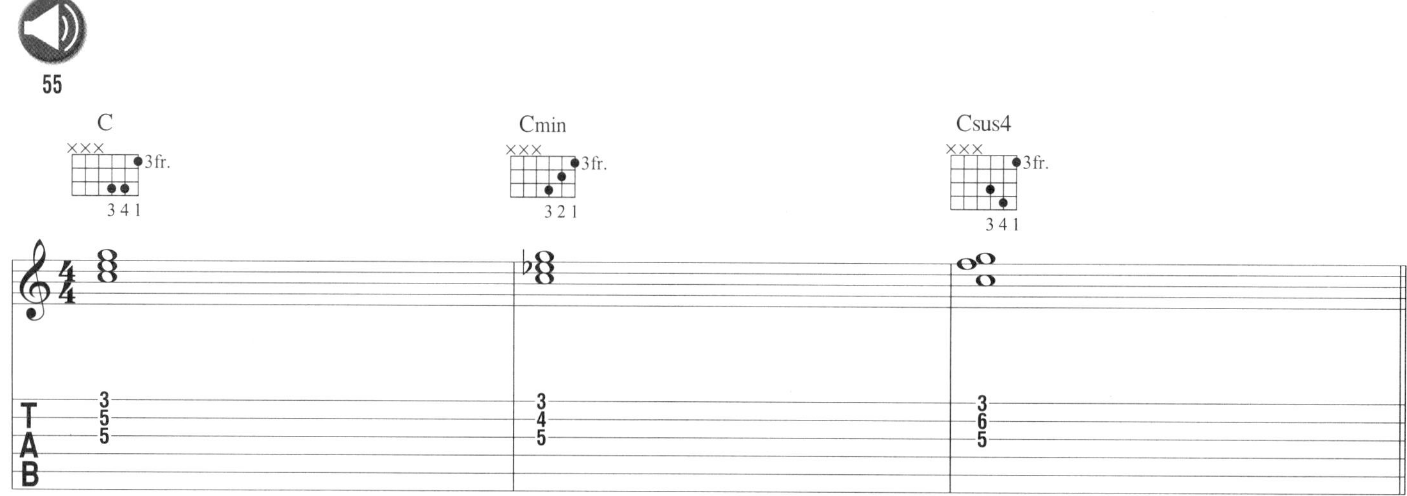

FIG. 9.1. Comparison of Major, Minor, and Suspended Triads

The intervallic structure of a sus4 chord is as follows. Note the outer boundary of the perfect fifth is the same as with major and minor triads, but with the middle tone a perfect fourth above the root and a major second below the fifth of the chord.

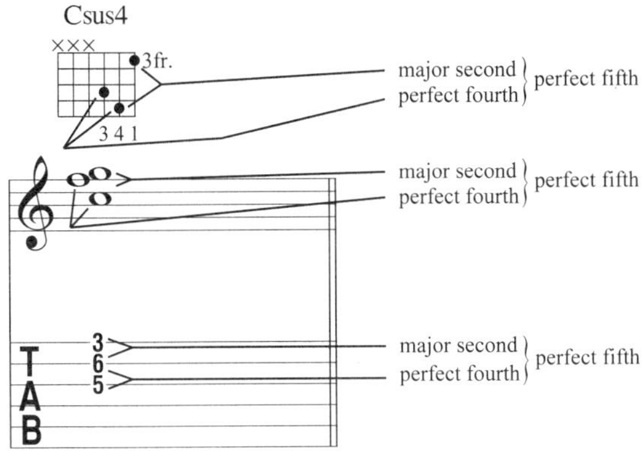

FIG. 9.2. Csus4 Triad Intervals

Although the sus4 most often resolves to major, it can certainly resolve to minor, or it can just leave the "suspended" or unresolved feeling in the listener. For string set ③②①, the 4 is found on the second string; on strings ④③②, the 4 is found on the third string. The chord suffixes sus and sus4 will be interchangeable terms throughout this book.

SUS4 SPREAD TRIAD VOICINGS

It's possible to voice sus4 triads as spread triads. Returning to our cards: Replacing the 3 card with the 4 card, we can derive a spread sus chord. The second tone is moved up one octave.

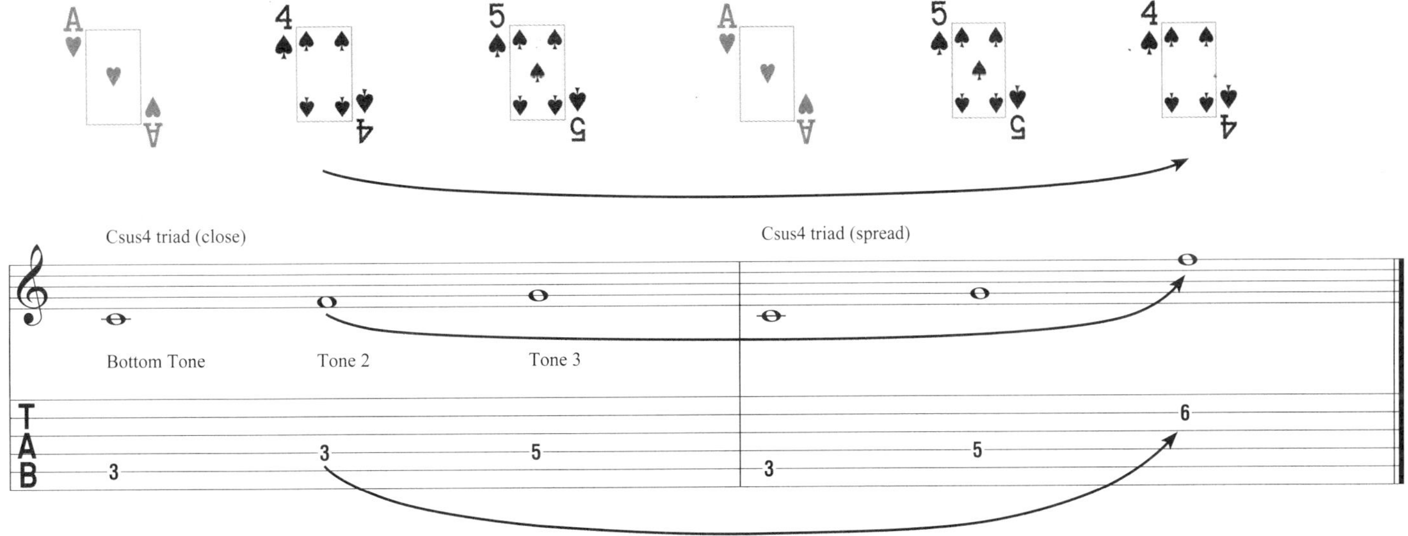

FIG. 9.3. Csus4 with Playing Cards

The G can be played as ③ open or at ④ fret 5. In this figure, for convenience, the G is first played as ③ open and then at ④ fret 5. Spread triads have several options for fingering, and this one is the easiest to perform for most guitarists.

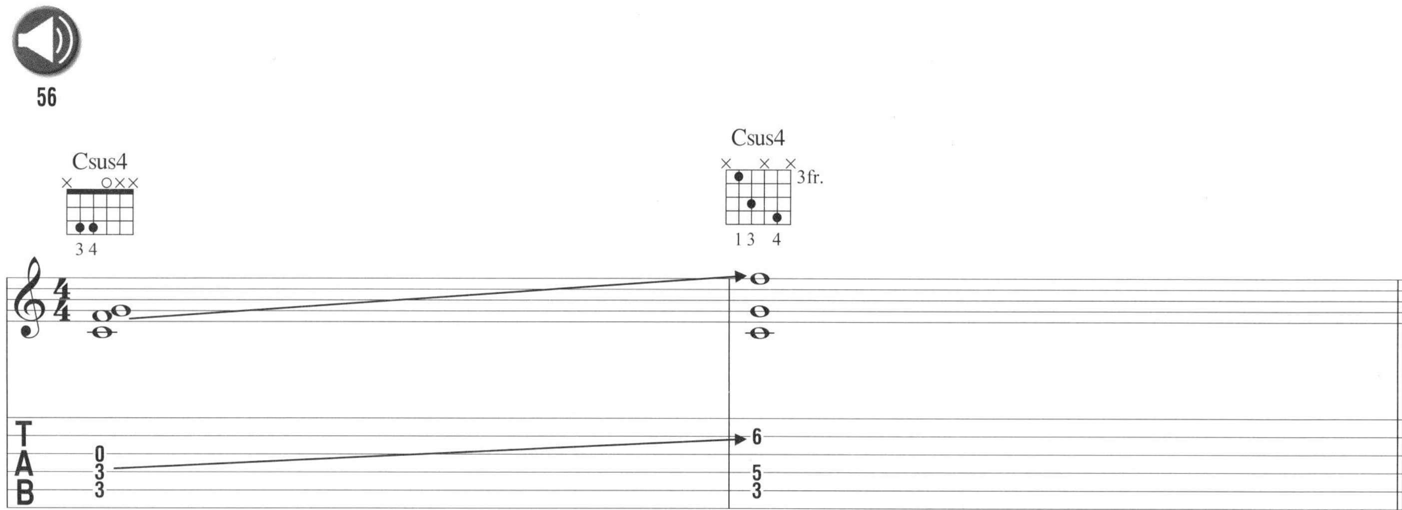

FIG. 9.4. Csus4 with Notation

Running through the raise 2 process, here is the Csus4 triad in close, and then spread positions.

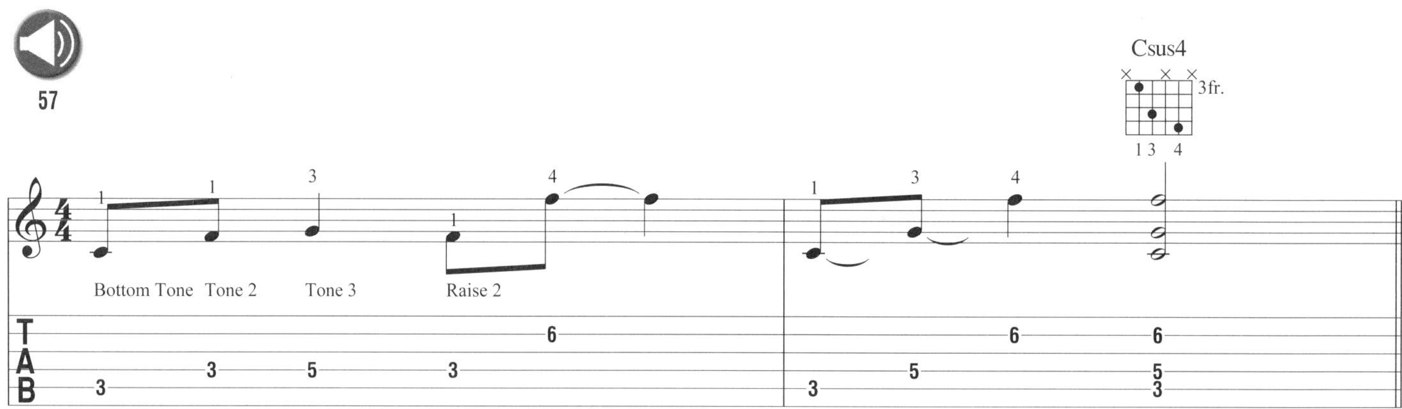

FIG. 9.5. Csus4 Raise 2

Exercise 9.1. Sus4 Triads on ④③② and ③②①

58, 59

Practice sus4 triads on strings ④③② and ③②①, moving in perfect fourths through twelve keys.

Straight 8ths ♩ = 82

Csus4 8fr. 3 4 1 — Fsus4 8fr. 3 4 1 — B♭sus4 6fr. 3 4 1 — E♭sus4 6fr. 3 4 1 — A♭sus4 4fr. 3 4 1 — D♭sus4 4fr. 3 4 1 — F♯sus4 2fr. 3 4 1

Bsus4 2fr. 3 4 1 — Esus4 7fr. 3 4 1 — Asus4 5fr. 3 4 1 — Dsus4 5fr. 3 4 1 — Gsus4 3fr. 3 4 1 — Csus4 3fr. 3 4 1 — Csus4 8fr. 3 4 1

Csus4 8fr. 3 4 1 — Fsus4 8fr. 3 4 1 — B♭sus4 6fr. 3 4 1 — E♭sus4 6fr. 3 4 1 — A♭sus4 4fr. 3 4 1 — D♭sus4 4fr. 3 4 1 — F♯sus4 2fr. 3 4 1 — Bsus4 2fr. 3 4 1

Esus4 7fr. 3 4 1 — Asus4 5fr. 3 4 1 — Dsus4 5fr. 3 4 1 — Gsus4 3fr. 3 4 1 — Csus4 3fr. 3 4 1 — Csus4 8fr. 3 4 1 — Csus4 8fr. 3 4 1

FIG. 9.6. Exercise 9.1. Sus4 Triads on ④③② and ③②①

Exercise 9.2. Suspended Triads in Close and Spread Voicings

Play through the following twelve-bar blues-based exercise to explore sus4, major, and minor triadic shapes. Work to perform the rhythms as notated and demonstrated. In bar 13, the triads are in spread voicings. If those are too challenging, you can simply repeat the voicings in the first twelve bars. Either way, this exercise will help you to develop flexibility with your voicings and develop strength in your fretting hand.

60, 61

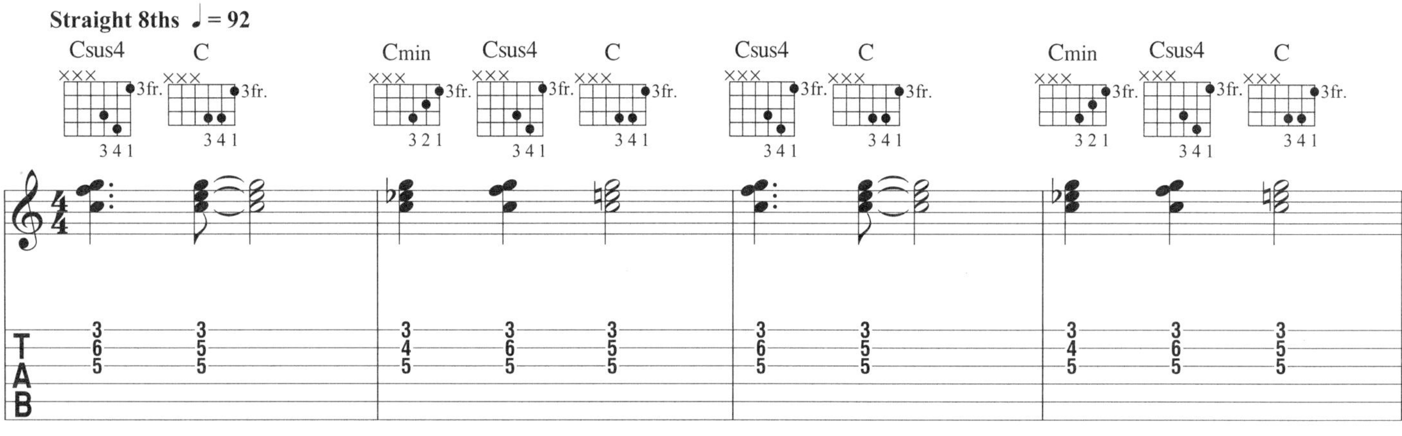

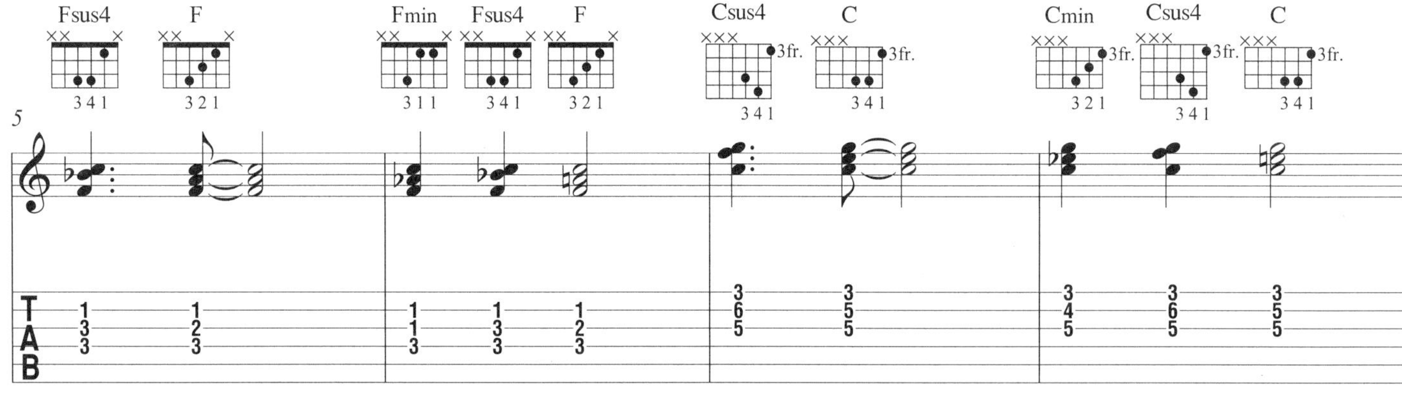

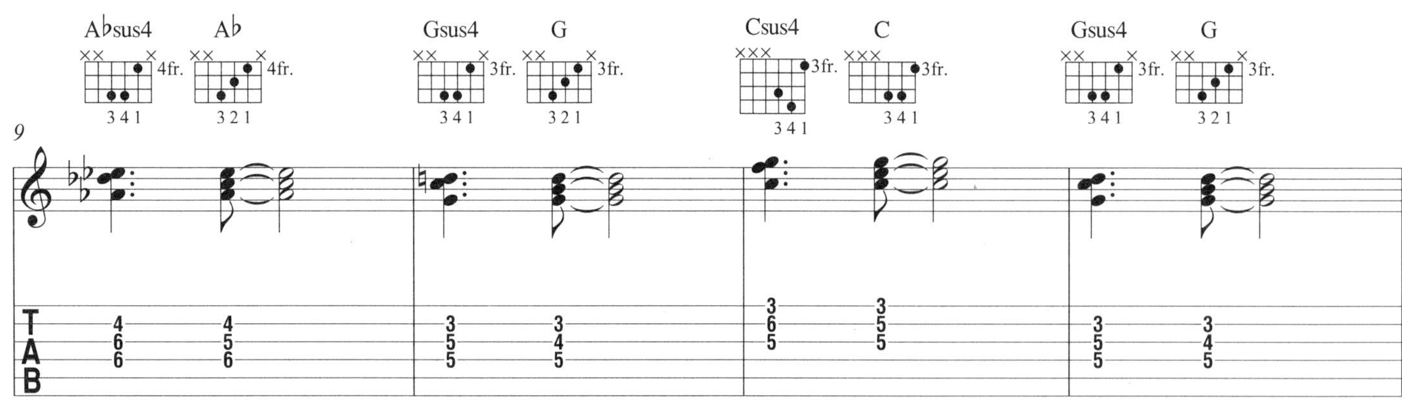

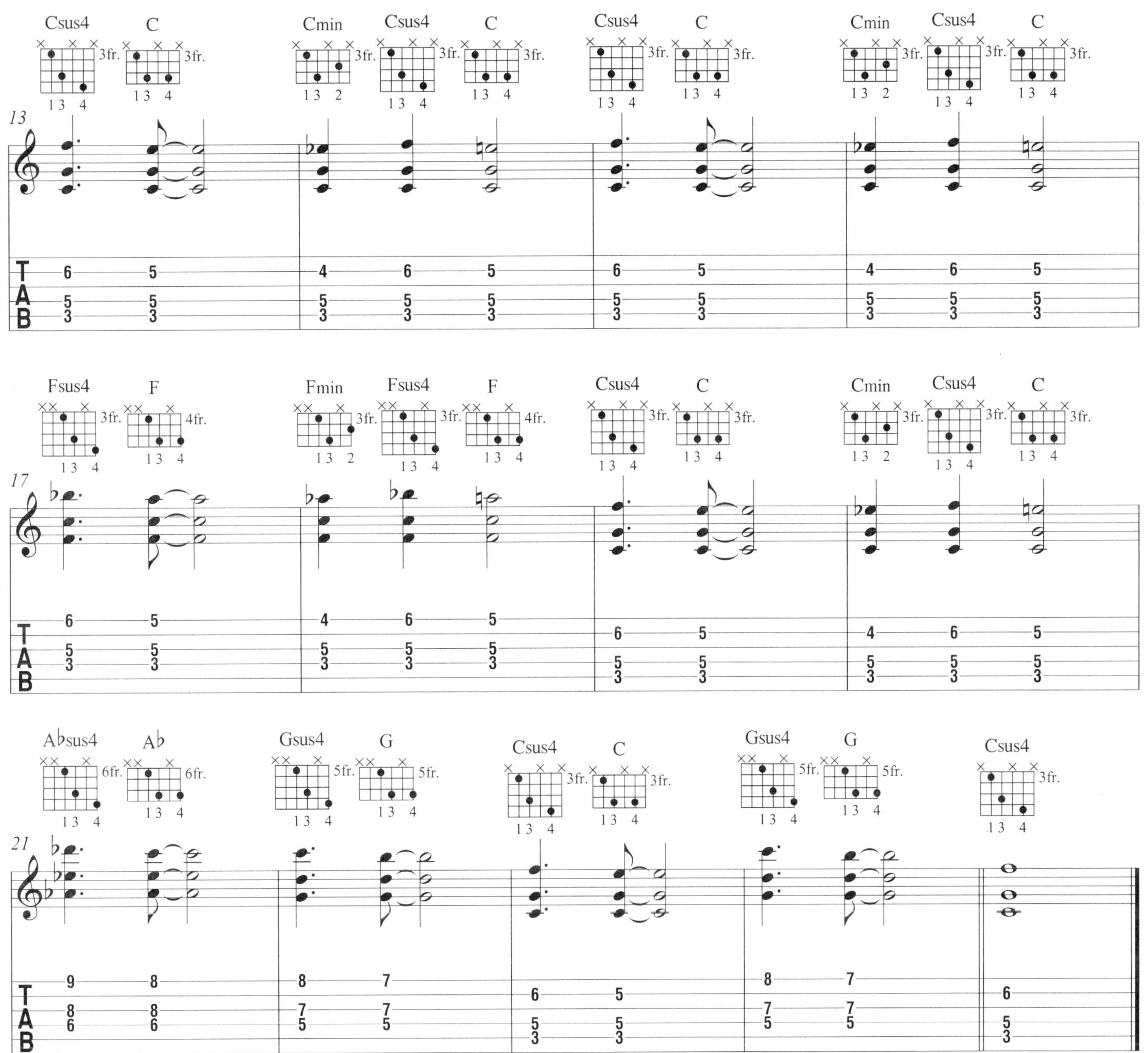

FIG. 9.7. Exercise 9.2. Suspended Triads in Close and Spread Voicings

LESSON 10

Diminished and Augmented Triads

DIMINISHED TRIADS

62

A diminished triad consists of two minor thirds. Cdim is C Eb Gb. Diminished triads can be seen as similar to minor triads but with a b5. If you know a voicing for Cmin, it's simple to build a Cdim triad by simply lowering the 5 of the minor chord.

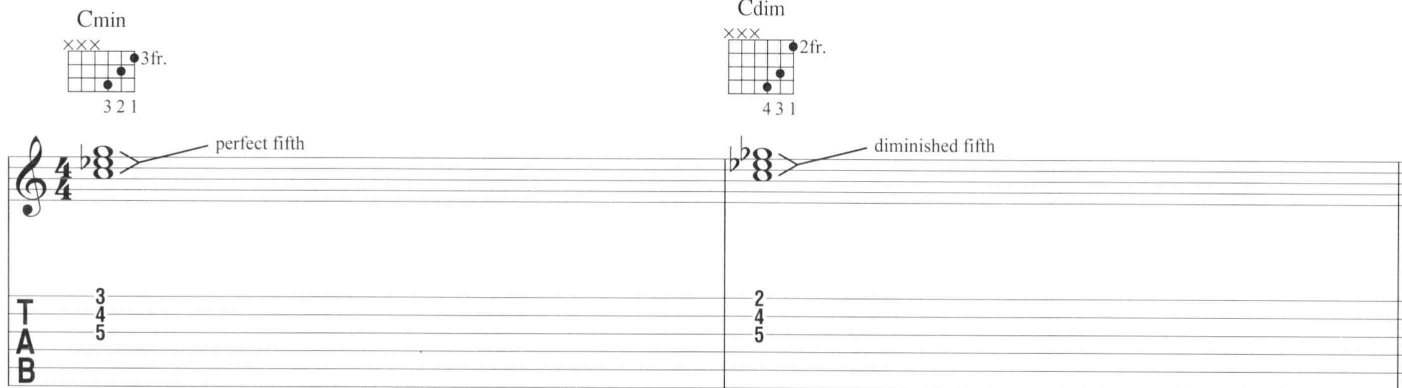

FIG. 10.1. Minor and Diminished Triads Compared

The root position diminished triad consists of two minor thirds. The diminished fifth interval, found from the root to the ♭5, is likely the reason for the triad's name.

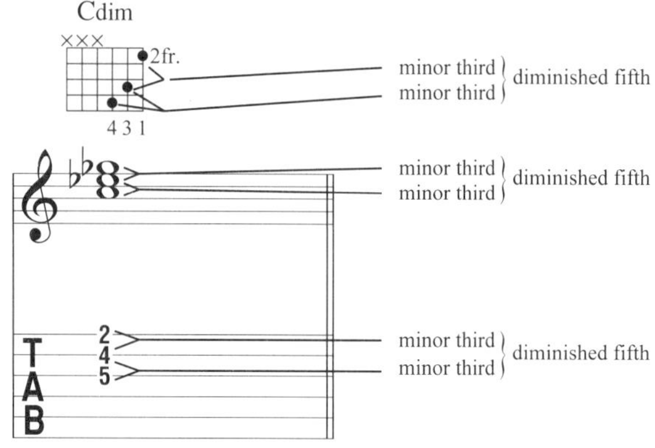

FIG. 10.2. Intervals of C Diminished

Diminished triads may seem to be chord blocks that don't apply to their style of music and will never will—an unrealistic deep dive into chord voicings in the back pages of a guitar book.

Q: *Why study diminished triads?*

A: You're already playing them all of the time! If you've ever played this voicing for D7, you've played a chord that contains a concealed diminished triad.

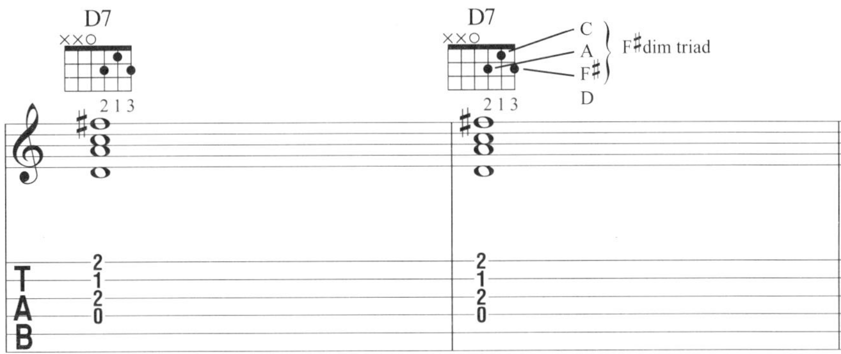

FIG. 10.3. F♯dim Triad within D7 Chord

A D7 contains the notes D F♯ A C. The notes of an F♯dim triad are F♯ A C. It is impossible to play a complete D7 without the three notes of the F♯dim triad. It's possible to look at a D7 chord as F♯dim played with a D added in the bass. In Berklee nomenclature, D7 contains two *lower structure triads*: D and F♯dim. Every standard dominant chord has two triadic residents: a major triad from root and a diminished triad built from its third.

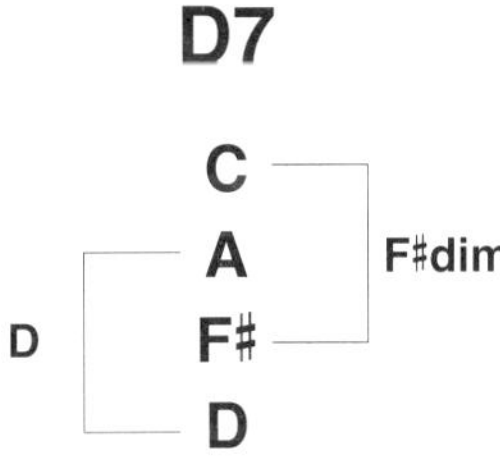

FIG. 10.4. D7 Lower Structure Triads

If you are playing on a D7 vamp with another guitarist, it's redundant (and musically cluttered) for both of you to play the same voicing in the same part of the fretboard. Open up the sound and other dimensions of harmonic sound by exploring the F♯dim triad (and its inversions) while the other guitarist stays on a standard D7.

64, 65

Exercise 10.1. Diminished Triads on ④③② and ③②①

FIG. 10.5. Exercise 10.1. Diminished Triads on ④③② and ③②①

Diminished Spread Triad Voicings

To build a spread diminished triad shape, start in close position, then raise the second tone from the bottom up an octave.

FIG. 10.6. Routine for Building Cdim Spread

66, 67

Exercise 10.2. Building Spread Diminished Triads

Practice diminished triads in spread voicings around twelve keys.

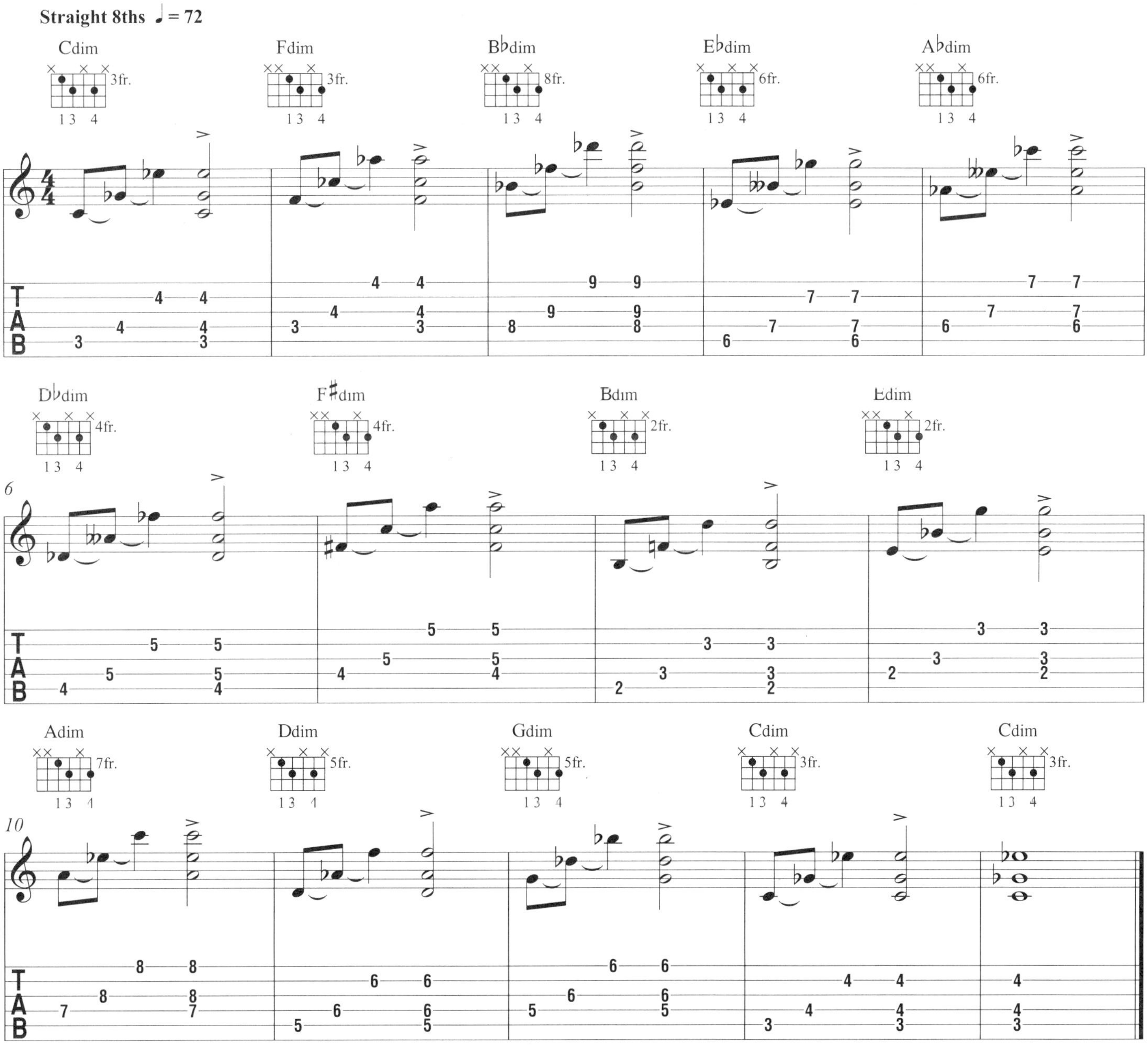

Straight 8ths ♩ = 72

Cdim Fdim B♭dim E♭dim A♭dim D♭dim F♯dim Bdim Edim Adim Ddim Gdim Cdim Cdim

FIG. 10.7. Exercise 10.2. Building Spread Diminished Triads

AUGMENTED TRIADS

The augmented triad consists of two major thirds. Built from C, that yields C E G♯. The notes are the same as a major triad with a sharped fifth. The G♯ is an augmented fifth away from C, hence the name. Wherever you can play a major triad on the neck, raising the fifth of the chord will result in an augmented triad.

68

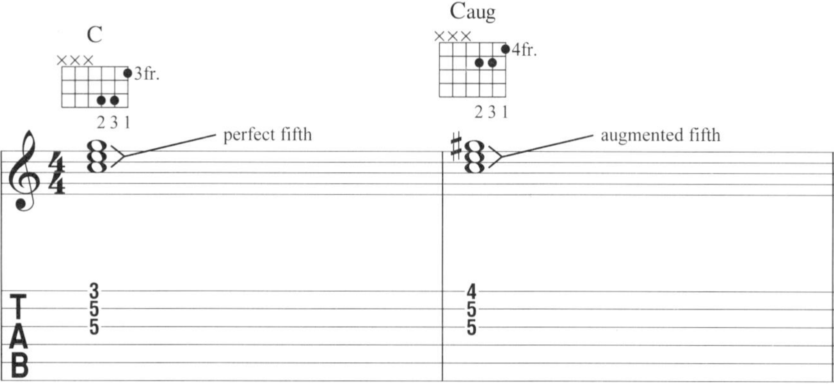

FIG. 10.8. Major and Augmented Comparison

The augmented triad is unique in that it is made up of two major thirds. The augmented fifth is one half step larger than we've seen in any of the triad shapes so far.

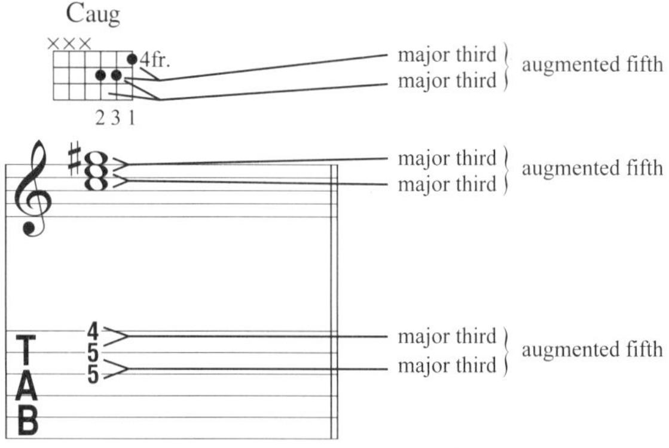

FIG. 10.9. Intervals Contained in Augmented Triad

Augmented Spread Triad Voicings

Move the second voice up one octave, resulting in a spread Caug triad in root position.

69

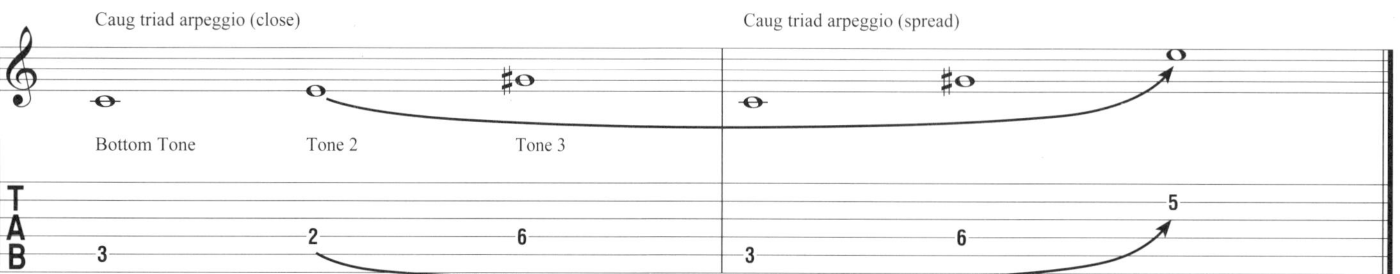

FIG. 10.10. Augmented Triad Spread

Exercise 10.3. Major/Augmented Spread Triad Blues

This exercise will help you to solidify your command of spread augmented triad shapes, and their close relationship with major triad shapes. Watch out for the × marks on these shapes, being careful to ensure that there are no extra strings trespassing, lessening the impact of these beautiful, pure sounds. Use the arch in your fretting fingers to mute the unwanted string sounds.

70, 71

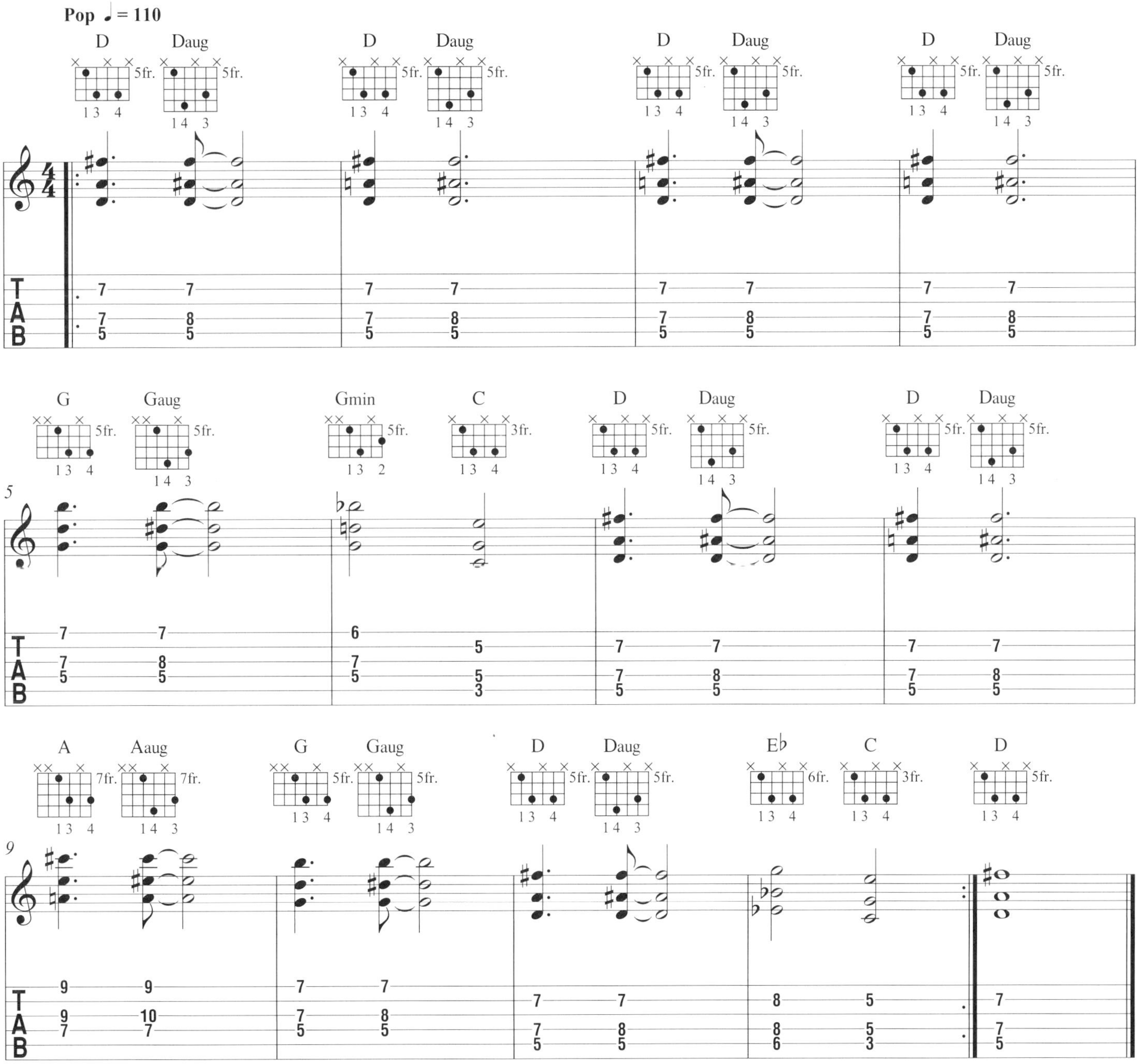

Pop ♩ = 110

D Daug D Daug D Daug D Daug

G Gaug Gmin C D Daug D Daug

A Aaug G Gaug D Daug E♭ C D

FIG. 10.11. Exercise 10.3. Major/Augmented Spread Triad Blues

LESSON 11

Triads Up the Fretboard

It's great to have options when we're playing triads on the fretboard. This makes it so you have tons of options wherever you are. You'll be able to find a nearby chord wherever your hand happens to be—but, of course, it takes some time, effort, and understanding to get there.

"Up and down" the fretboard refers to going up the neck from lower fret numbers to higher frets and down the neck from higher frets to lower frets.

We go "up" to higher fret numbers and "down" to lower fret numbers. It's important to have mobility up and down the neck, while staying on the same string groups, changing registers.

It's also important to be able to stay in the same region of the fretboard, while varying the string sets that we use. When we go "across" the fretboard, we go from the higher pitched strings to the lower pitched strings or from the lower pitched strings to the higher pitched strings, while staying in the same general region of fret numbers.

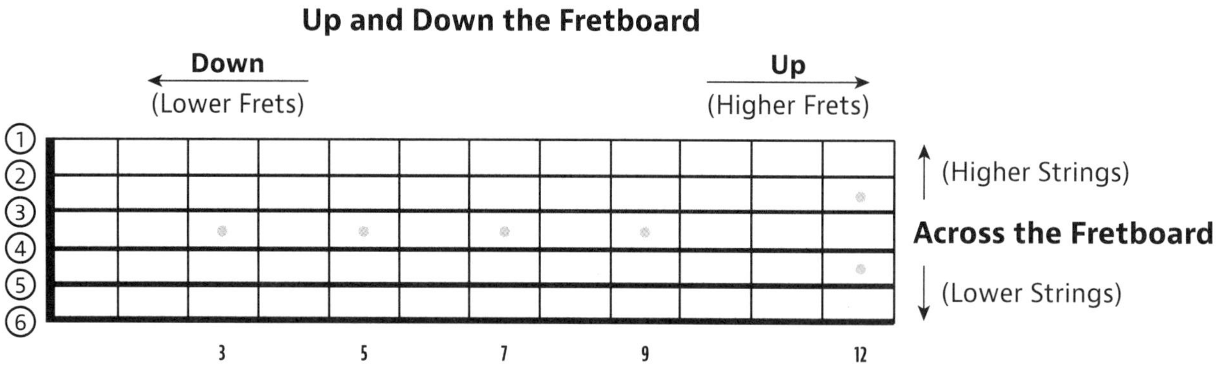

Up and Down the Fretboard

Down (Lower Frets)

Up (Higher Frets)

(Higher Strings)

Across the Fretboard

(Lower Strings)

① ② ③ ④ ⑤ ⑥

3 5 7 9 12

FIG. 11.1. Up and Down vs. Across the Fretboard

We'll be working on voicing shapes across the fretboard in the next chapter.

MAJOR TRIAD INVERSIONS UP THE FRETBOARD

Time to work out with inversions of a C triad in all inversions. Let's look at the root position, first inversion, and second inversions of a C triad, using our Inversions Generator format.

Chord Voicings (Low to High)

Any Major Triad			
Root Position	**First Inversion**	**Second Inversion**	
5	R	3	Lead
3	5	R	
R	3	5	Bottom Note

Chord Tones in Close Position Order

FIG. 11.2. Inversion Generator with Interval Names

Let's play the three inversions of C major on strings ③②①. On the top string set ③②①, root position is playable in third position, first inversion in eighth position, and second inversion in twelfth position.

The lowest tone is raised one octave to get to the next inversion. Notice which approach works better for you: the voicing stacks in the table (figure 11.2) or the notation (figure 11.3)? The answer can involve either approach.

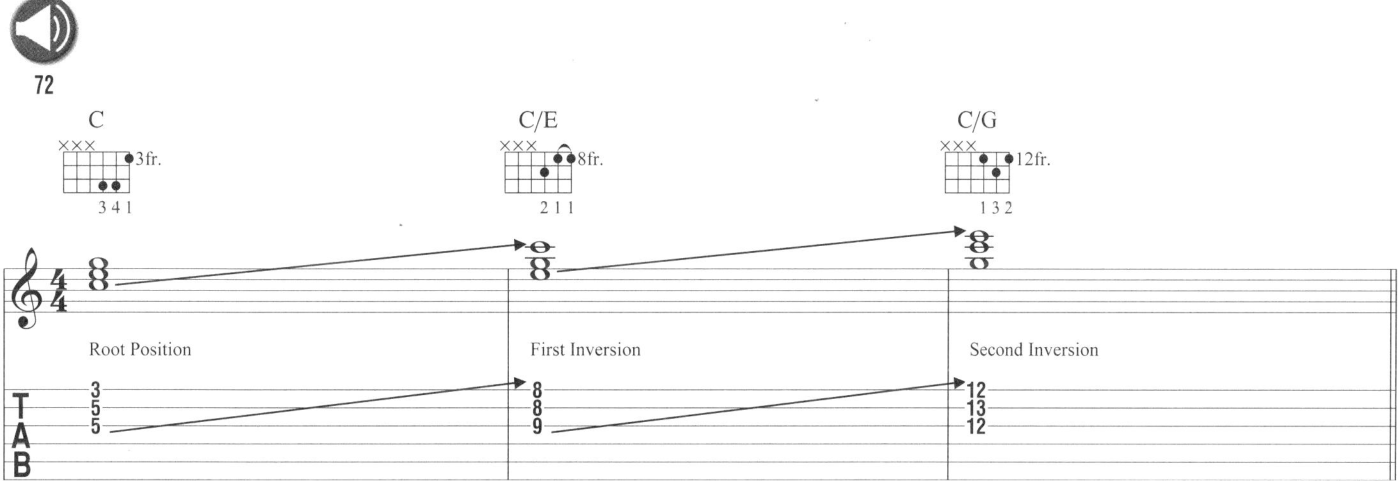

FIG. 11.3. C Major Triad Inversions on ③②① Up the Fretboard

Exercise 11.1. Major Triads in Four Keys on ③②①

Taking the keys of C, B♭, E♭, and B, practice playing all of the inversions of the major triad, always starting from root position. Ensure that you're focusing on the strings that are to be played, while avoiding the ×-marked strings.

73, 74

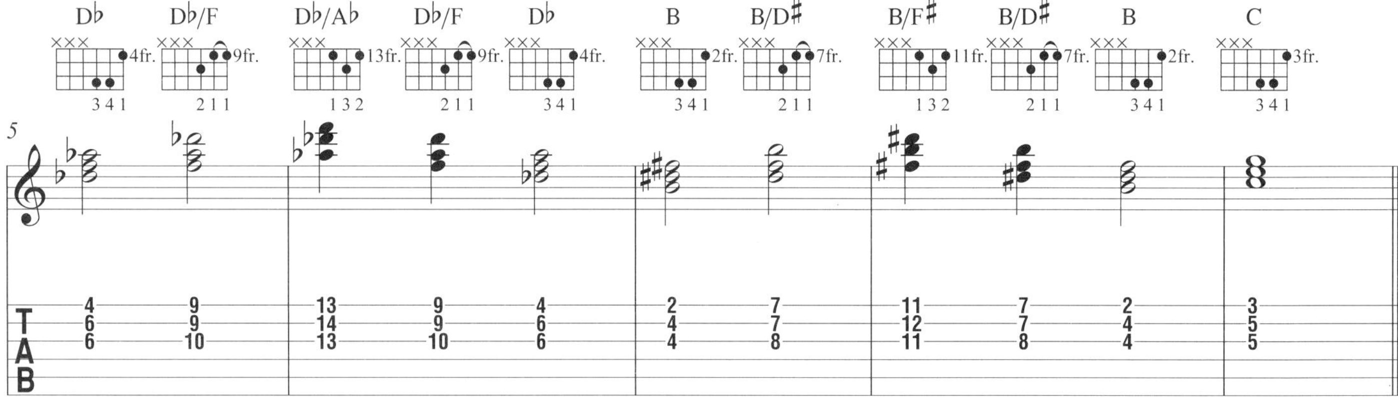

FIG. 11.4. Exercise 11.1. Major Triads in Four Keys on ③②①

Next, play the inversions of G major on ④③②.

75

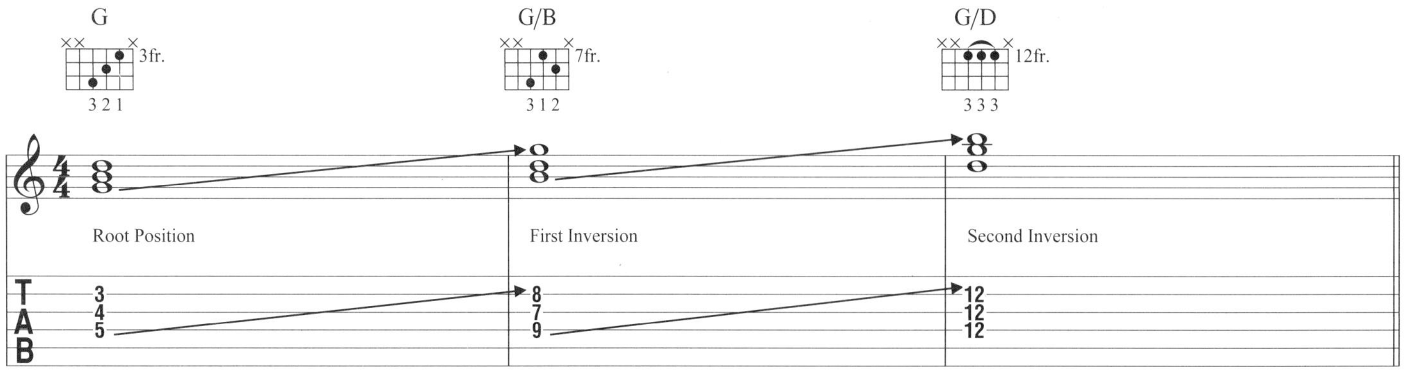

FIG. 11.5. G Major Triad on ④③②

Exercise 11.2. Major Triads on ④③② in Four Keys

Now on ④③②, run through the major triads in four more keys.

76, 77

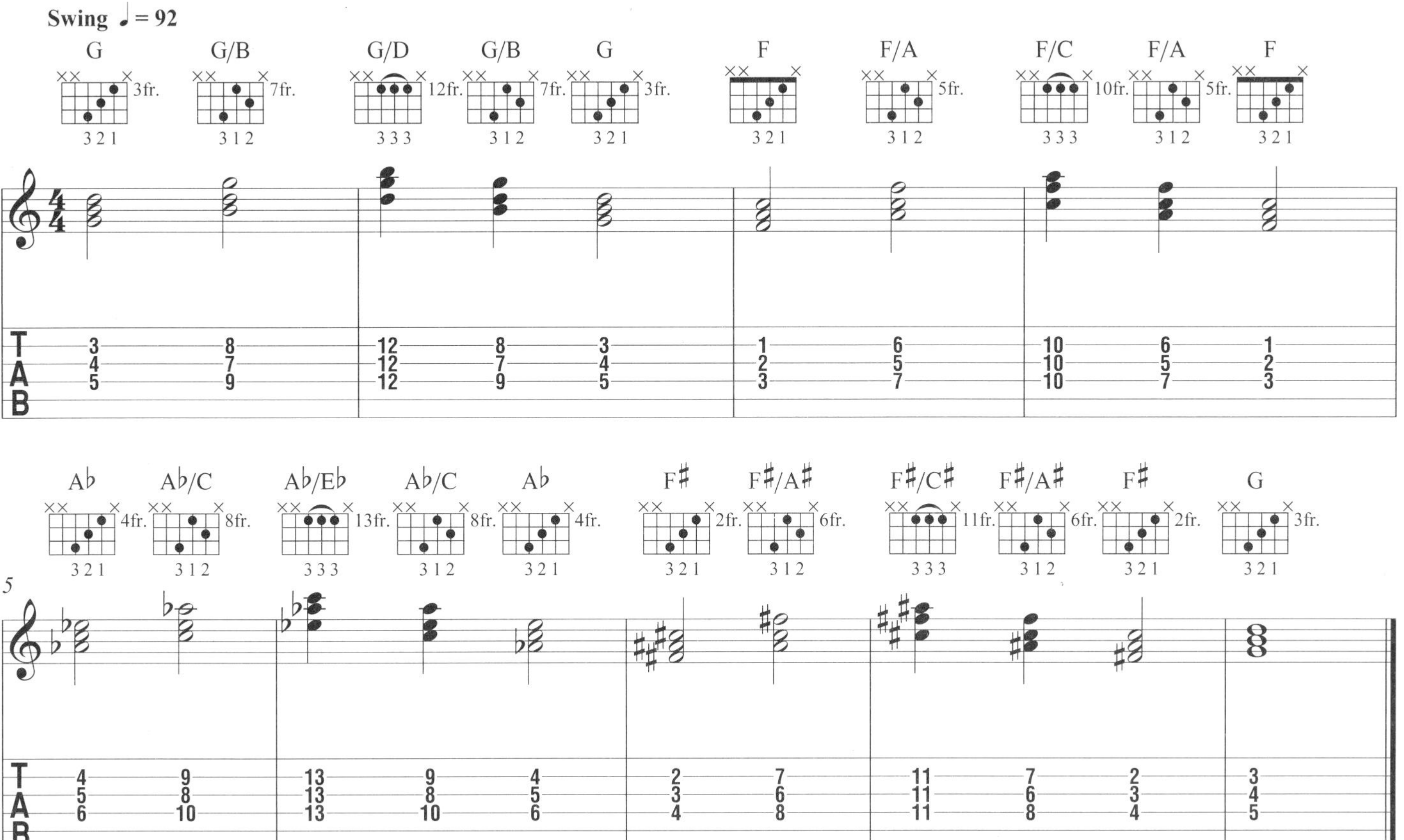

FIG. 11.6. Exercise 11.2. Major Triads on ④③② in Four Keys

MINOR TRIAD INVERSIONS UP THE FRETBOARD

Let's check out the inversions of minor, traveling up the fretboard. Bearing major triads in mind, it's relatively simple to flat the 3 and build the C minor triad, in first and second inversions.

Chord Voicings (Low to High)	Any Minor Triad			
	Root Position	**First Inversion**	**Second Inversion**	
	5	R	♭3	Lead
	♭3	5	R	
	R	♭3	5	Bottom Note
	Chord Tones in Close Position Order			

FIG. 11.7. Inversion Generator for Minor Triads on Strings ③②①

Minor Triads on Strings ③②①

Keep track of the note names in each of these shapes to gain control of C minor on ③②①. Use the Inversion Generator or use the notation. The bottom pitch is moved up one octave to get the next inversion. Keeping track of the root found in each shape can help you to gain control of these shapes.

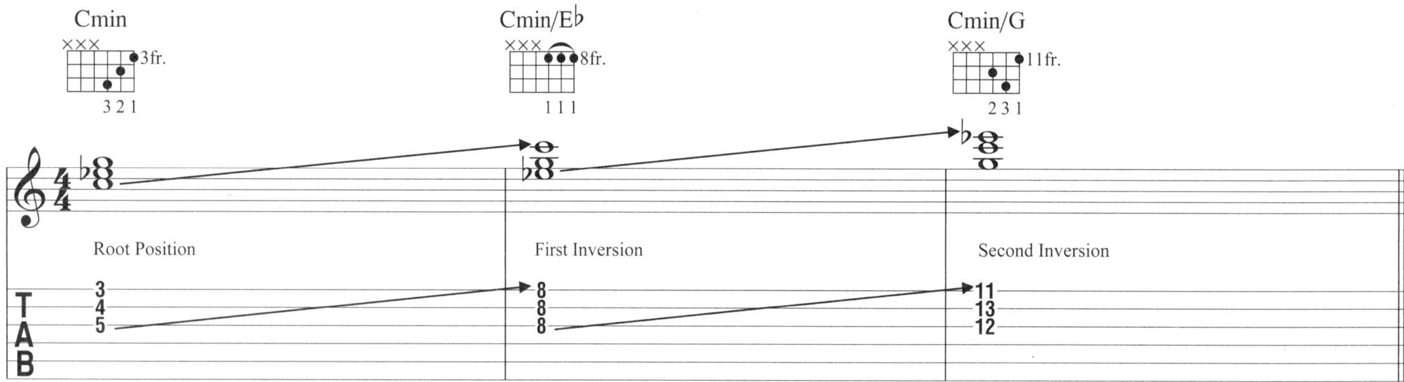

FIG. 11.8. Cmin Triad on ③②①

Minor Triads on Strings ④③②

The shapes of these voicings look a bit different on the second string set, but root, ♭3, and 5 are pretty easily found. The number of shapes we're working with may seem overwhelming, but keeping track of the root in each shape can help.

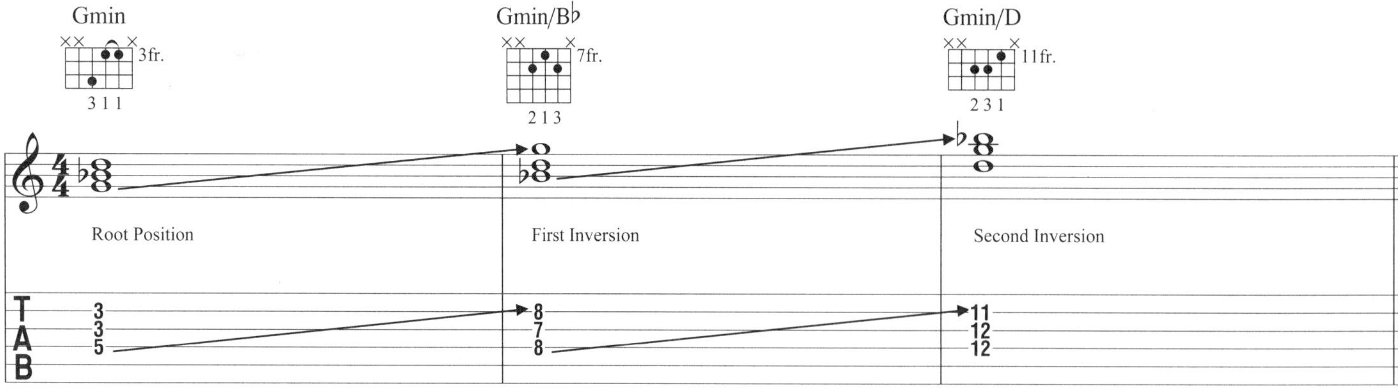

FIG. 11.9. Gmin Triad on ④③②

DIMINISHED TRIADS UP THE FRETBOARD ON ③②① AND ④③②

Relating the diminished to minor triads is very helpful. Find the fifth of the minor chord, and move it down one fret.

Chord Voicings (Low to High)	Cdim			
	Root Position	First Inversion	Second Inversion	
	♭5 (G♭)	R (C)	♭3 (E♭)	Lead
	♭3 (E♭)	♭5 (G♭)	R (C)	
	R (C)	♭3 (E♭)	♭5 (G♭)	Bottom Note

Chord Tones in Close Position Order

FIG. 11.10. Inversion Generator for Cdim

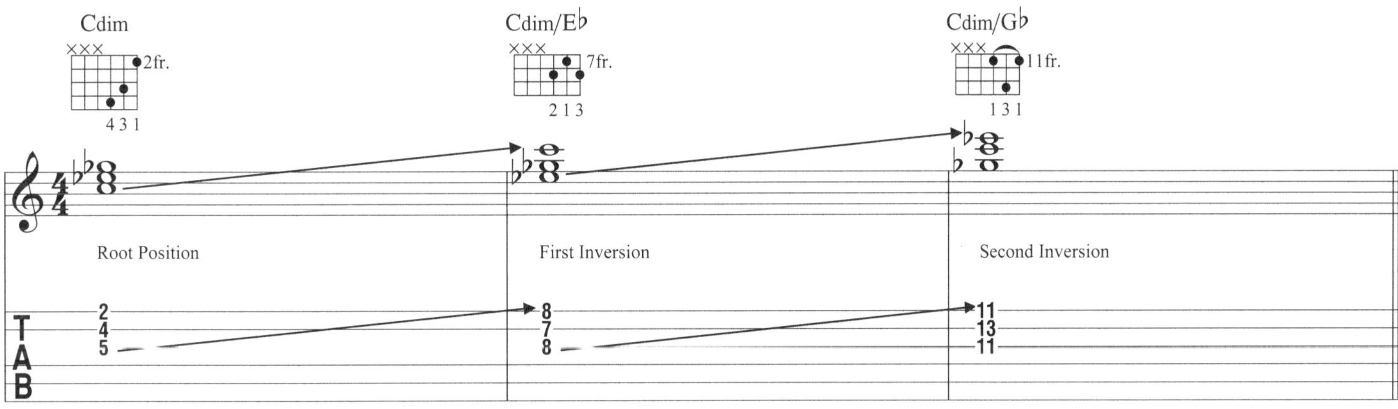

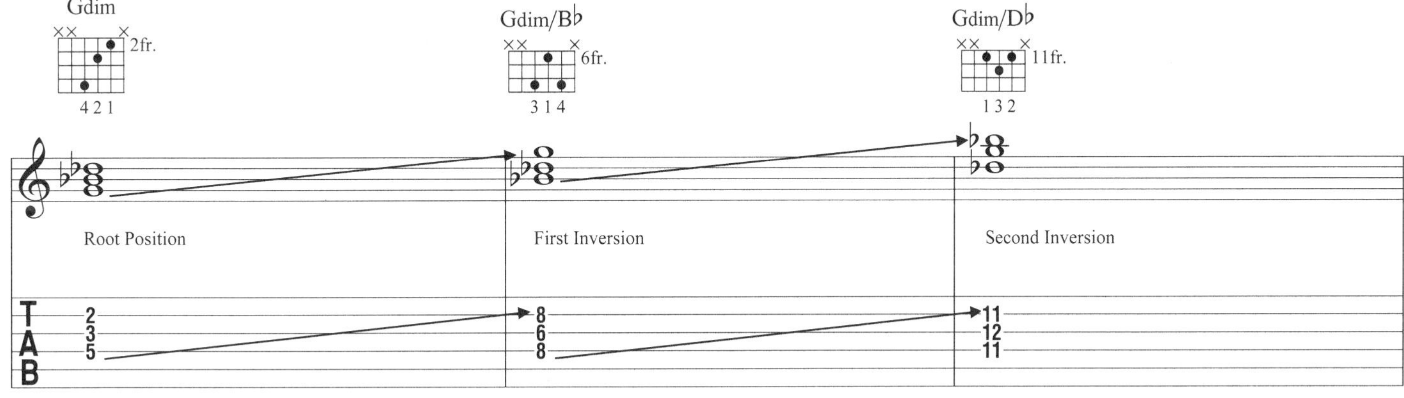

FIG. 11.11. Cdim on ③②① and Gdim on ④③②

AUGMENTED TRIADS UP THE FRETBOARD ON ③②① AND ④③②

Chord Voicings (Low to High)	Caug			
	Root Position	First Inversion	Second Inversion	
	♯5 (G♯)	R (C)	3 (E)	Lead
	3 (E)	♯5 (G♯)	R (C)	
	R (C)	3 (E)	♯5 (G♯)	Bottom Note
	Chord Tones in Close Position Order			

FIG. 11.12. Inversion Generator for Augmented Triad

The augmented chord quality is unique in the world of triads. When moving up the fretboard, the shape is the same for root, first inversion, and second inversion. How is this so? Twelve half steps in one octave, four half steps in a major third interval, three notes in a triad. As long as you stay to the same string set, all the inversions contain the same configuration of fingers. The challenge is to hit the correct voicing when shifting to the next inversion. The easiest way is to spell the augmented triad in your mind and target the next voicing with accuracy. For example, get the shape of the first voicing for Caug, and spell the triad: C E G♯. The correct frets are 5, 9, and 13.

81

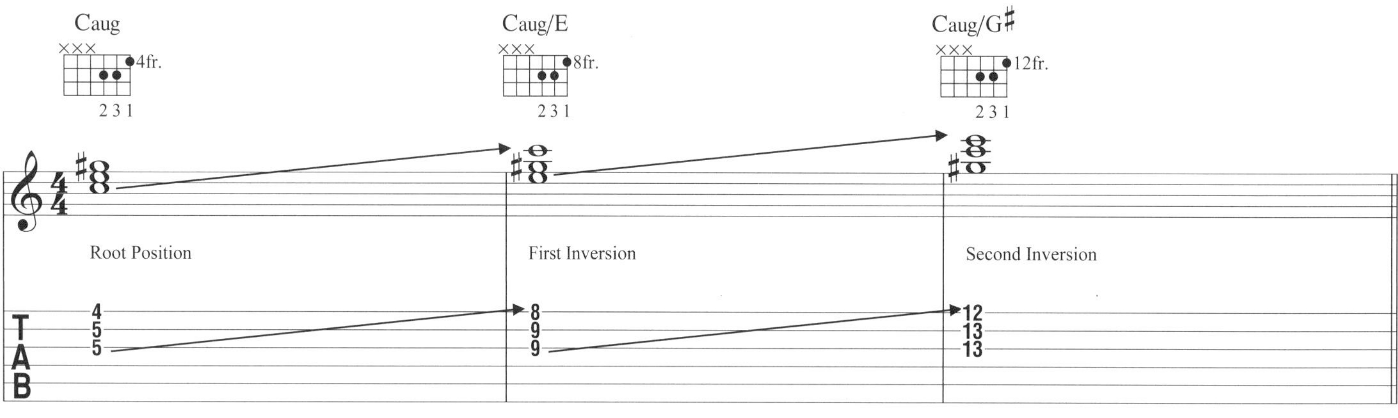

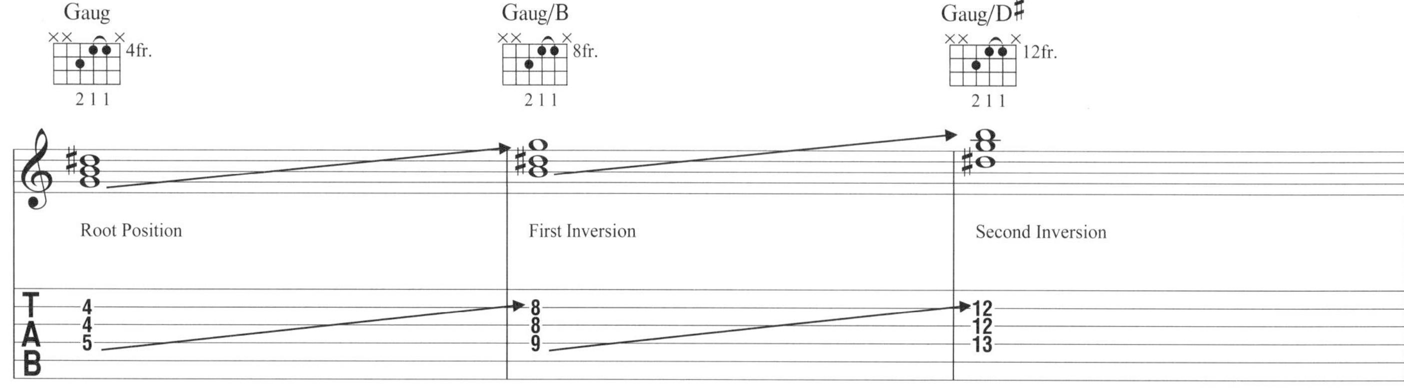

FIG. 11.13. Augmented Triads on ③②① and ④③②

SUS4 TRIADS UP THE FRETBOARD ON ③②① AND ④③②

Chord Voicings (Low to High)

sus4			
Root Position	First Inversion	Second Inversion	
5	R	4	Lead
4	5	R	
R	4	5	Bottom Note

Chord Tones in Close Position Order

FIG. 11.14. Inversion Generator for sus4 Triad

82

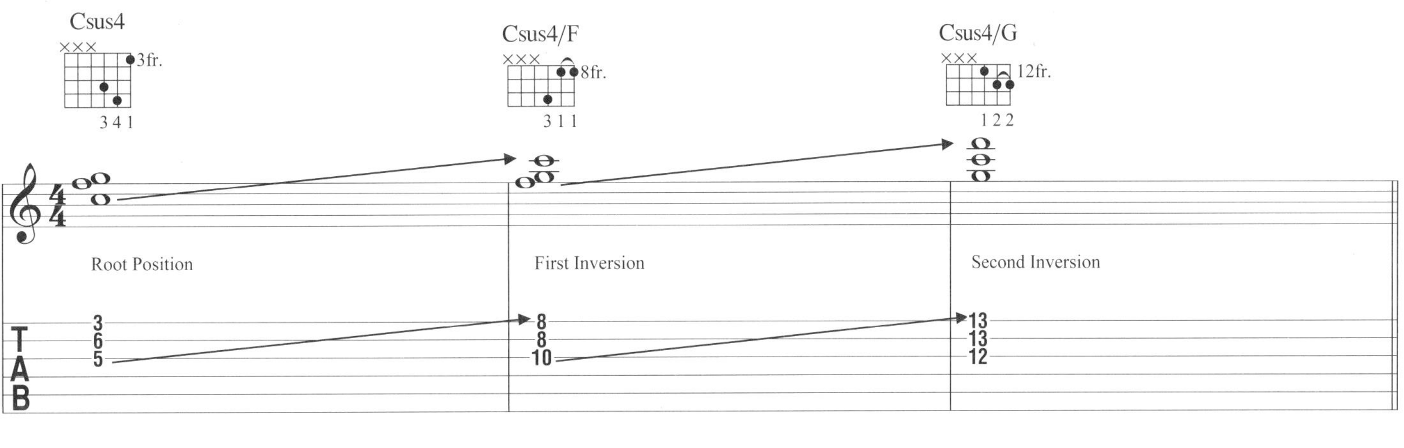

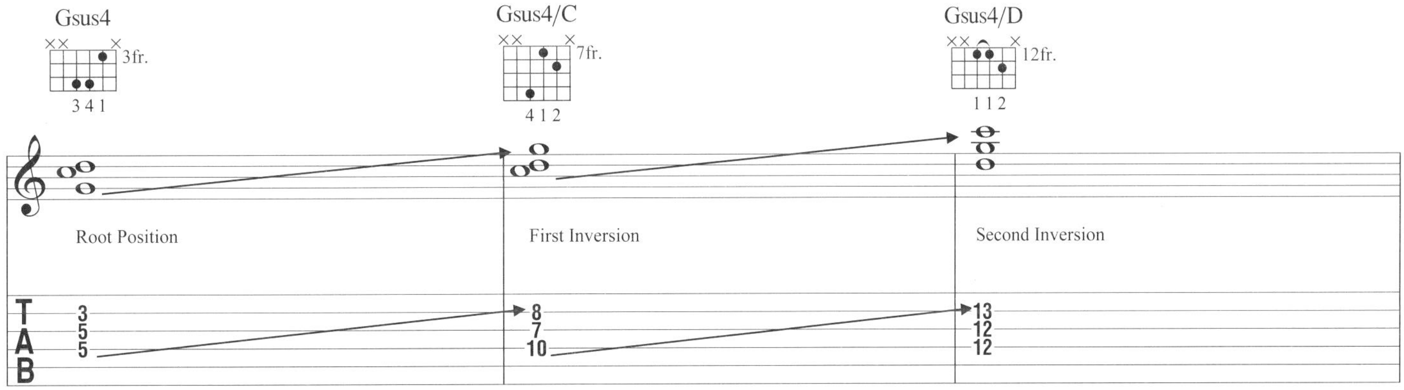

FIG. 11.15. Suspended Triads on ③②① and ④③②

Exercise 11.3. Mixed Triads Up and Down the Fretboard

Use this exercise to gain some fluency with major, minor, diminished, and augmented triads on ③②① and ④③②. It's challenging, but worth the effort. Play with good time, while looking ahead to the next voicing shape.

83, 84

Reggae ♩ = 72

Gmin/B♭ (3fr., 1 1 1) | Gmin/D (6fr., 2 3 1) | Gmin (10fr., 3 2 1) | Gmin/D (6fr., 2 3 1) | Gmin/B♭ (3fr., 1 1 1) | F/A (2 1 1) | Gmin/B♭ (3fr., 1 1 1)

5

Gmin (3fr., 3 1 1) | Gmin/B♭ (7fr., 2 1 3) | Gmin/D (11fr., 2 3 1) | Gmin/B♭ (7fr., 2 1 3) | Gmin (3fr., 3 1 1) | F (3 2 1) | Gmin (3fr., 3 1 1)

9

Cmin (3fr., 3 2 1) | Cmin/E♭ (8fr., 1 1 1) | Cmin/G (11fr., 2 3 1) | Cmin/E♭ (8fr., 1 1 1) | Cmin (3fr., 3 2 1) | B♭ (3 4 1)

FIG. 11.16. Exercise 11.3. Mixed Triads Up and Down the Fretboard

LESSON 12

Triads Across the Fretboard

Let's look at the concept of inverting chords on the guitar by moving the top chord tone down an octave, moving voicings across, and somewhat diagonally, across the fretboard.

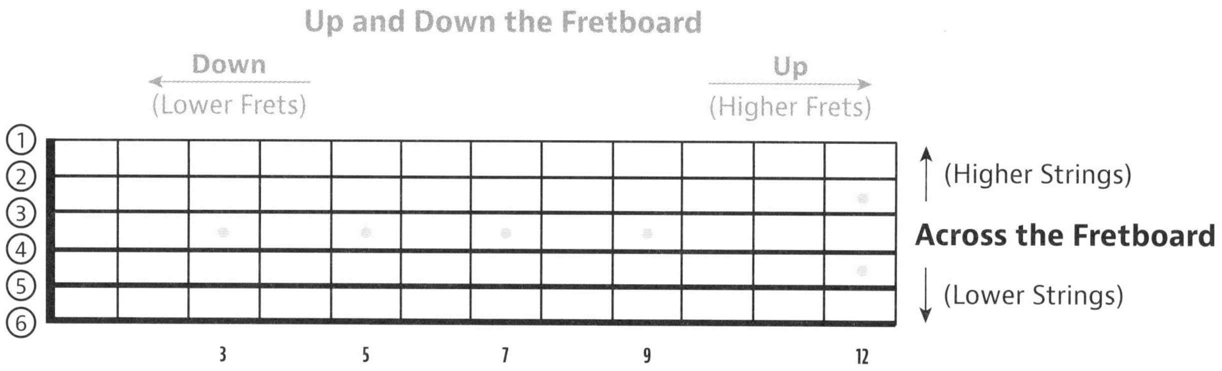

Up and Down the Fretboard

Down (Lower Frets)

Up (Higher Frets)

① ② ③ ④ ⑤ ⑥

(Higher Strings)

Across the Fretboard

(Lower Strings)

3 5 7 9 12

FIG. 12.1. Across the Fretboard

Look at a C major triad, played in root position, progressively moving the highest pitch down one octave. The G on ① is transferred down an octave to ④, then the E is moved from ② to ⑤, followed by the C moving from ③ to ⑥. Note the recommended changes of fingering. The shapes are moving.

85

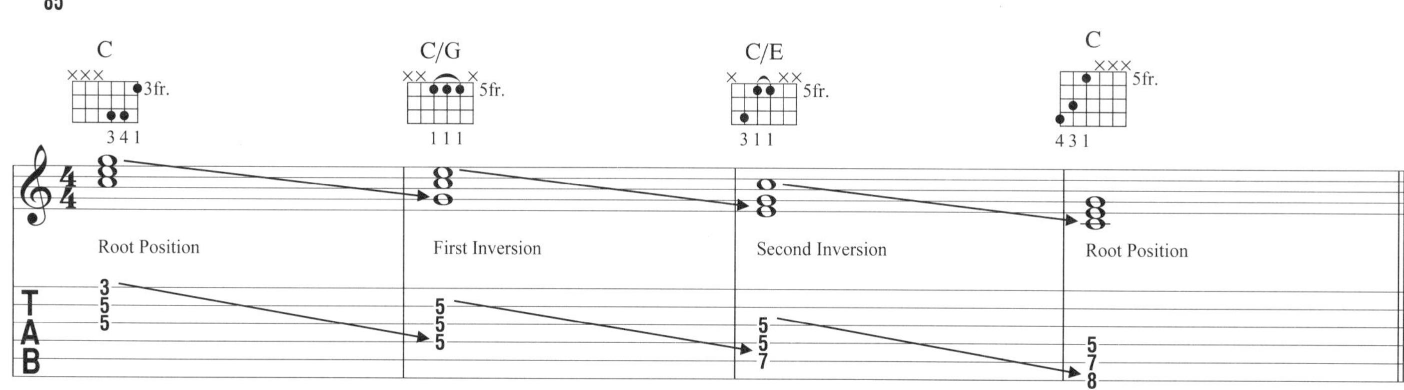

FIG. 12.2. C Major Triad Across the Fretboard

SOLID TAKE: GAINING FLUENCY WITH INVERSIONS

With practice and time, playing the various inversions becomes more natural. It's easiest when you're able to quietly spell the triad, maintaining awareness that the root is the anchor of the triad you're inverting. Remember, muscle memory is an overly simplified way of describing technical fluency—your muscles can't spell chords! It will become automatic with time and repetition. Also, there are some wide stretches on ⑥⑤④, and it's tempting to assume that your hands are too small or that the material is too difficult. Substantial change takes persistence and calendar time. Stay with it!

Here are the C minor and C augmented triads played across the fretboard.

86

(a) Minor Triad Across the Fretboard

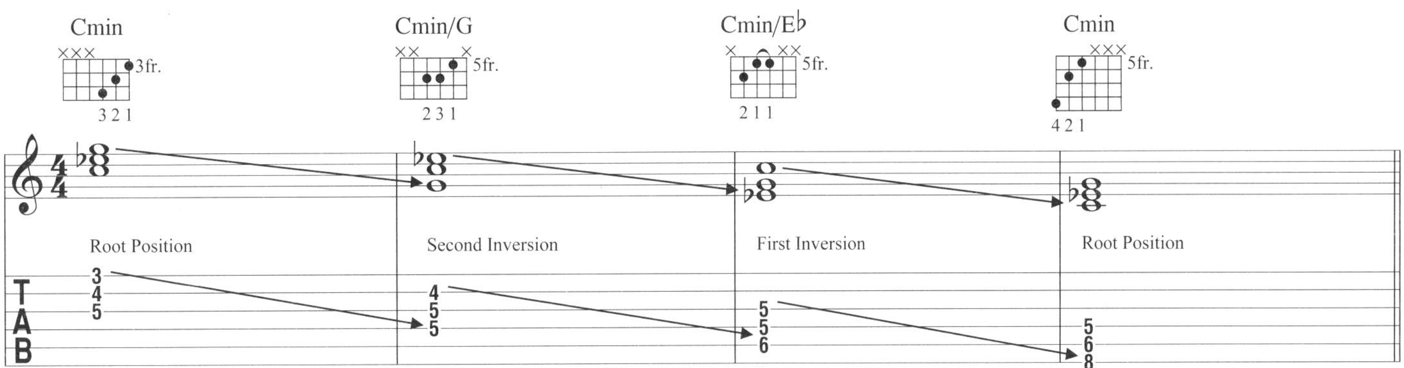

(b) Augmented Triad Across the Fretboard

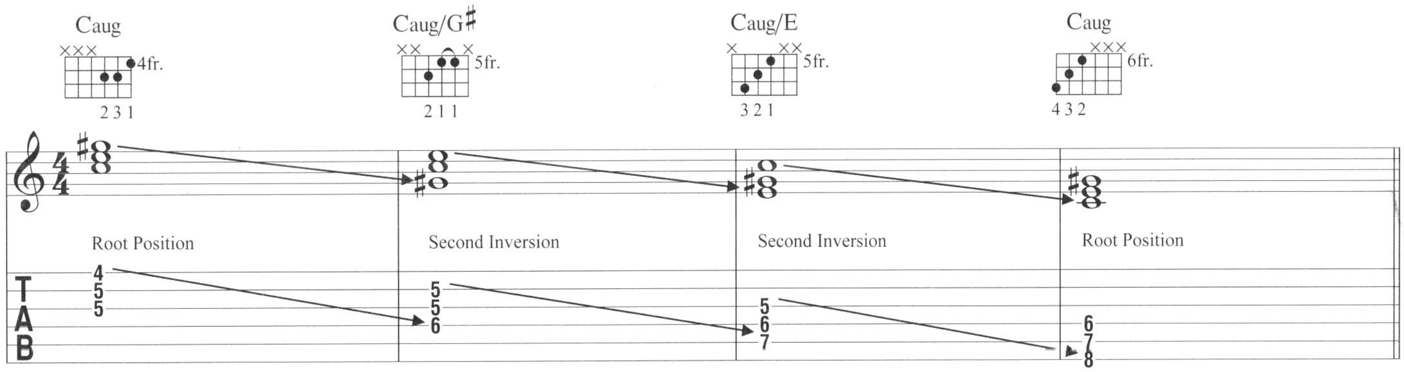

FIG. 12.3. Cmin and Caug Across the Fretboard

Diminished Triad Across the Fretboard

Play the diminished triad across the fretboard, transferring the highest note of the triad down an octave to give you the next inversion. Please note that the inversion on the bottom three strings is not included in the upcoming exercise. It's a pretty difficult stretch and beyond the reach of many guitarists—but it's notated here in case you'd like to try it.

87

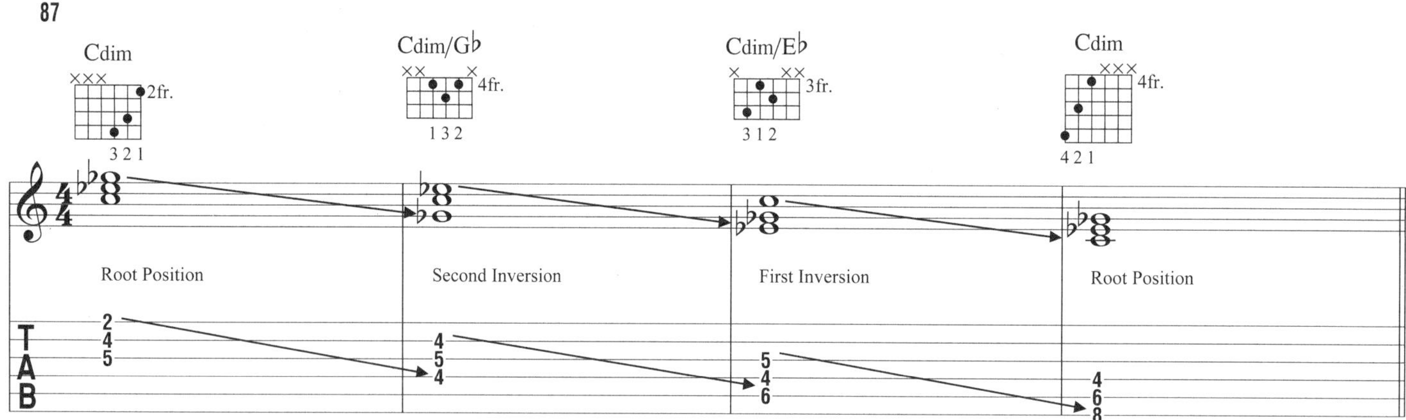

FIG. 12.4. Cdim Across the Fretboard

Sus4 Triad Across the Fretboard

Finally, run through the various inversions of the sus4 triad. Again, the stretches are difficult but not unattainable.

88

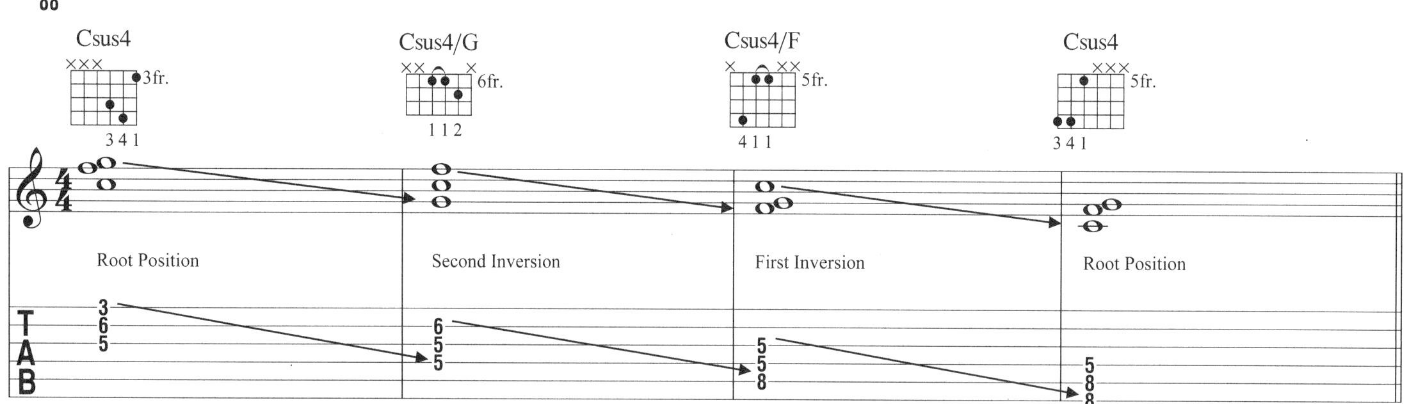

FIG. 12.5. Csus4 Across the Fretboard

Exercise 12.1. Triad Qualities Across the String Sets

This exercise should help you to get a firm grasp of all of the triad qualities we've covered in many inversions. Pay careful attention to the fingerings and be diligent about visualizing the shape of the upcoming voicing. Imagine the musical moment and match the sound in your mind rather than to "think with your fingers," grabbing around the fretboard until you find the right notes.

89, 90

Look in your mind before you leap with your fingers!

Reggae ♩ = 92

Cmin | Cmin/G | Cmin/E♭ | Cmin | Cmin/E♭ | Cmin/G | Ddim | Ddim/A♭ | Ddim/F

5 E♭aug | E♭aug/B | E♭aug/G | E♭aug | E♭aug/G | E♭aug/B | Fmin | Fmin/C | Fmin/A♭

9 G | G/B | G/D | G | Gsus4 | Gsus4/C | G

13 Cmin | Cmin/G | Cmin/E♭ | Cmin/G | Cmin

FIG. 12.6. Exercise 12.1. Triad Qualities Across the String Sets

LESSON 13

Power Chords

Few things make the guitar sound more monstrously powerful than "power" chords. There's nothing like the sound of a heavily distorted solid-body guitar cranked to the max with a hard-pounding beat coming from electric bass and drums.

The quality of these chords is often notated as "5," as in E5, A5, and D5. This is due to the fifth and the root making up the only contents of the chord. Traditionally, power chords are neither major nor minor, and they are played with the bottom pitch on string ⑥ or ⑤. Even though these somewhat primitive voicings have served as the entry point for many beginning guitarists, they are somewhat difficult to play flawlessly. Power chords, when played with heavy distortion, contain many rich overtones, creating a wall of sound. When played poorly, extra open strings can clash with the harmony of the moment and disrupt continuity when going through a sequence of power chords. Four-part chords are not nearly as effective with heavy distortion, since the overtones in more complex voicings can conflict with each other, sounding muddy and less defined.

POWER CHORDS: BIG SOUND, TWO TONES

Let's get back to basics! The "power chord," notated as a root name followed by a 5, includes just the root and fifth, but no third or seventh. Often, the octave root is on top, as well—only two chord tones total, even though three notes are sounded. Root-5-root is all that you need for a power chord, and the sound can be huge. Here is an E5, found in two positions on the neck:

91

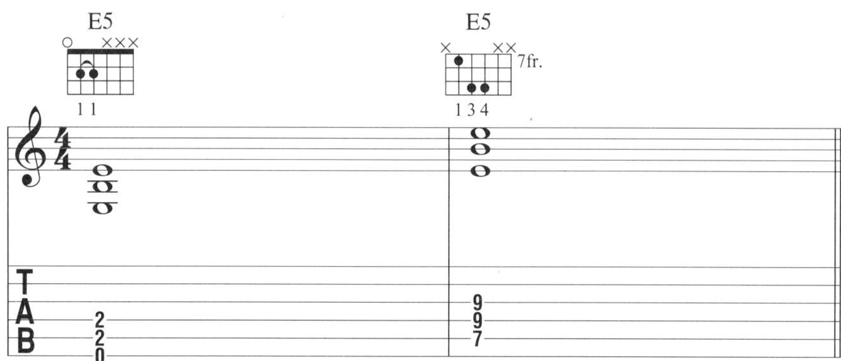

FIG. 13.1. Two Options for E5 Power Chord

92, 93

Exercise 13.1. Power Chords through the Circle of Fourths

Play through these root-5-root voicings (with or without distortion).

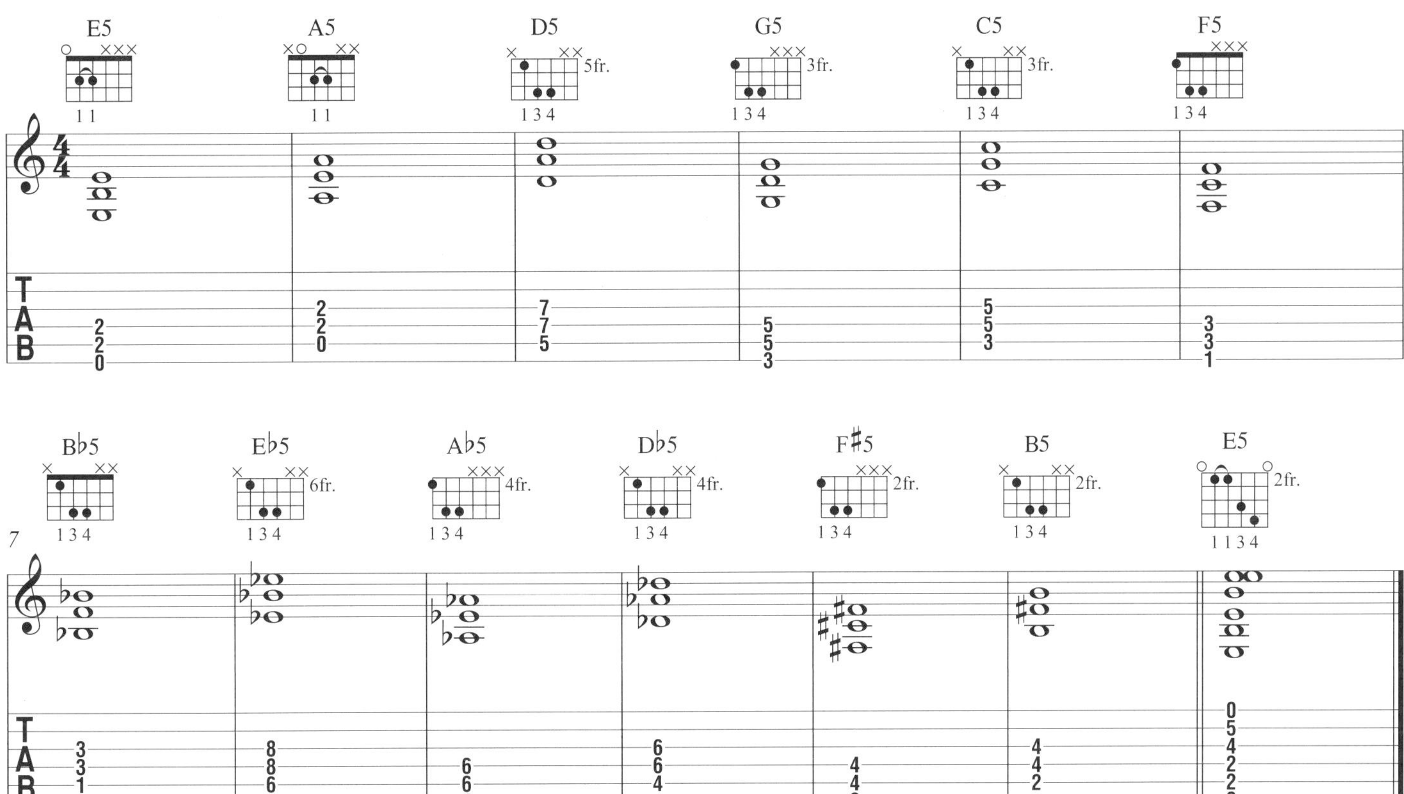

FIG. 13.2. Exercise 13.1. Power Chords through the Circle of Fourths

The longer the string, the better the sound. Masters of guitar tone, such as Jimi Hendrix, Jimmy Page, Paul Kossoff, Bonnie Raitt, Billy Gibbons, and many others, make use of open strings.

Consider the key and whether an open string will fit into your power chord voicings.

These power chords use open strings. Muting the unwanted strings is the challenge here.

94

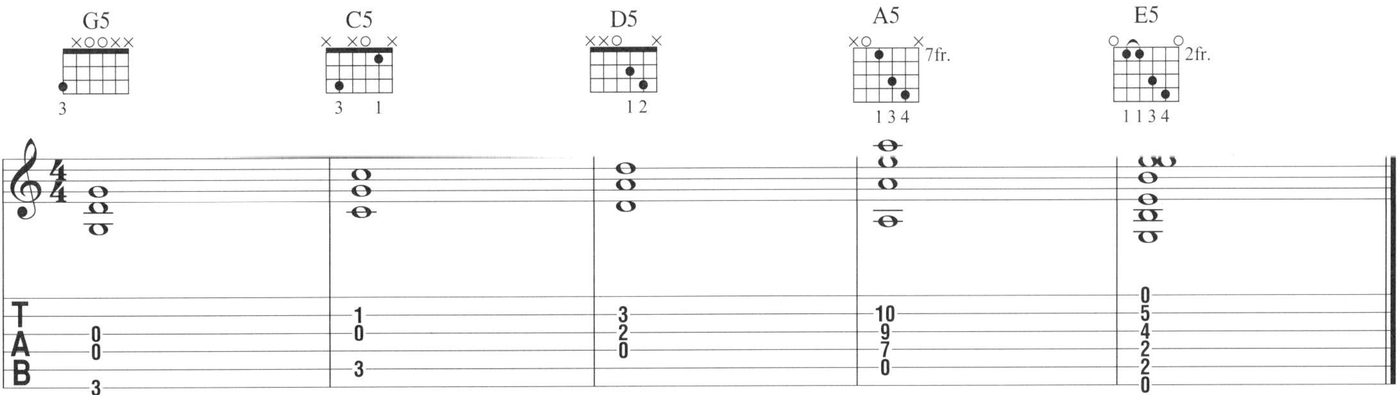

FIG. 13.3. Power Chords with Open and Muted Strings

Exercise 13.2. Power Chords

Play with the backing track, ensuring that your subdivision matches up with the recorded performances of the bass and drums tracks. From bar 9 to the end, every eighth note is being performed on the guitar. In the first section, the eighth note subdivision is implied, but there are only two attacks: on beat 1 and on the "and" of beat 2. Although stylistically much different, the 1920s song "Charleston" (recorded by James P. Johnson and many others) repeats this rhythm throughout. If you think or say the lyric, "Charles-ton," you may find it easier to hit beat 1 and then wait for the proper amount of time to accurately play the second attack. Find the rhythm, feel the proper time to attack, and flow in your performance!

95, 96

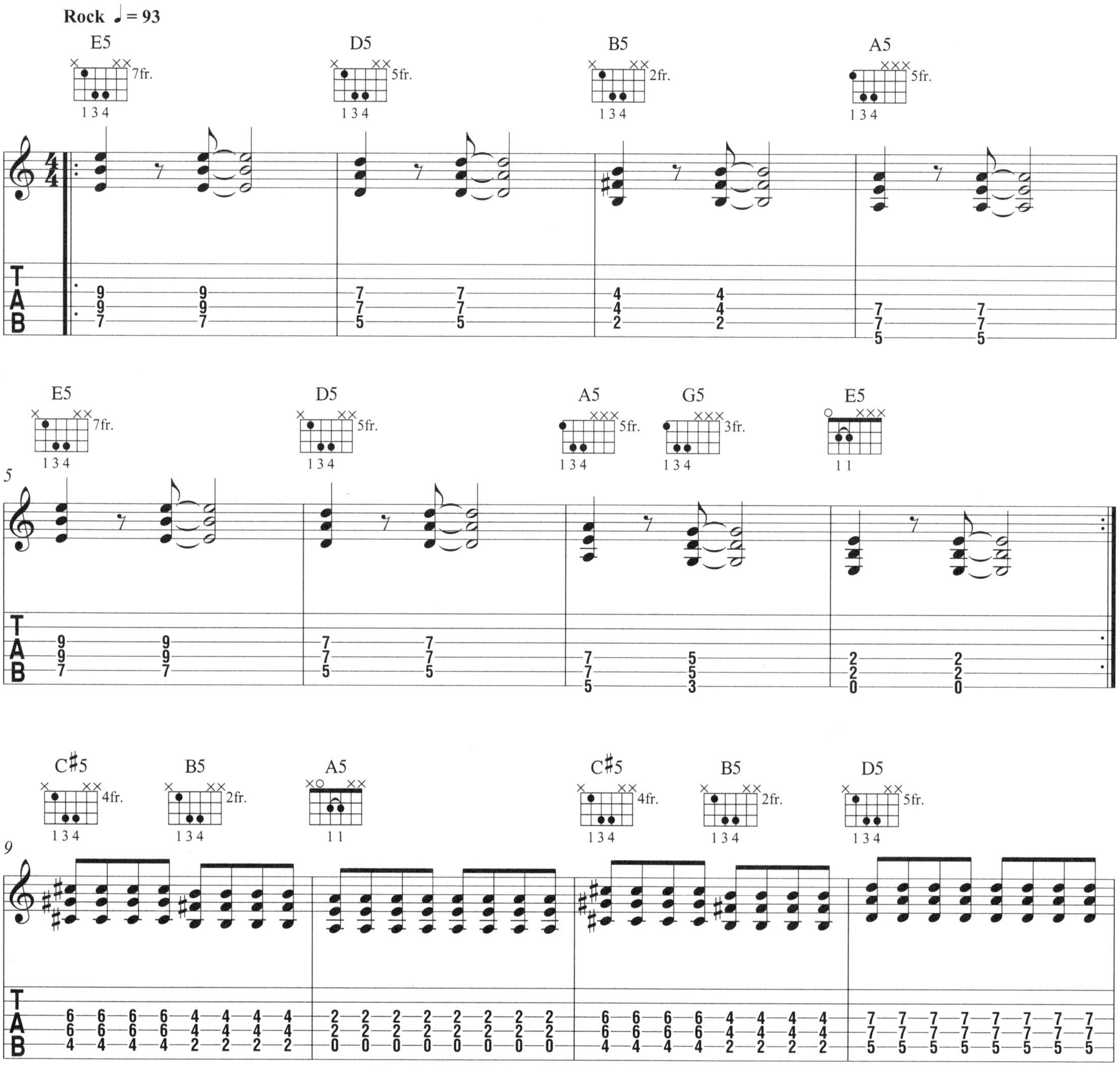

Rock ♩= 93

E5 (7fr., 134) D5 (5fr., 134) B5 (2fr., 134) A5 (5fr., 134)

5

E5 (7fr., 134) D5 (5fr., 134) A5 (5fr., 134) G5 (3fr., 134) E5 (11)

9

C♯5 (4fr., 134) B5 (2fr., 134) A5 (11) C♯5 (4fr., 134) B5 (2fr., 134) D5 (5fr., 134)

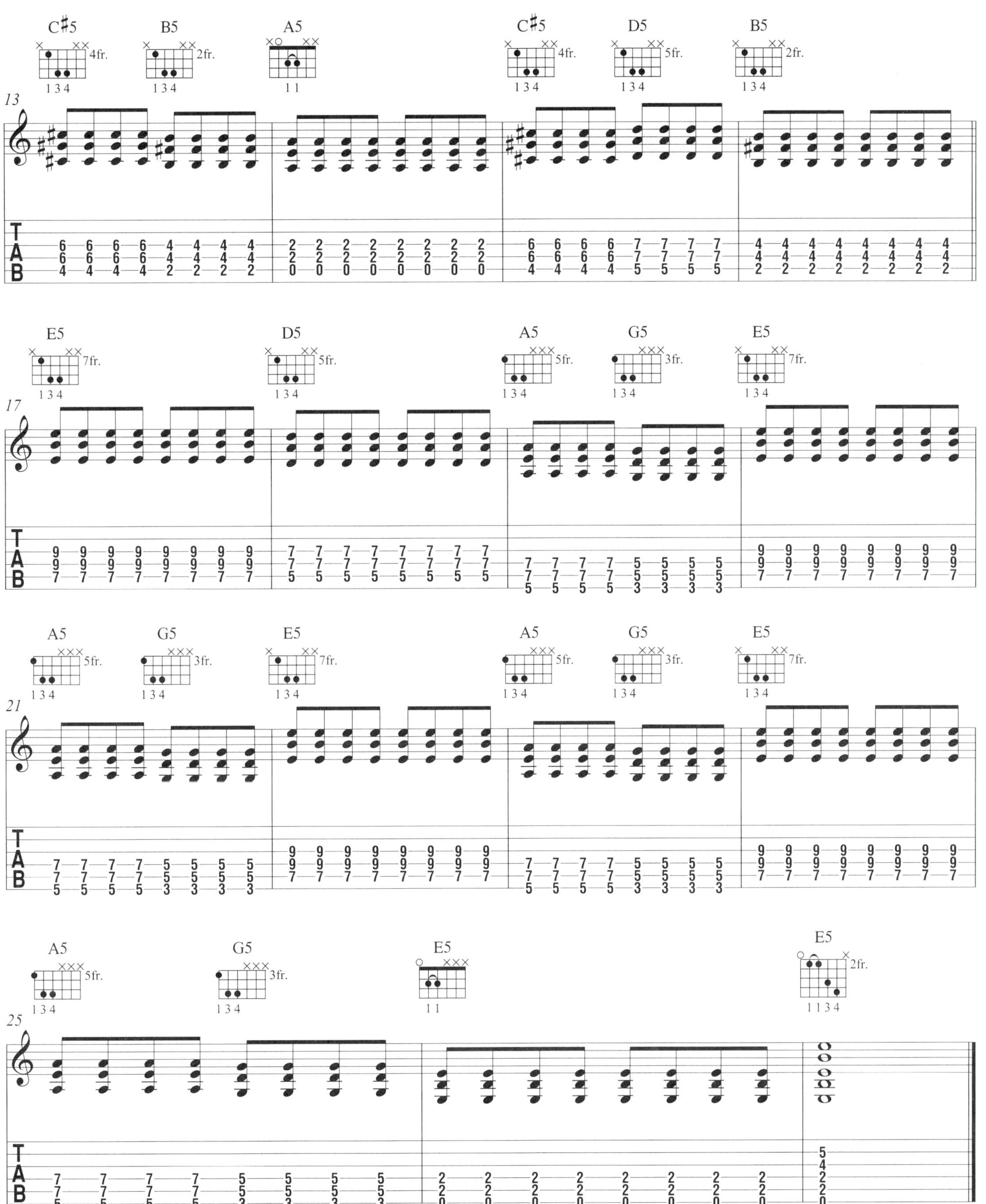

FIG. 13.4. Exercise 13.2. Power Chords

LESSON 14

Barre Chords

The term "barre" can be defined as using one finger to press down multiple strings across a single fret of the fretboard. Clip-on capos are often used by guitarists to give a solid, mechanical replacement for the fretboard's nut.

Barre chords represent a huge amount of the vocabulary used by guitarists in rock and pop music. Although they may be a bit tough on your fretting fingers at first, the many applications of these shapes make the effort well worthwhile. If you've had experience with these chords, you may find that the various exercises will give you greater facility and command of the material.

BARRE CHORDS: BIG SOUND, THREE OR FOUR TONES

The following voicings appear on countless rock and rhythm 'n' blues recordings. The power chord's root and fifth are found in the bottom of each of the following variations. These voicings are moveable shapes, and guitarists choose ⑥ or ⑤ based on the closest, most convenient option at the moment.

97

Dominant 7

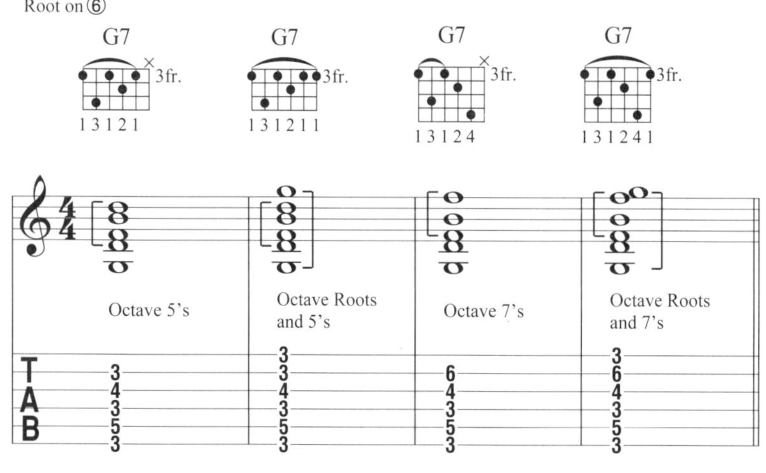

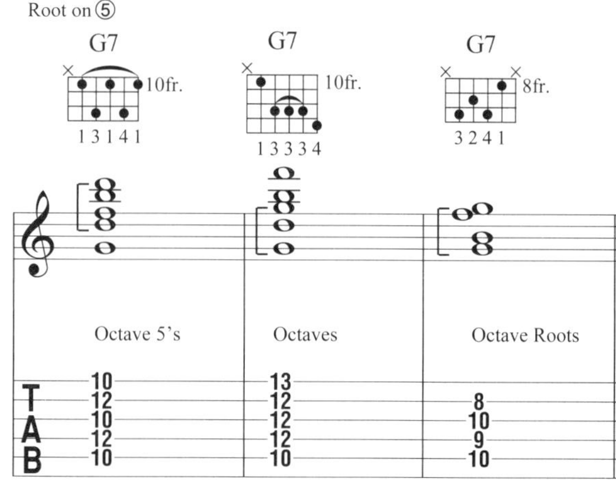

FIG. 14.1. Dominant 7 (G7) Barre Chord Options

Major

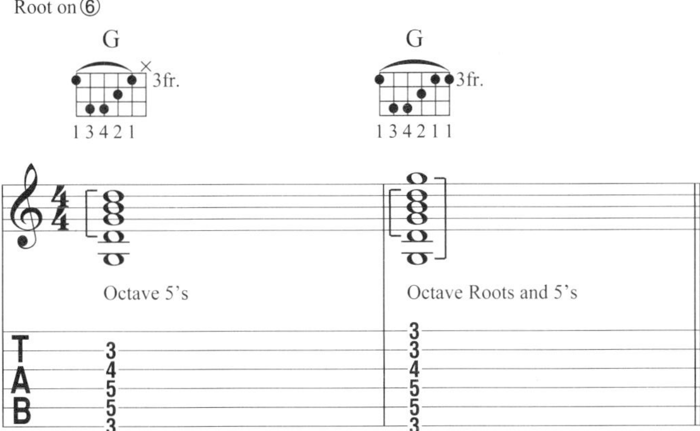

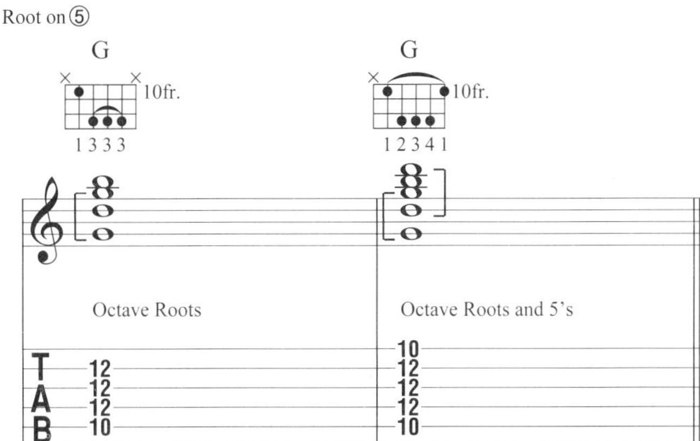

FIG. 14.2. Major (G) Barre Chord Options

Minor

99

Adjusting the third in the major chord forms provides options for minor.

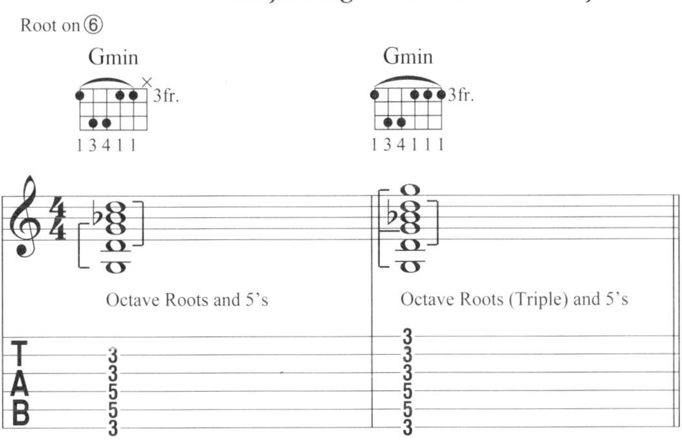

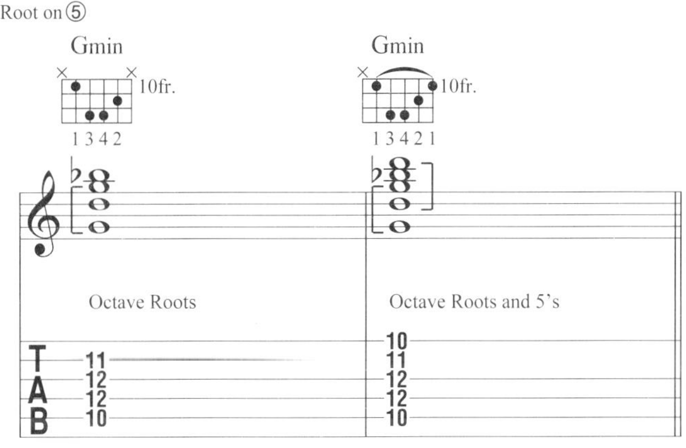

FIG. 14.3. Minor (Gmin) Barre Chord Options

Minor 7

Root on ⑥

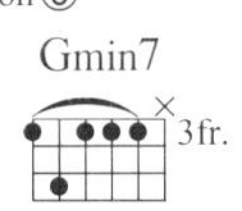

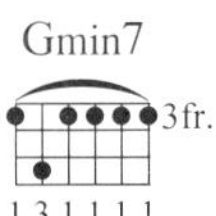

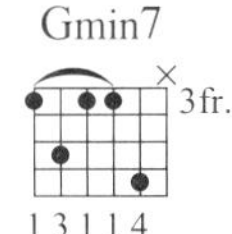

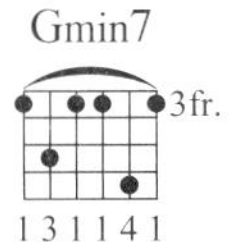

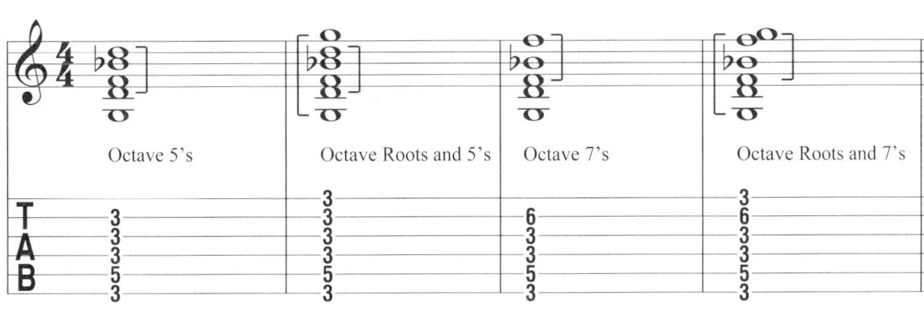

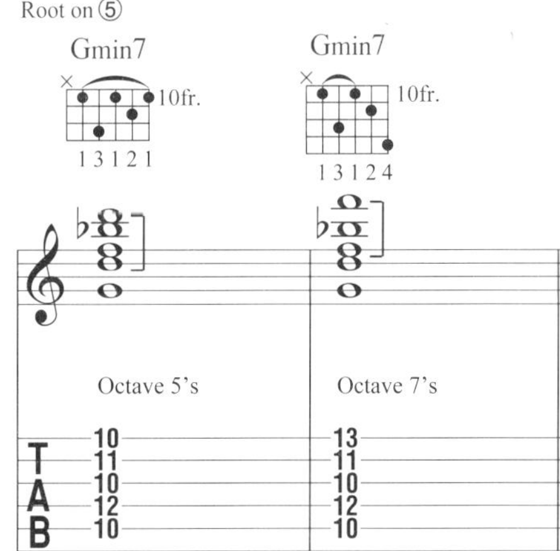

FIG. 14.4. Minor 7 (Gmin7) Barre Chord Options

BARRE CHORDS: SO MANY VARIATIONS

Why are there so many variations? That's a hard one to answer, other than to say that guitarists have been finding their own way to play the instrument for hundreds of years.

Some song hooks are written around a particular voicing; some players gravitate toward certain sounds with habitual signature chord grips. Doubling voices or leaving them out won't necessarily make any of these voicings "wrong" or even less sophisticated than the voicings we've been developing; they're just different shades of the same basic colors.

Hopefully, this book is introducing some new sounds that haven't occurred to you before, and you'll actually put them into your musical vocabulary. Breaking the chords down to essential fundamentals will allow you to build variations that will make sense to any listener.

Exercise 14.1. Barre Chord Practice

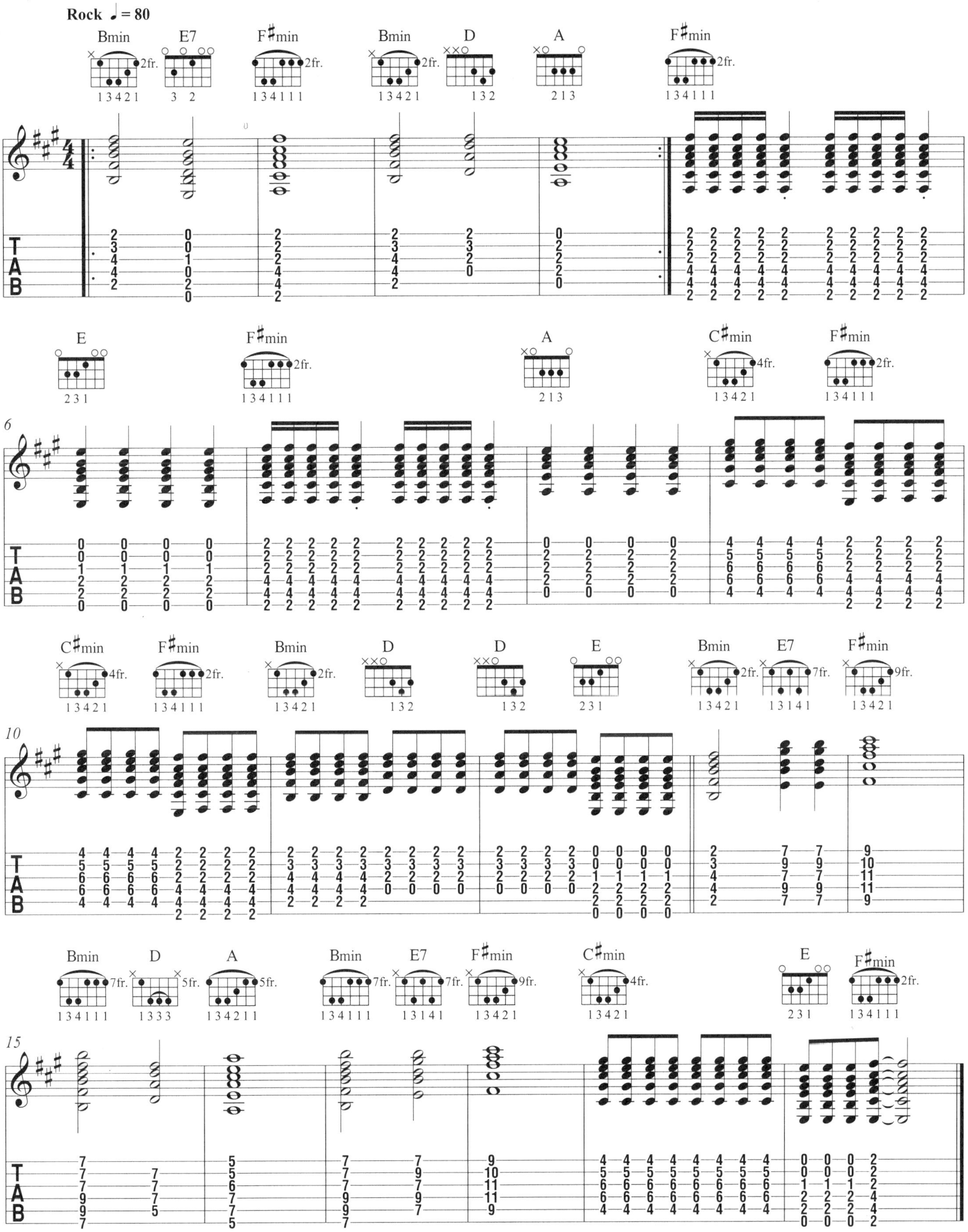

FIG. 14.5. Exercise 14.1. Barre Chord Practice

LESSON 15

Four-Part Chords: Root Position Drop 2 Using Raise 2 Approach

It's time to expand our harmonic knowledge to include several new colors using four voices. We've been working with the triad using root, 3, and 5. Now we can add the 7 to the basic sound, arriving at a four-part chord. Four-part chords can be tricky to manage on the fretboard, so guitarists often use the drop 2 configuration, dropping the next-to-the-highest note in a chord down an octave to become the lowest note in the chord.

This results in voicings that fit well on four adjacent strings. Drop 2 voicing configurations are commonplace in the vocabulary of pianists in jazz and/or rhythm 'n' blues influenced music, and arrangers often use them with voicings using horns or vocalists.

Whenever you discover and focus on a new shape on the fretboard, it takes practice to make that new voicing a part of your playing vocabulary. This lesson is going to give you plenty of practice in constructing and playing these voicings. We are going well beyond simple, reflexive "grips" on the fretboard.

Let's look at a drop 2 voicing that you may already know.

103

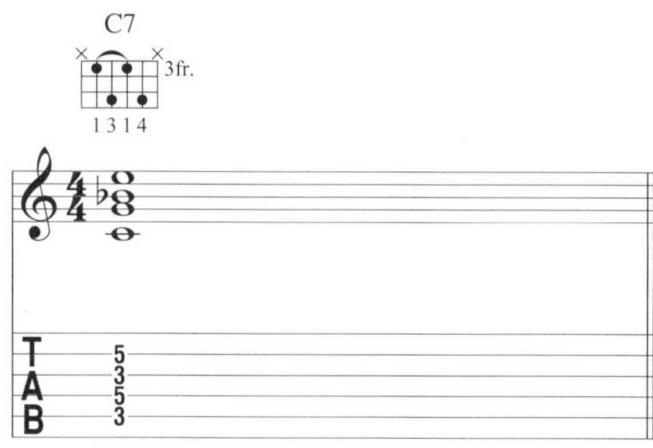

FIG. 15.1. Basic Drop 2 Chord Shape for C7

THE RAISE 2 APPROACH

Drop 2 works well on the guitar, but since it is more intuitive to build voicings from the bottom up, it's easier to build in a process called "raise 2." Let's look at how we can build voicings using the raise 2 approach.

DROP 2 VOICINGS: FOUR ADJACENT STRINGS ⑤④③②

Arpeggiate a close position spelling of a C7 chord, taking notice of the second chord tone from the bottom. That tone, in this case and E, is to be moved up, producing a great easy-to-play voicing. Let's put this onto the guitar, considering the bottom, second, third, and fourth voice, from lowest pitch to the highest.

104

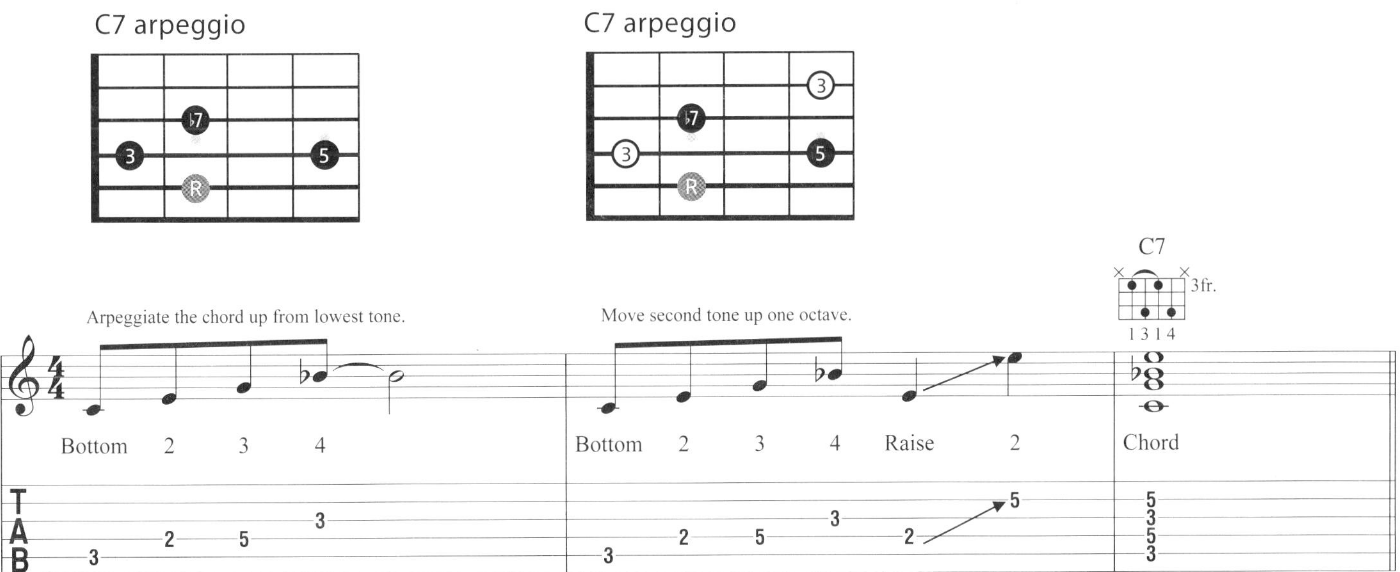

FIG. 15.2. Step-by-Step Building of a Drop 2 Chord Shape for C7

RAISE 2 AND DROP 2: TWO ROUTES TO THE SAME DESTINATION

Let's look at C7 in all inversions, each in close position.

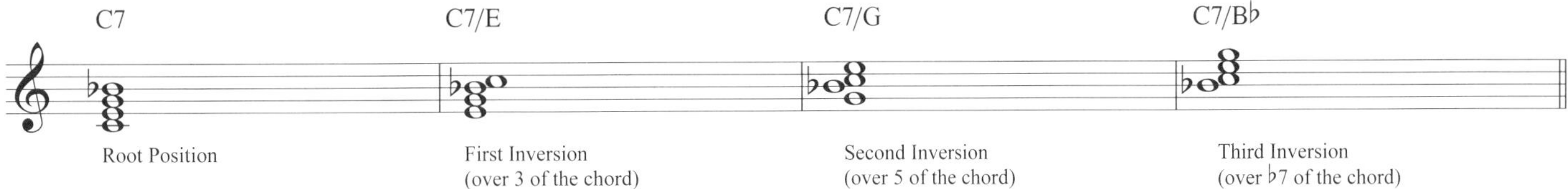

FIG. 15.3. Four Inversions of C7 in Close Position

If you try to play the preceding voicings, you'll quickly see why guitarists have worked to find more practical ways to play four-part voicings. Raise 2 is the key.

In figure 15.4, you will see both approaches to a root position voicing.

- **Raise 2:** Using the root position chord, move the second voice from the bottom up one octave.
- **Drop 2:** Using the second inversion chord (C7/G), move the second voice from the top down one octave.

They result in the same configuration of chord tones.

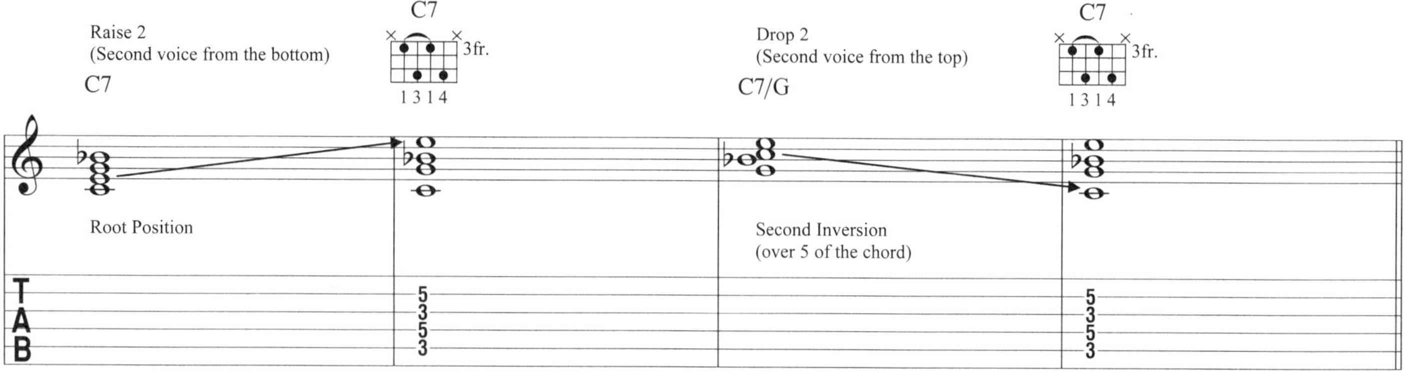

FIG. 15.4. Raise 2 and Drop 2 to Build the Same C7 Configuration

Both raise 2 and drop 2 approaches are effective. Arrangers and pianists often prefer building voicings from the top voice to the bottom, using drop 2, when they are harmonizing a melodic lead line. Generally, most guitarists prefer to build voicings from the bottom to the top, making the raise 2 approach easier to understand and play. The *Chords 101* approach emphasizes the bottom-to-top approach to build voicings: raise 2!

Exercise 15.1. Building Raise 2 Voicings on ⑤④③②

105, 106

Let's put the fifth string root voicing (⑤④③②) to work, with a twelve-bar blues framework. It's a recording of a blues in C with a simple rhythmic pattern played throughout. You will need to play the basic dominant 7 shape on the roots C, F, G, and D♭.

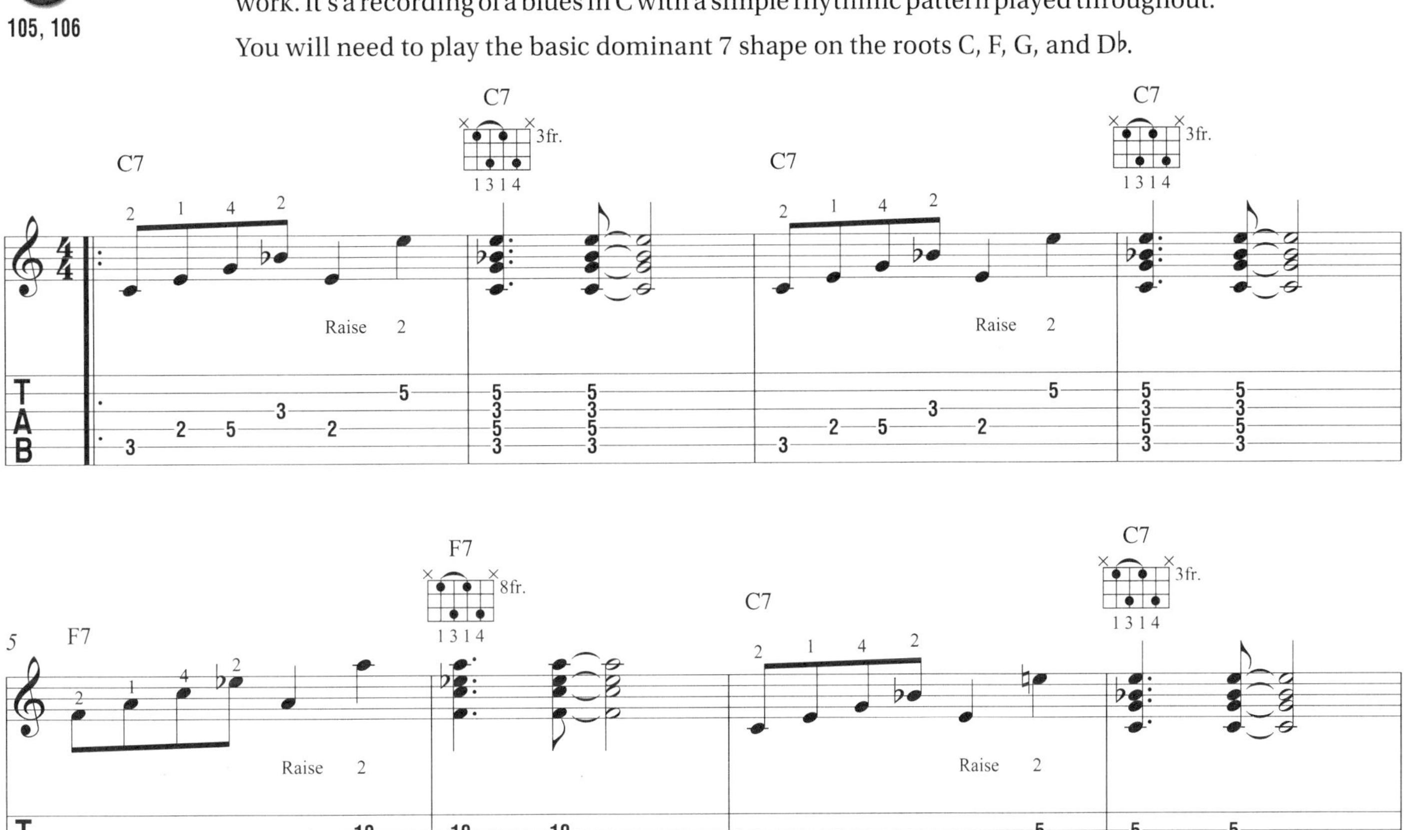

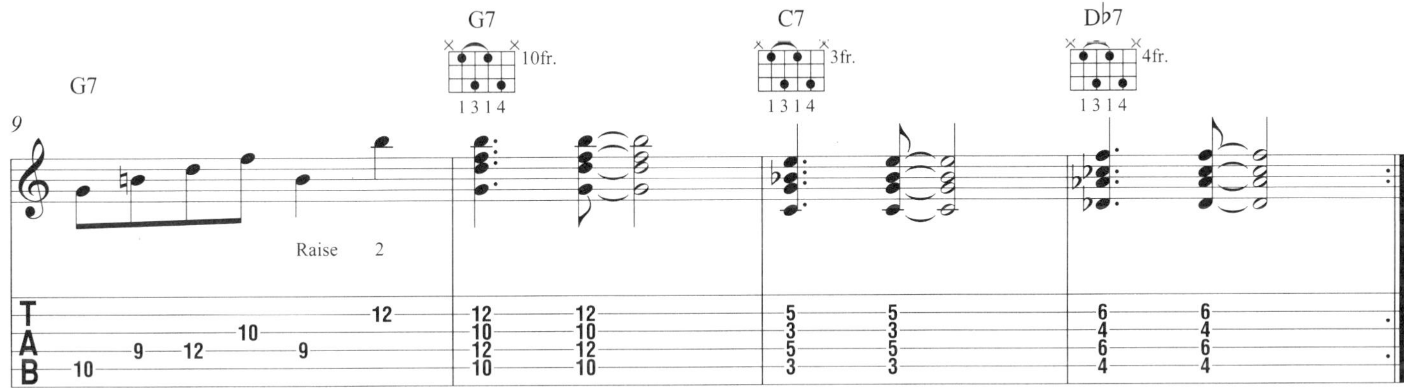

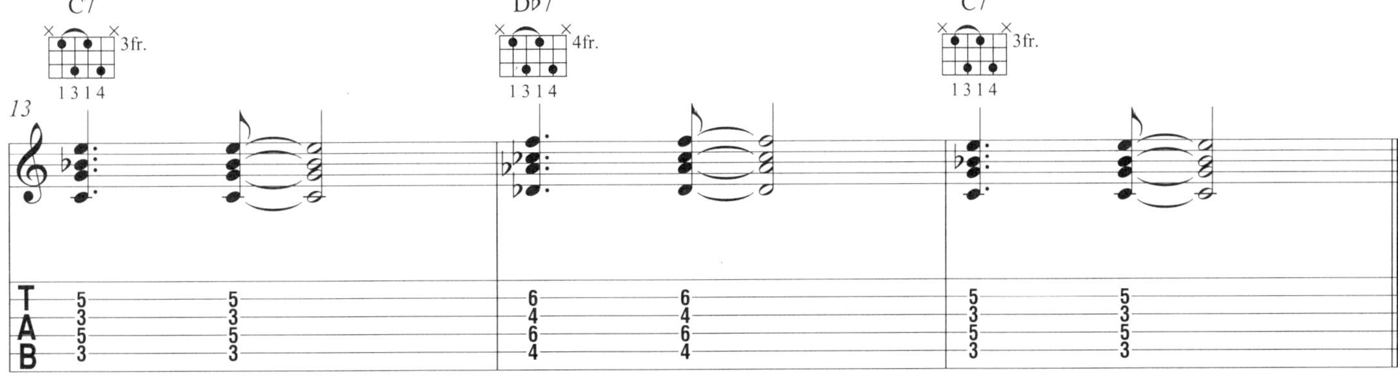

FIG. 15.5. Exercise 15.1. Building Raise 2 Voicings on ⑤④③②

Exercise 15.2. Raise 2 Voicing Practice with Four-Part Chords

107, 108

Let's use the same approach, including dom7, maj7, min7, and min7♭5 arpeggios. The following exercise will put you on track.

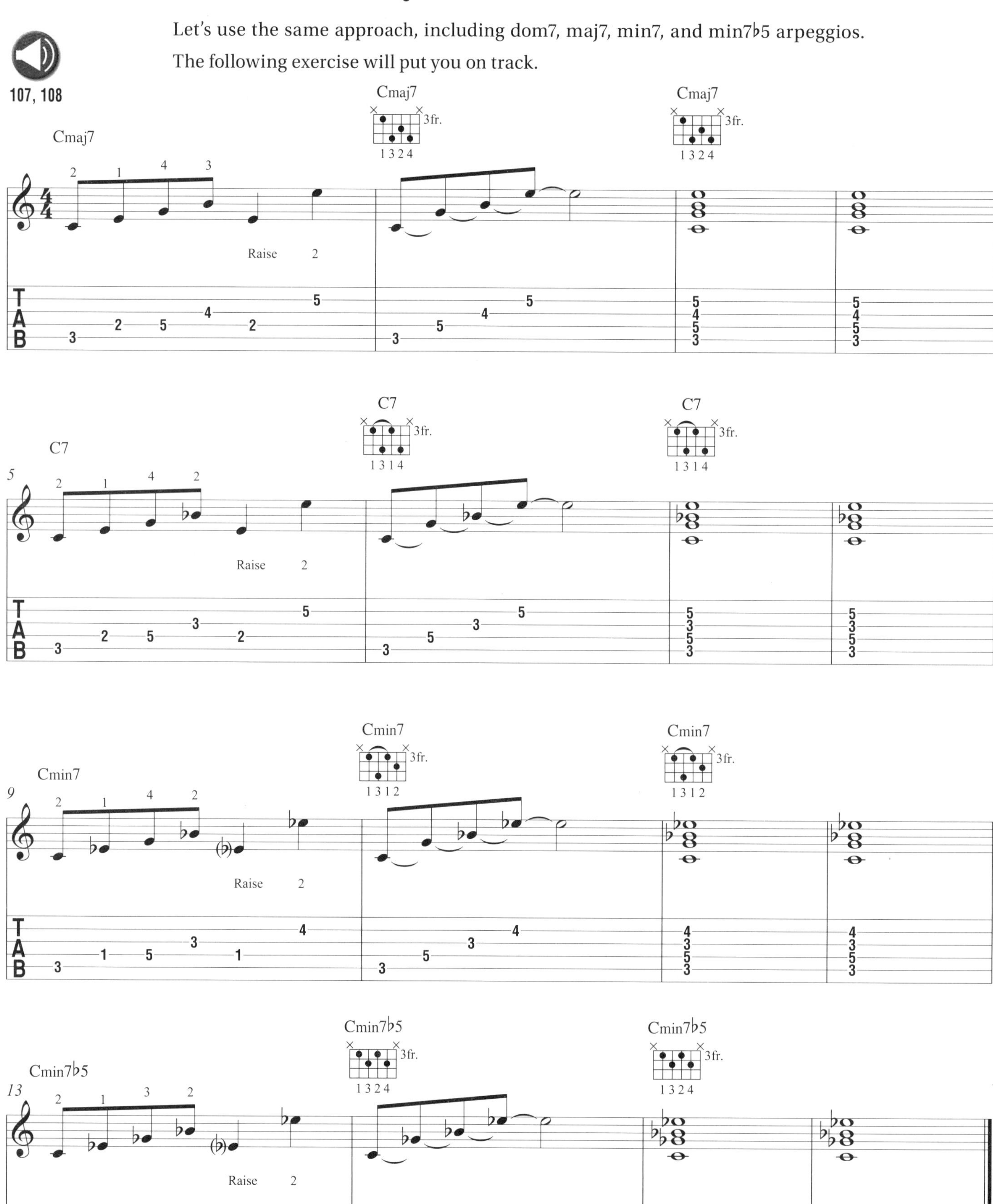

FIG. 15.6. Exercise 15.2. Raise 2 Voicing Practice with Four-Part Chords

COMMON PRACTICE WITH SEVENTH CHORD SYMBOLS

Chord symbols represent harmonic sounds in shorthand. These short names are meant to indicate a set of sounds to be realized by the player. Ideally, chord symbols are meant to be abbreviations for chords that musicians already know. It takes a while to link the names with the feel and sound of the chords. If you're just beginning to learn chord symbols, you may be trying to find logic in the names of each one of these abbreviations—there is logic involved! But, sometimes, it all boils down to memorizing a few things.

C7 vs. Cmaj7

As we've seen, it's possible to think of chord tones and use raise 2 to get chord voicings. Many find it easier to relate one chord form to another.

C7 and Cmaj7 look like similar chords, and they are, seeing as there is only one different note between the two. Both consist of major triads with added sevenths. The difference between C7 and Cmaj7 is found in the quality of the seventh chord degree. C7 consists of C E G B♭, and Cmaj7 is C E G B♮. Here they are in their drop 2, root position shape:

109

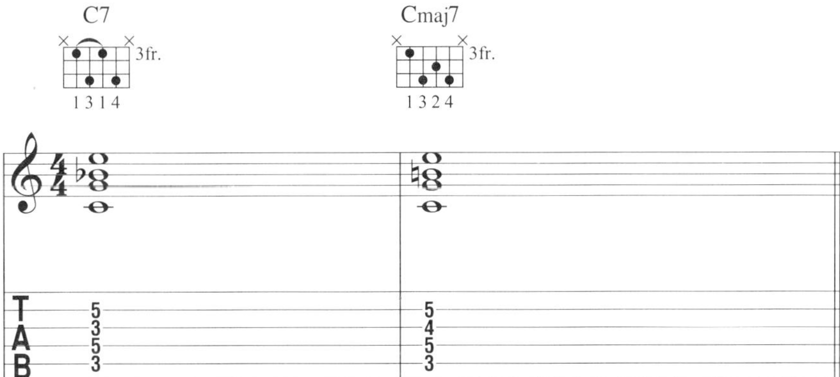

FIG. 15.7. Relating Drop 2 Shapes on ⑤④③②

Drop 2 voicings with the root on ⑤ feature the 5 of the chord on ④, the 7 on ③ and the 3 on ②. Here are five voicings, all found through variations of the C7 chord form in third position. Play through the following shapes, noticing how switching one or two fingers can make a dramatic difference. Compare the shapes and notice the differences and similarities of the various colors.

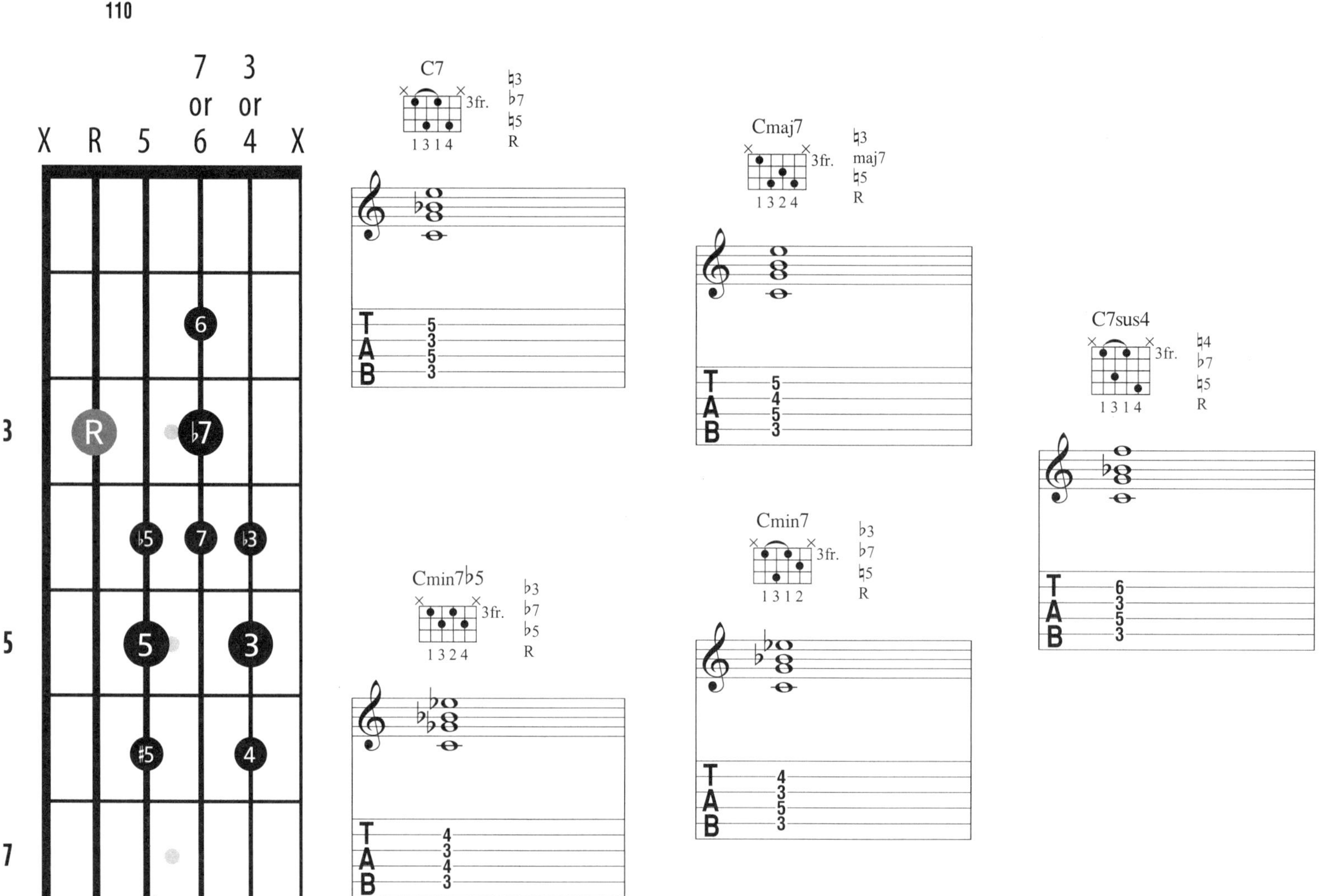

FIG. 15.8. Comparison of Drop 2 Chord Qualities

Keeping track of the quality of the 3, 5, and 7 allows you to gain control of all of these chord qualities.

Regarding chord fingering, you may have other ways of approaching these voicings (barre in place of multiple fingers, vice versa). Experienced guitarists vary fingering to best get from the voicing they have just played to the voicing they're about to play.

Exercise 15.3. Relating Drop 2 Chords ⑤ Root

111, 112

In this chord exercise, take special care with the sound of the chord precisely at the point of the chord change. Think ahead, and concentrate on each upcoming chord shape.

FIG. 15.9. Exercise 15.3. Relating Drop 2 Chords ⑤ Root

LESSON 16

Drop 2 Crossovers: Moving Chord Shapes Across String Sets

In standard tuning, the guitar is traditionally tuned in perfect fourth intervals, except in the case of ③ and ②. The major third interval found between ③ and ② makes life more comfortable for our fretting hand, but it makes things complicated when transferring specific voicings to different parts of the fretboard.

Chord voicings can be duplicated on different string sets, but we have to alter the *chord form* that we're playing to match the chord quality. Through use of *crossovers* (sometimes called "transfers"), we can take a chord voicing across the fretboard, moving it from one set of strings to another, changing the chord form to get the same voicing sound on two sets of strings. Increasing the options allows for smooth voice leading, avoiding the need for large, awkward position shifts.

Considering an Fmaj7 in eighth position on ⑤④③②, let's learn the crossover process to move the same configuration of chord tones to ④③②①.

113

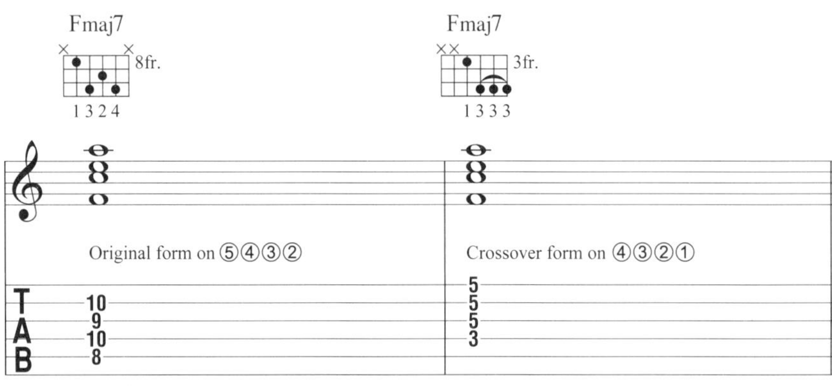

FIG. 16.1. Fmaj7 in Two Positions

Use the following steps to get started with the crossover process.

114

Fmaj7 8fr. 1 3 2 4 — Original form on ⑤④③② Move this precise form directly to ④③②①

Transitional form 8fr. 1 3 2 4 — Adjust tone on ② up one fret

B♭maj7 8fr. 1 3 3 3 — Adjusted form complete

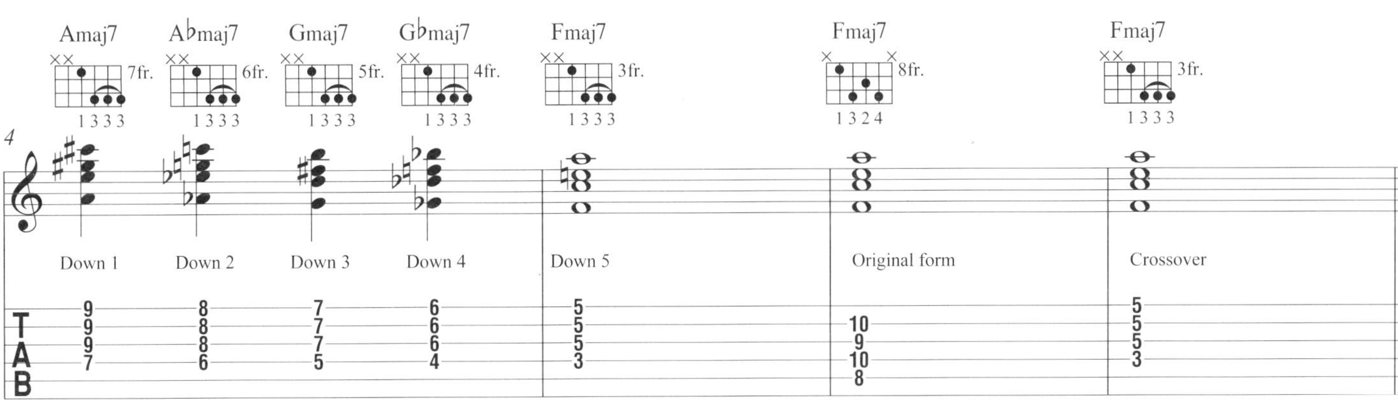

FIG. 16.2. Crossover Process Step-by-Step

SOLID TAKE: INTEGRATING CROSSOVERS

We have addressed some challenging concepts. The process of transferring voicings from one string set to another takes some time to understand, but it exponentially increases the number of chords at your fingertips. The concept of seventh-chord inversions is complicated to visualize on the guitar neck, and to top it off, extremely tough to execute on the fretboard. You must know by now that this is the type of work that will pay the highest dividends. The sheer number of voicings we're working with will require you to see the chord tones on the neck—helping you to evolve beyond memorized chord "grips" and into the realm of seeing chord tones in their functional role. Keep up the good work!

CROSSOVER PROCESS

1. Play original form on ⑤④③②.
2. Migrate this shape from ⑤④③② to ④③②① without changing the fingering/chord form.
3. Move the chord tone on ② one fret higher to compensate for the major third between ③ and ②.
4. Move the "new" shape down five frets (or up seven frets) to find the same chord voicing. The choice to move up or down is based on where you're starting on the fretboard.

If you "run out of neck" in the lower positions and you don't have room to go down five frets, go up seven frets to find the same voicing type in a higher position. See the process that follows.

115

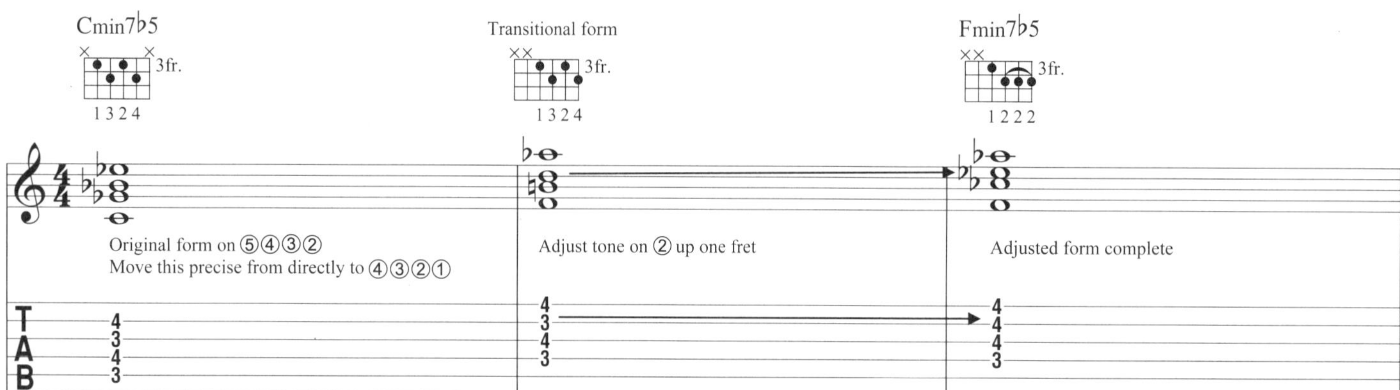

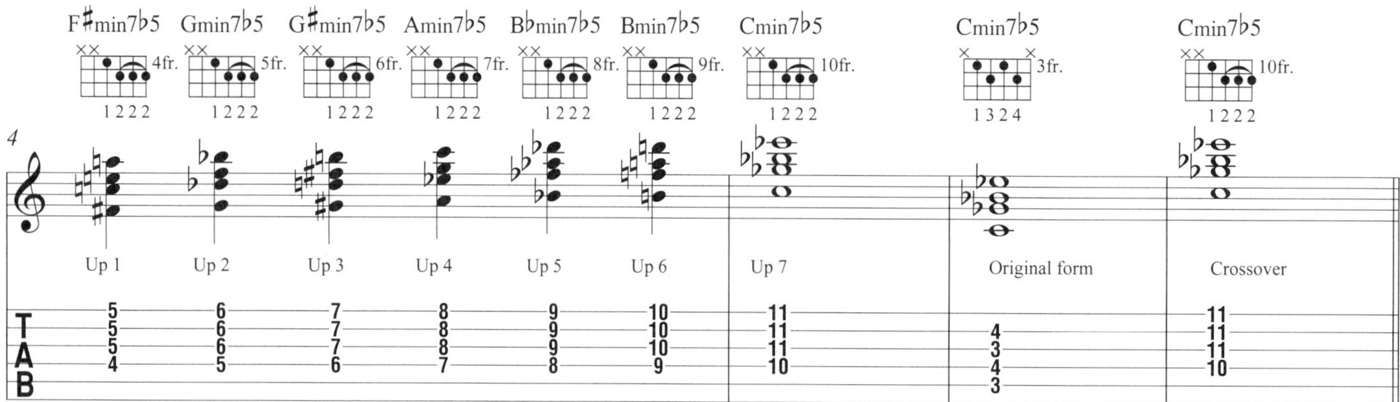

FIG. 16.3. Crossover Process Moving Up the Fretboard

Exercise 16.1. Diatonic Chords and Crossovers in B♭ and E♭

116, 117

Extending the concept of crossovers to larger diatonic sections, play through the diatonic chords of the keys B♭ and E♭, working to maintain the volume balance of each tone in every chord.

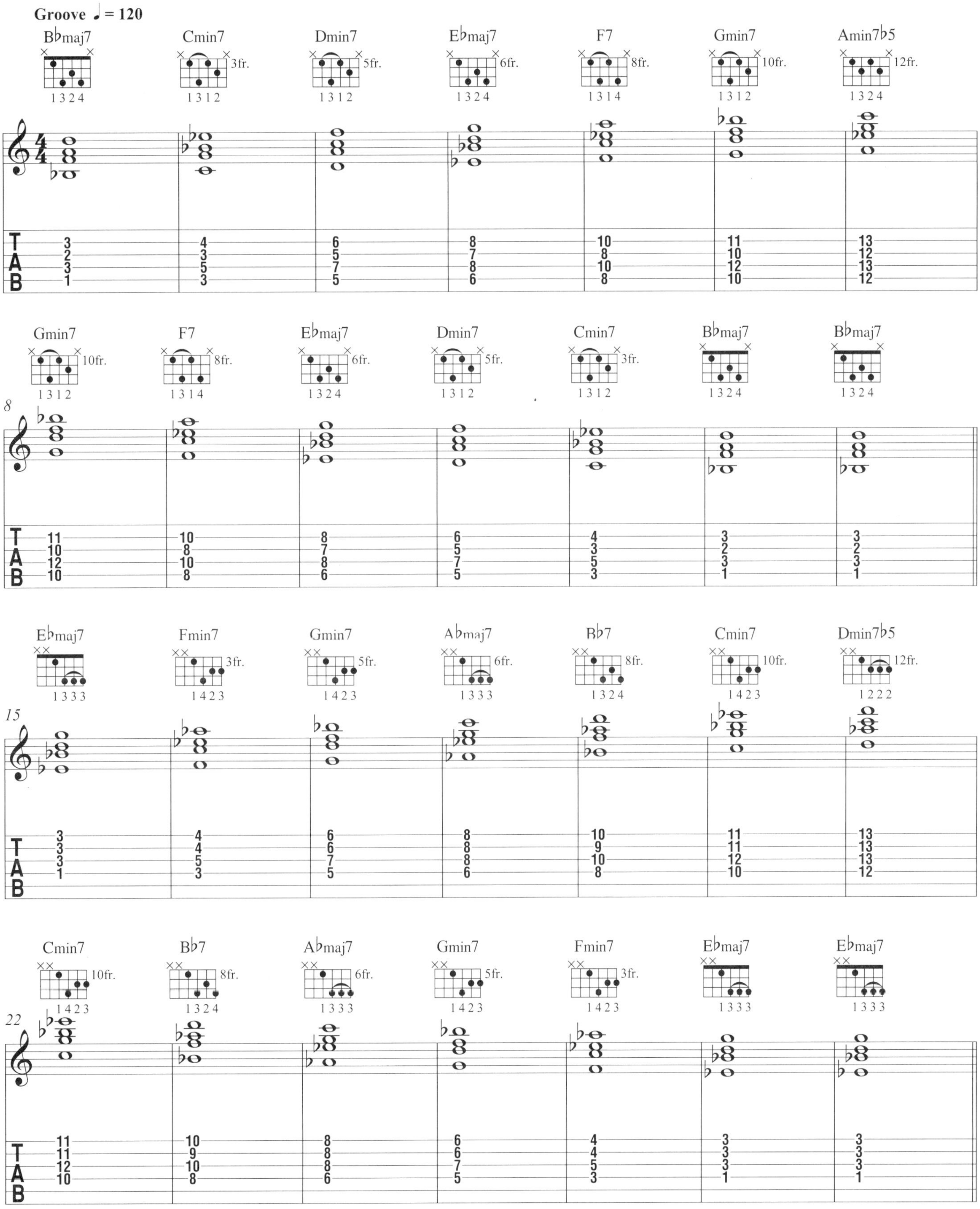

Groove ♩ = 120

B♭maj7 Cmin7 Dmin7 E♭maj7 F7 Gmin7 Amin7♭5

Gmin7 F7 E♭maj7 Dmin7 Cmin7 B♭maj7 B♭maj7

E♭maj7 Fmin7 Gmin7 A♭maj7 B♭7 Cmin7 Dmin7♭5

Cmin7 B♭7 A♭maj7 Gmin7 Fmin7 E♭maj7 E♭maj7

FIG. 16.4. Exercise 16.1. Diatonic Chords and Crossovers in B♭ and E♭

Exercise 16.2. Drop 2 Crossovers Sequence in C and F

118, 119

Play through the voicings with the backing track and work out with the crossover concept with the exercise, Drop 2 Crossovers from ⑤④③② to ④③②①.

Extending the concept of crossovers to diatonic sections with some larger chord leaps, play through the diatonic chords of the keys B♭ and E♭, working to maintain the volume balance of each tone in every chord.

Bossa Nova ♩ = 82

⑤④③②

Cmaj7 (3fr., 1324) – Dmin7 (5fr., 1312) | Emin7 (7fr., 1312) – Fmaj7 (8fr., 1324) | G7 (10fr., 1314) – Emin7 (7fr., 1312) | Dmin7 (5fr., 1312) – Bmin7♭5 (2fr., 1324)

Cmaj7 (3fr., 1324) – Emin7 (7fr., 1312) | Fmaj7 (8fr., 1324) – Dmin7 (5fr., 1312) | G7 (10fr., 1314) – Emin7 (7fr., 1312) | Dmin7 (5fr., 1312) – Bmin7♭5 (2fr., 1324)

④③②①

Fmaj7 (3fr., 1333) – Gmin7 (5fr., 1423) | Amin7 (7fr., 1423) – B♭maj7 (8fr., 1333) | C7 (10fr., 1324) – Amin7 (7fr., 1423) | Gmin7 (5fr., 1423) – Emin7♭5 (2fr., 1222)

Fmaj7 (3fr., 1333) – Amin7 (7fr., 1423) | B♭maj7 (8fr., 1333) – Gmin7 (5fr., 1423) | C7 (10fr., 1324) – Amin7 (7fr., 1423) | Gmin7 (5fr., 1423) – Emin7♭5 (2fr., 1222) | Fmaj7 (3fr., 1333)

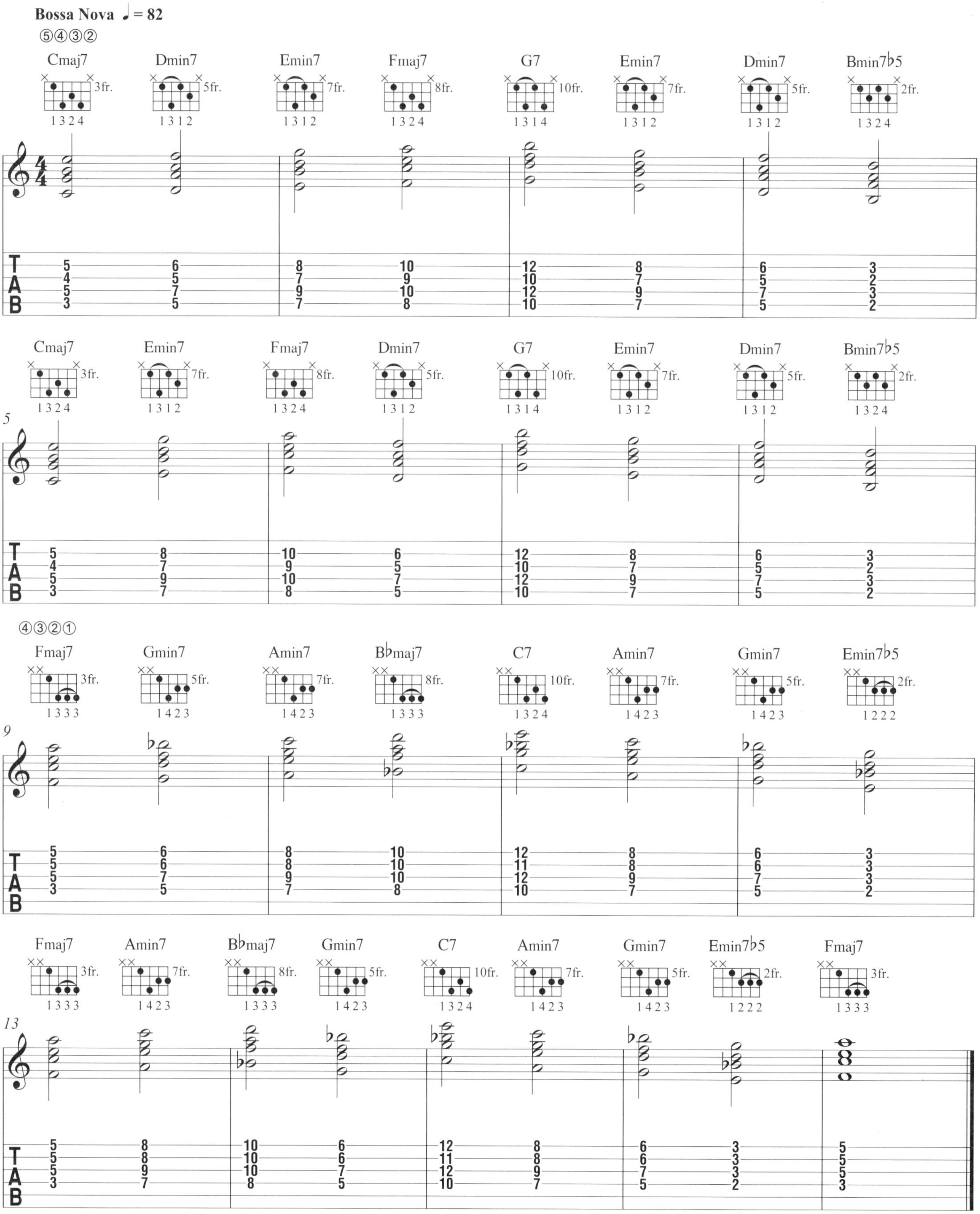

FIG. 16.5. Exercise 16.2. Drop 2 Crossovers Sequence in C and F

LESSON 17

Four-Part Chords: Inverting Drop 2

Inverting drop 2 chord voicings is a challenge for guitarists—both theoretically and physically. Guitarists often assume that inverting a four-part chord is just like working with triads. Inverting triads involves the bottom chord tone leapfrogging to the top.

Inversion of four-part chords is much more complicated—worthy of some focus here. In drop 2 voicing inversions, each tone moves to the nearest chord tone. Root moves to 3, 3 moves to 5, 5 moves to 7, and 7 moves to root. Graphing the tones out with an "Inversion Generator" table has proven helpful to many student (see figure 17.1).

Root Position		First Inversion		Second Inversion		Third Inversion
3	→	5	→	7	→	Root
7	→	Root	→	3	→	5
5	→	7	→	Root	→	3
Root	→	3	→	5	→	7

FIG. 17.1. Inversions of Drop 2 Chords

Drop 2 Seventh Chord Inversions

Please try to play through the voicings described in this lesson, looking at the inversion table that follows. C7 is fully explored here.

When moving through the inversions, notice that the chord tones travel up through the inversions as follows.

- R moves to the 3
- 3 moves to the 5
- 5 moves to the 7
- 7 moves to the R

120

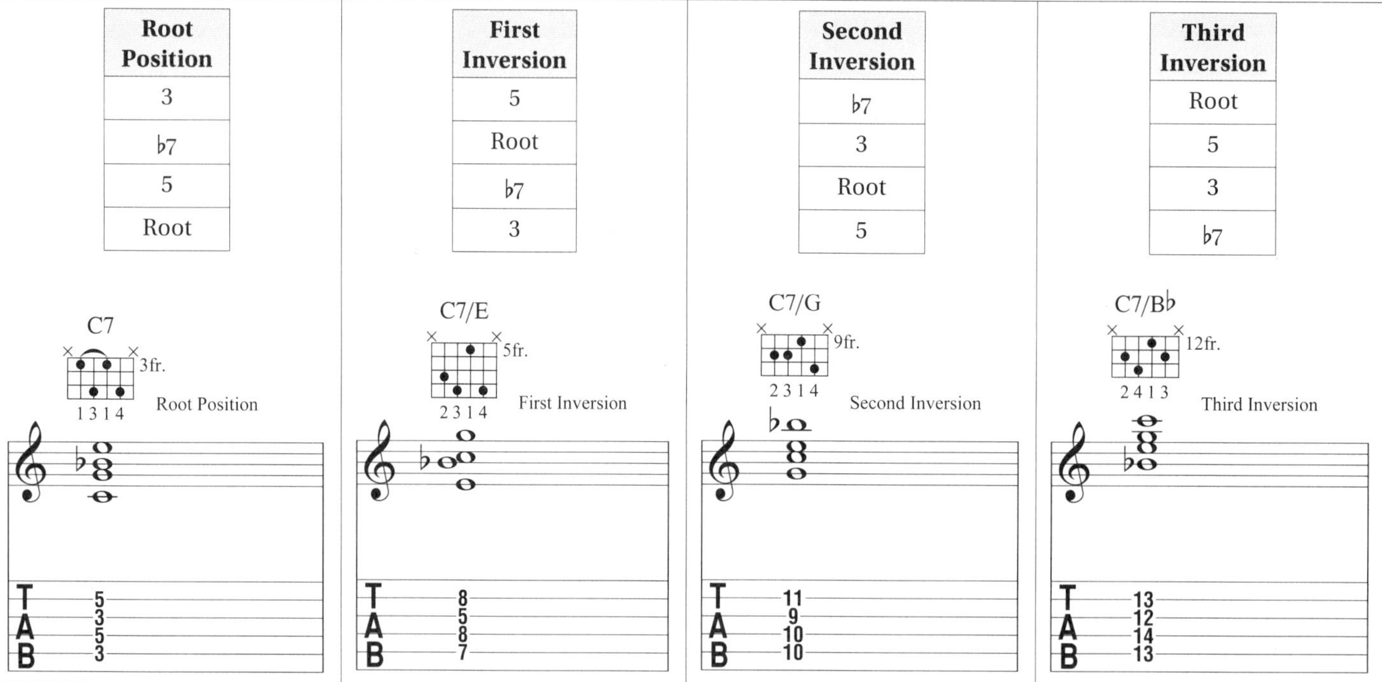

Chord Voicing in Raise 2

Any Drop 2 Dominant 7 Chord				
Root Position	**First Inversion**	**Second Inversion**	**Third Inversion**	
3	5	♭7	Root	Lead
♭7	Root	3	5	
5	♭7	Root	3	
Root	3	5	♭7	Bottom Note

Chord Tones in Close Position

Chord Voicing in Raise 2

C7 Drop 2				
Root Position	**First Inversion**	**Second Inversion**	**Third Inversion**	
E	G	B♭	C	Lead
B♭	C	E	G	
G	B♭	C	E	
C	E	G	B♭	Bottom Note

Chord Tones in Close Position

Root Position
3
♭7
5
Root

First Inversion
5
Root
♭7
3

Second Inversion
♭7
3
Root
5

Third Inversion
Root
5
3
♭7

FIG. 17.2. Drop 2 Inversions for C7

Exercise 17.1. Drop 2 Inversions

This exercise gives you some experience with playing dominant 7, minor 7, minor 7♭5, and major 7 in all inversions. Play through the following exercise. String groups ⑤④③② and ④③②① are mixed for more practical fingering of the voicings. This may be challenging, but try to follow the fingerings as presented.

121, 122

Shuffle Groove ♩ = 100

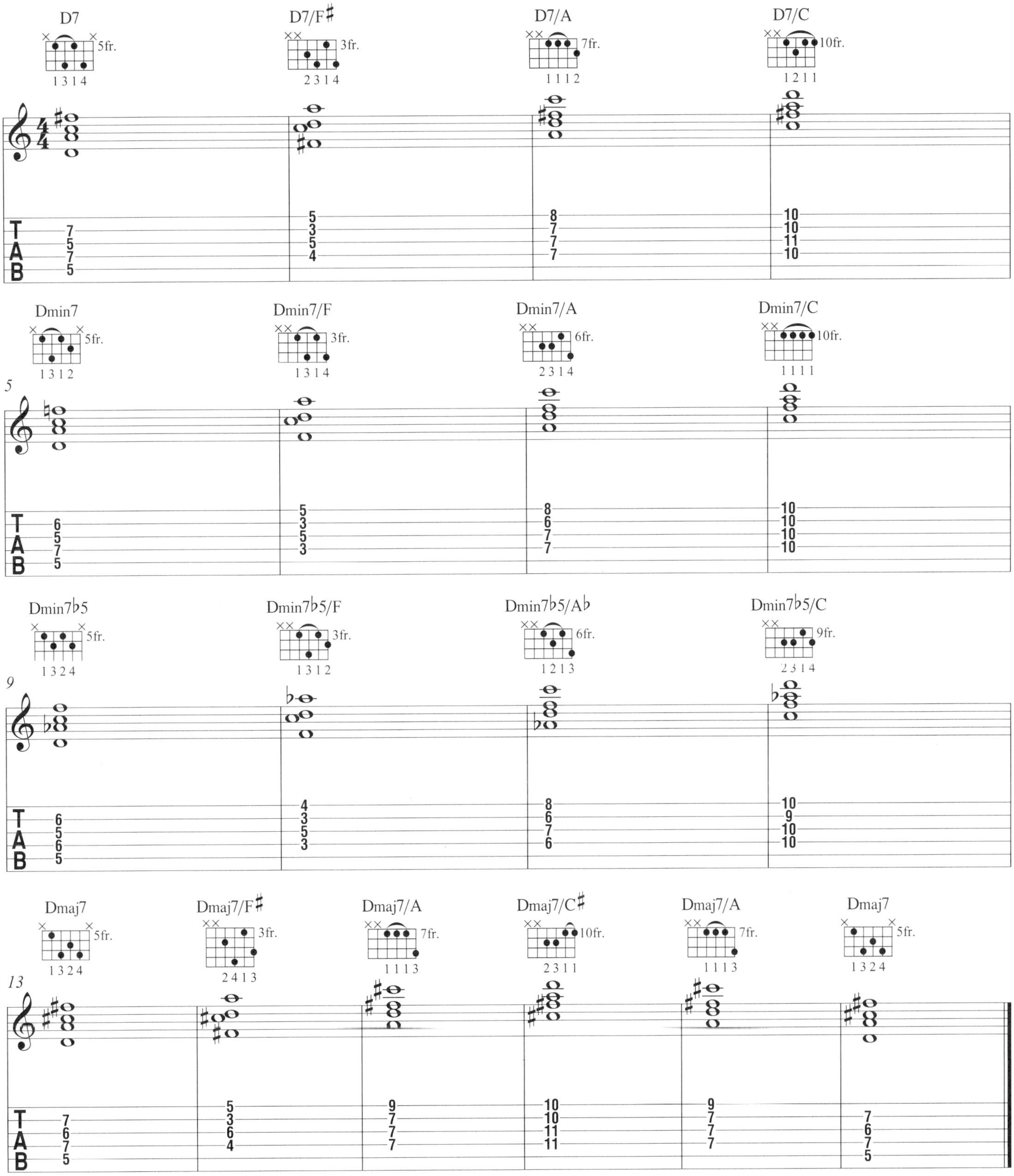

D7 (5fr., 1 3 1 4) | D7/F♯ (3fr., 2 3 1 4) | D7/A (7fr., 1 1 1 2) | D7/C (10fr., 1 2 1 1)

5 Dmin7 (5fr., 1 3 1 2) | Dmin7/F (3fr., 1 3 1 4) | Dmin7/A (6fr., 2 3 1 4) | Dmin7/C (10fr., 1 1 1 1)

9 Dmin7♭5 (5fr., 1 3 2 4) | Dmin7♭5/F (3fr., 1 3 1 2) | Dmin7♭5/A♭ (6fr., 1 2 1 3) | Dmin7♭5/C (9fr., 2 3 1 4)

13 Dmaj7 (5fr., 1 3 2 4) | Dmaj7/F♯ (3fr., 2 4 1 3) | Dmaj7/A (7fr., 1 1 1 3) | Dmaj7/C♯ (10fr., 2 3 1 1) | Dmaj7/A (7fr., 1 1 1 3) | Dmaj7 (5fr., 1 3 2 4)

FIG. 17.3. Exercise 17.1. Drop 2 Inversions

We will be making much more use of the concept of drop 2 inversions in the upcoming chapters, but working through exercise 17.1 will be very helpful preparation.

LESSON 18

Diminished 7 Drop 2 Chords

Diminished 7 voicings have several functions, with a lot of harmonic applications. At times, the diminished chord functions as a dominant chord, helping the harmonic progression to feel as if it should move forward with greater momentum. At other times, the diminished chord provides a rich, contrasting color to a tonic chord. You will encounter the diminished chord most frequently in standard jazz tunes, but it crops up frequently in blues progressions and in other musical styles as well.

The diminished 7, sometimes called fully diminished 7, is unique in several ways:

1. The chord tones are all a minor third apart, making inversions of voicing types relatively easy on the fretboard. Inverting diminished triads is difficult, inverting dim7 (on the same set of strings) is a snap!
2. VIIdim7 in minor keys can be seen as a first inversion dom7♭9 chord.
3. Idim7 functions as a delayed resolution chord, which often resolves to a tonic Imaj7 chord.

Chord tones are root, ♭3, ♭5, ♭7. Spelling diminished 7 chords involves stacking minor thirds. The double-flat found on the 7 is enharmonic to the note found a major sixth above the root, and to avoid double-flats, the major 6 is often used when spelling the diminished 7 chord.

See the bottom line of the Inversion Generator blocks that follow to see the close position version of this chord type. The easiest way to spell dim7 is to think: root, ♭3, ♭5, 6. Drop 2 diminished 7 chords are built in the same way as the others, using the raise 2 process.

123

Chord Voicing in Raise 2

Any Raise 2 Diminished Seventh Chord				
Root Position	**First Inversion**	**Second Inversion**	**Third Inversion**	
♭3	♭5	♭♭7 (6)	Root	Lead
♭♭7 (6)	Root	♭3	♭5	
♭5	♭♭7 (6)	Root	♭3	
Root	♭3	♭5	♭♭7 (6)	Bottom Note

Chord Tones in Close Position

Chord Voicing in Raise 2

Cdim7 Raise 2				
Root Position	**First Inversion**	**Second Inversion**	**Third Inversion**	
E♭	G♭	B♭♭ (A)	C	Lead
B♭♭ (A)	C	E♭	G♭	
G♭	B♭♭ (A)	C	E♭	
C	E♭	G♭	B♭♭ (A)	Bottom Note

Chord Tones in Close Position

Root Position
♭3
♭♭7 (6)
♭5
Root

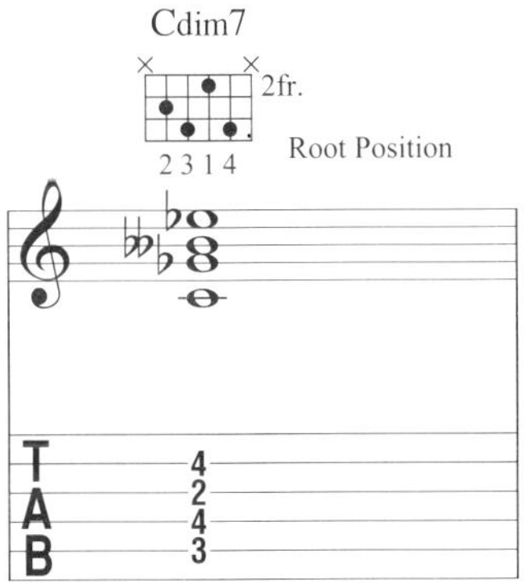

First Inversion
♭5
Root
♭♭7 (6)
♭3

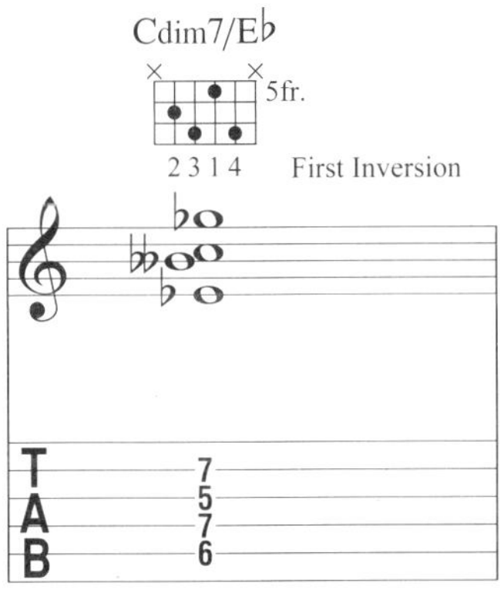

Second Inversion
♭♭7 (6)
♭3
Root
♭5

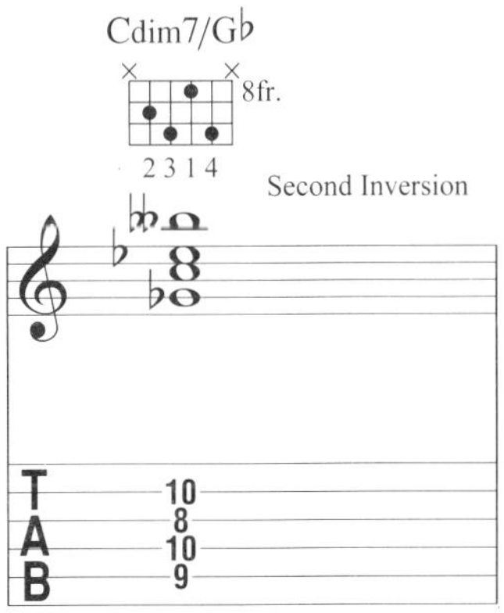

Third Inversion
Root
♭5
♭3
♭♭7 (6)

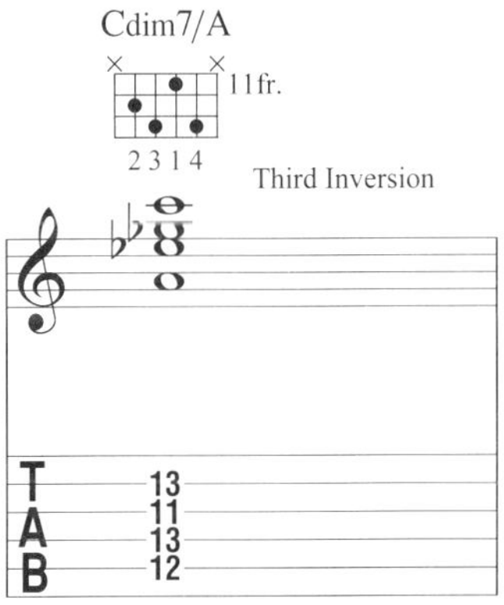

FIG. 18.1. All Inversions of Cdim7 with Intervals and Chord Tones Identified

Use the raise 2 process to get a drop 2 shape in the following way:

1. Arpeggiate the chord, noting the second tone from the bottom.
2. Raise the second tone one octave.
3. Play the raise 2 chord form (same configuration as drop 2).

124

FIG. 18.2. Raise 2 for Cdim7

Using the crossover process, we can move from ⑤④③② to ④③②①.

The steps:

1. Play the original chord form on ⑤④③②.
2. Move the shape directly from ⑤④③② to ④③②①, finding a transitional shape.
3. Raise the note on ② by one fret.
4. Take the new form up seven frets or down five frets to match the original root.

125

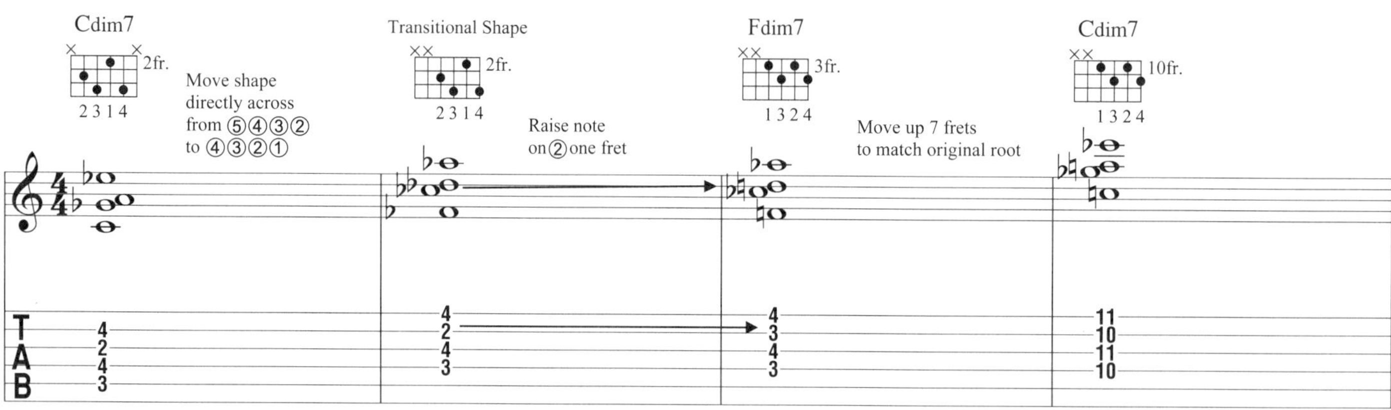

FIG. 18.3. Cdim7 as a Crossover From ⑤④③② to ④③②①

Diminished 7 voicings are unique in their ability to fortify dominant harmony. Placing a dim7 chord from the 3, 5, ♭7, or ♭9 of a dominant chord implies a dom7(♭9) sound. In figure 18.4, open ⑥ is used as a pedal point, and E7 is being enriched with G♯dim7 (3), Fdim7 (♭9), Ddim7 (♭7) and Bdim7 (5). We will be discussing alterations of dominant chords in a future chapter, but for now, play through figure 18.4.

126, 127

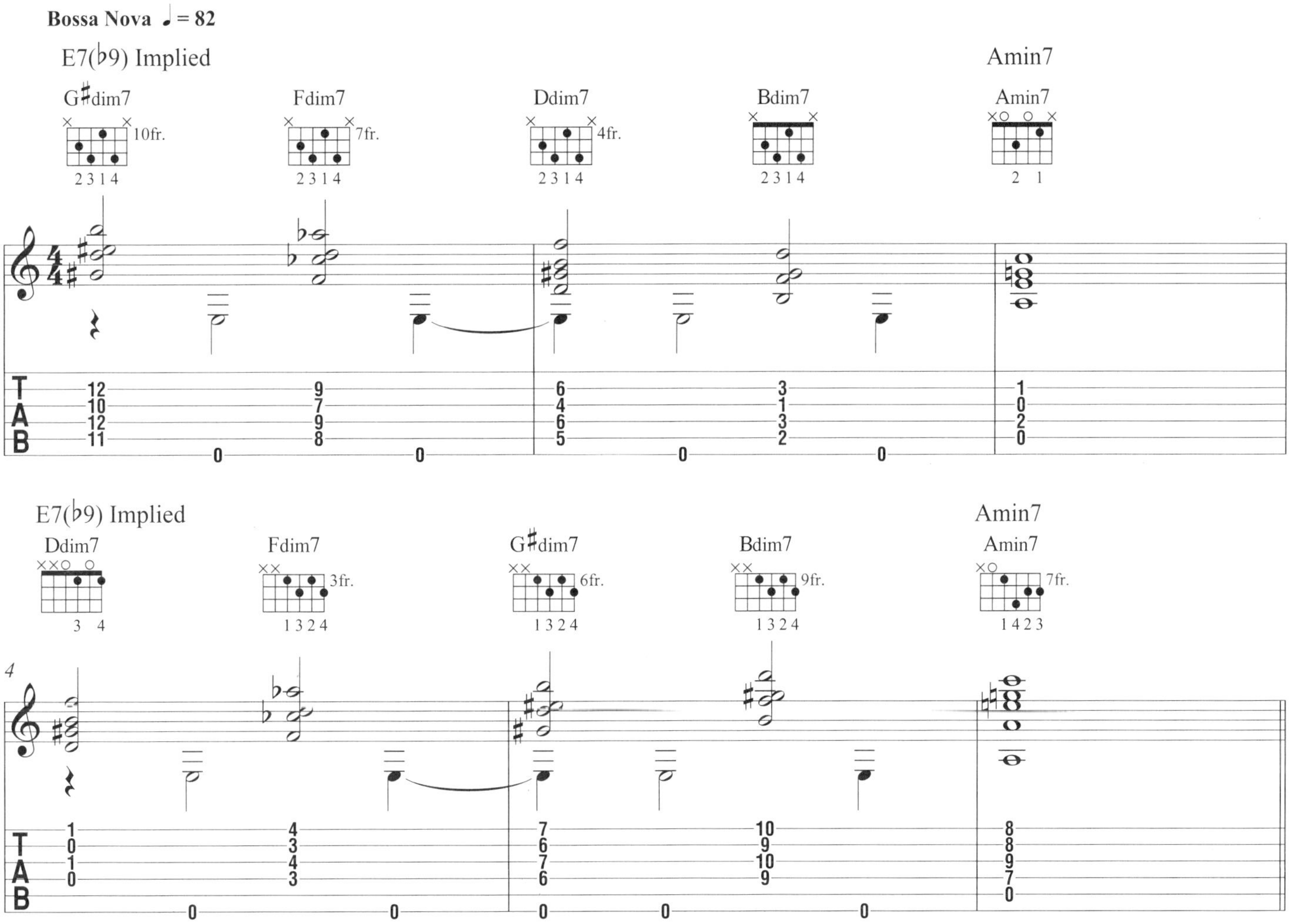

Bossa Nova ♩ = 82

E7(♭9) Implied — G♯dim7 (10fr.), Fdim7 (7fr.), Ddim7 (4fr.), Bdim7 — Amin7

E7(♭9) Implied — Ddim7, Fdim7 (3fr.), G♯dim7 (6fr.), Bdim7 (9fr.) — Amin7 (7fr.)

FIG. 18.4. Dim7 in Its Role as Dominant 7 Function

Exercise 18.1. Diminished 7 in Various Functions

Let's devote some practice to diminished voicings by playing through this exercise. I encourage you to do this exercise repeatedly until you have control of these chord shapes. In bars 19 to the end, listen for the diminished 7 chord in its dominant function as well as tonic diminished, resolving to tonic major 7.

128, 129

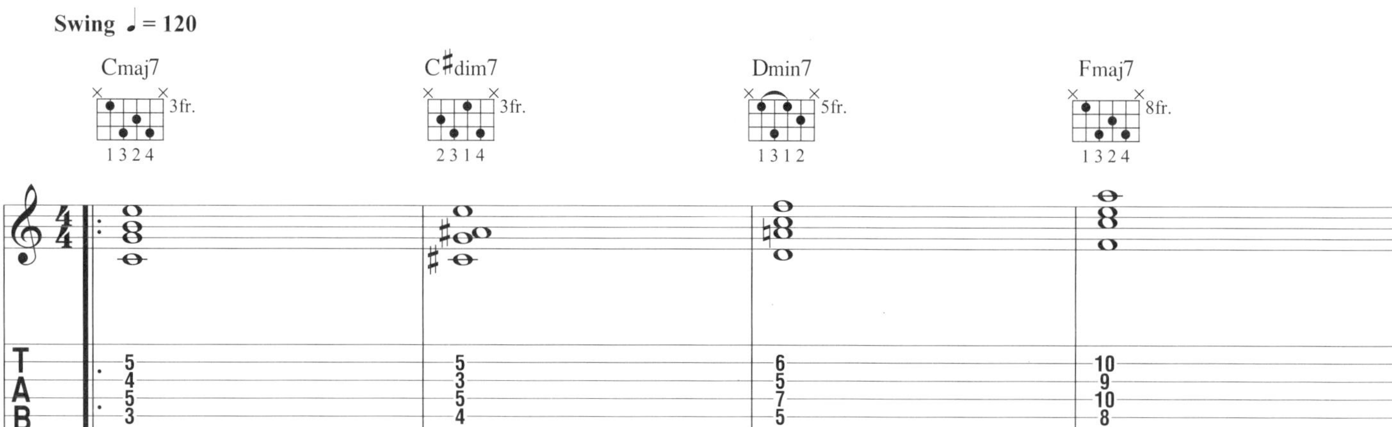

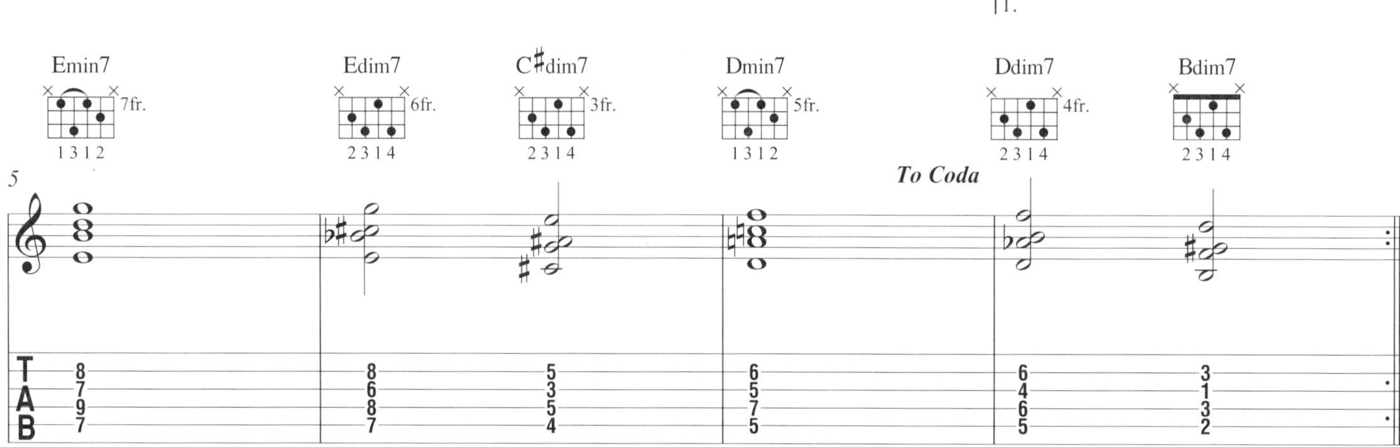

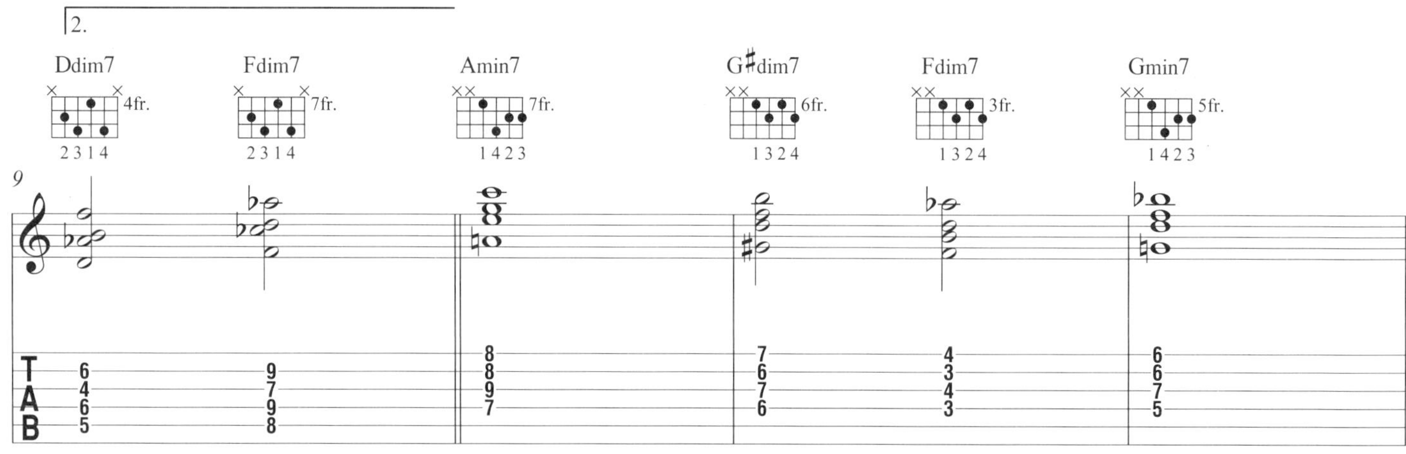

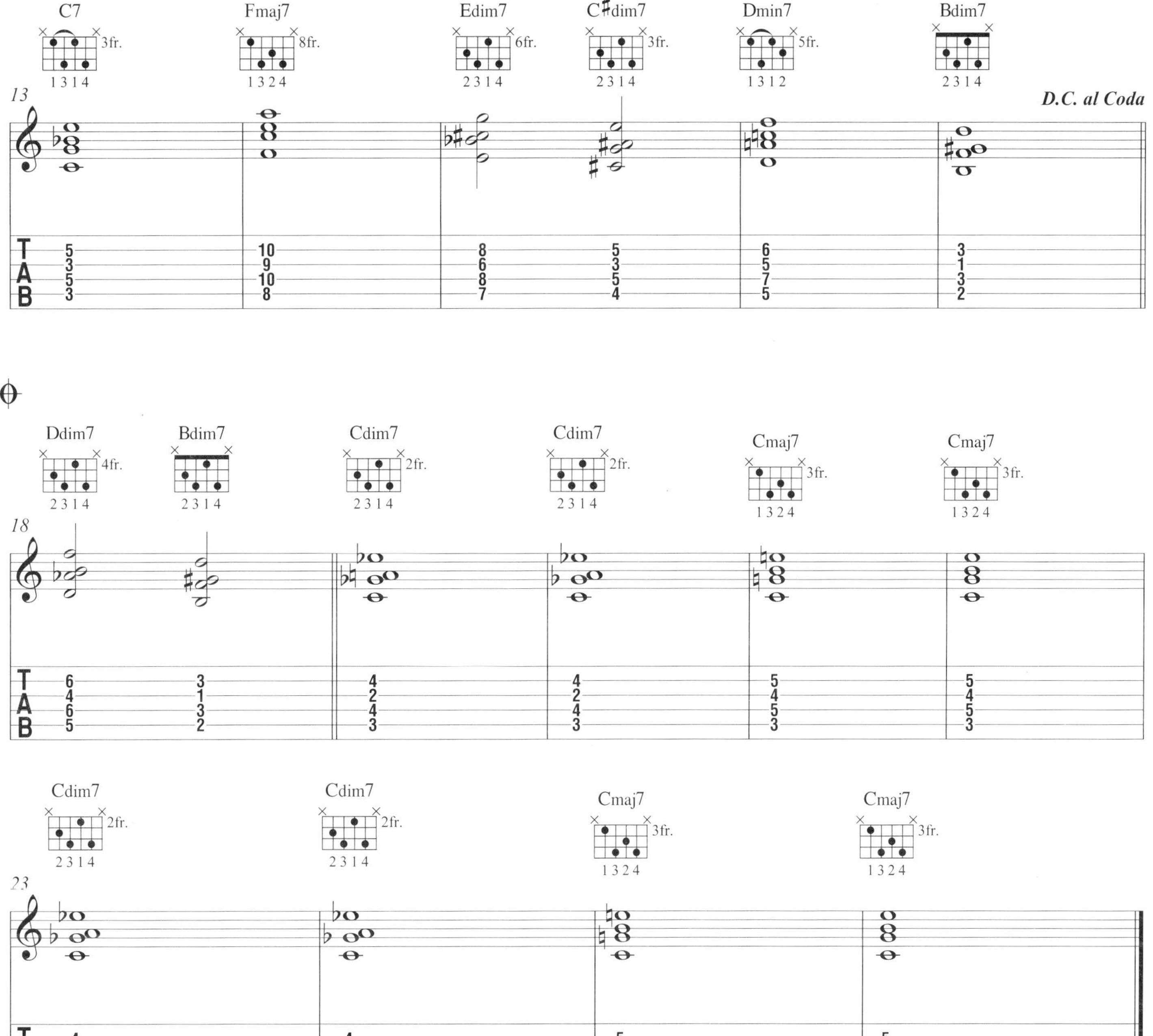

FIG. 18.5. Exercise 18.1. Diminished 7 in Various Functions

LESSON 19

Drop 3 Voicings Using Raise 2 and 3 Process

It's time to add the drop 3 configuration for four-part chords to our repertoire. These voicings consist of a bass note, a skipped string, and then three adjacent strings, in contrast to the drop 2 with its four adjacent strings.

To summarize:

Four-Part Chords Review:	**Four-Part Chords New:**
Drop 2 Voicings (built with raise 2 process)	Drop 3 Voicings (built with raise 2 and 3 process)
String sets: ⑤④③② and ④③②①	String sets: ⑥④③② and ⑤③②①

The drop 3 features a wider range from lowest to highest pitch, and you'll emerge with a greater understanding of the fretboard as a result of working on this set of versatile voicings.

DROP 3: BOTTOM STRING, SKIPPED STRING, THEN THREE ADJACENT STRINGS

Drop 3 voicings provide a contrasting shape on the fretboard, different than our set of drop 2 voicings. Drop 3 voicings are structures that have a fifth or sixth string on the bottom, skip a string, and then have three adjacent strings.

Let's use raise 2 and raise 3 to get G7 with root on ⑥. Arpeggiate the chord, move the second and third voices up one octave, and sound the chord, as demonstrated.

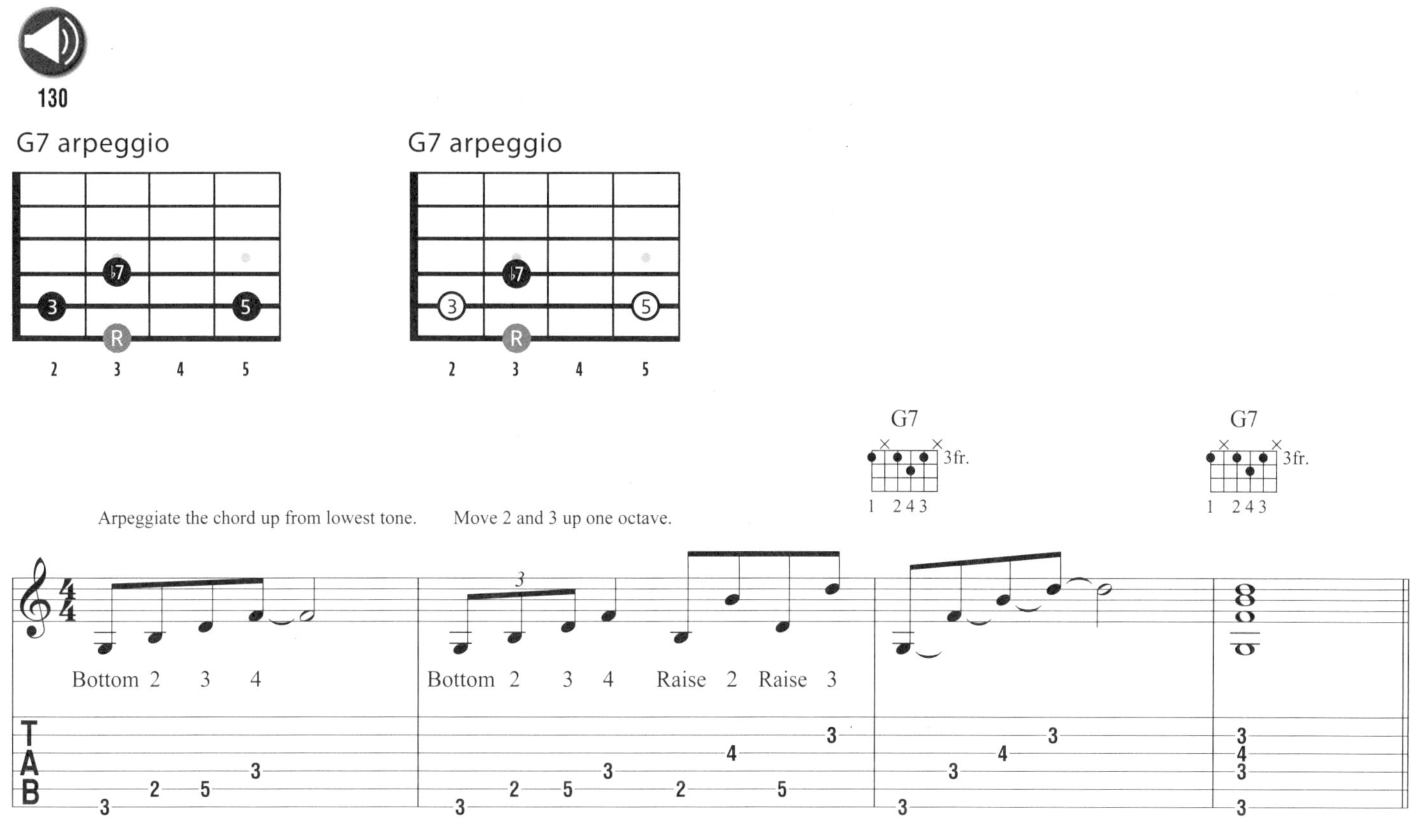

FIG. 19.1. Raise 2 and 3 Process for G7

Two Routes to the Same Voicing: Raise 2 and 3 versus Drop 3

The *Chords 101* approach to building voicings is to favor a *raise* process, rather than a *drop* process, since most guitarists have found it easier to build a root position voicing starting with a root position chord spelling.

Using standard notation, here is G7 in root position, followed by its three inversions.

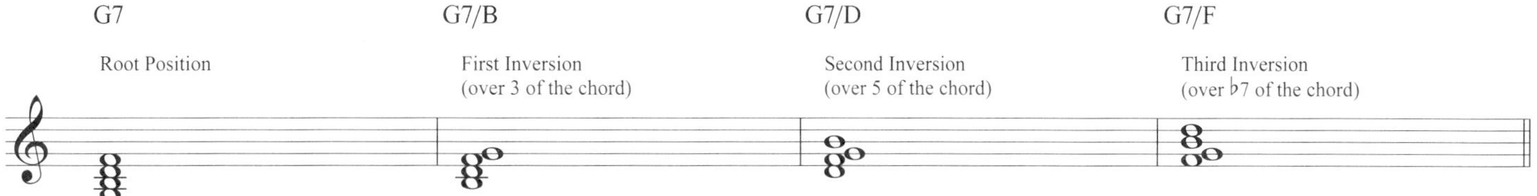

FIG. 19.2. G7 in All Inversions

With raise 2 and 3, we can build the root position voicing from the bottom up. To use drop 3, we need to start from the third inversion spelling of the chord. Here are the two routes to a drop 3 voicing for a G7 with root on ⑥.

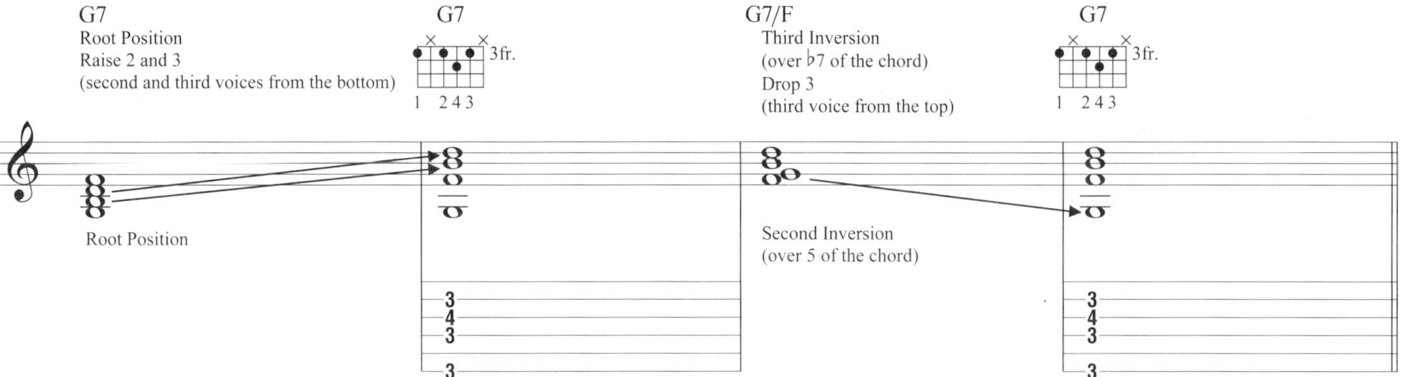

FIG. 19.3. G7 as Raise 2 and 3 and Drop 3

Here are the inversions of G7, as described by two inversion generator tables: first with interval names and then with G7 chord tones. In these tables, close position chords are in the rows, with raise 2 and 3 voicings in the columns. Remember, muted strings (×'s) are important to a clean, clear sounding of these chord voicings.

Any Raise 2 and 3 Dominant 7 Chord (Chord Voicing in Raise 2 and 3 / Chord Tones in Close Position)

	Root Position	First Inversion	Second Inversion	Third Inversion
Lead	5	♭7	Root	3
	3	5	♭7	Root
	♭7	Root	3	5
Bottom Note	Root	3	5	♭7

G7 Raise 2 and 3 (Chord Voicing in Raise 2 and 3 / Chord Tones in Close Position)

	Root Position	First Inversion	Second Inversion	Third Inversion
Lead	D	F	G	B
	B	D	F	G
	F	G	B	D
Bottom Note	G	B	D	F

Root Position
5
3
♭7
Root

G7 — 3fr. — 1 243 — Root Position — TAB: 3, 4, 3, 3

First Inversion
♭7
5
Root
3

G7/B — 5fr. — 3 142 — First Inversion — TAB: 6, 7, 5, 7

Second Inversion
Root
♭7
3
5

G7/D — 8fr. — 3 241 — Second Inversion — TAB: 8, 10, 9, 10

Third Inversion
3
Root
5
♭7

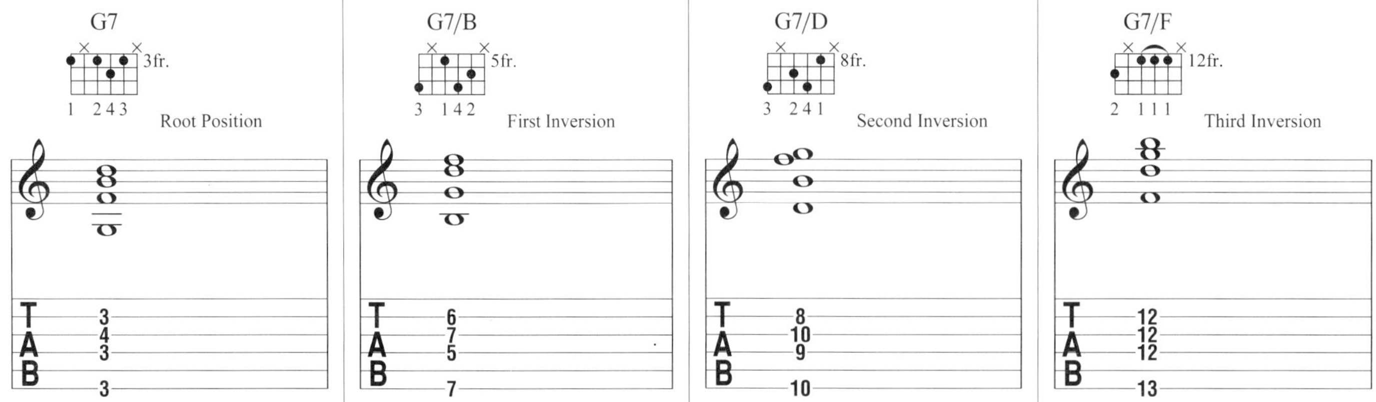

G7/F — 12fr. — 2 111 — Third Inversion — TAB: 12, 12, 12, 13

FIG. 19.4. Drop 3 G7 Inversions with Interval Names and Chord Tones

Let's look at some other chord qualities in their drop 3 configuration on ⑥④③②. Please note the structure of drop 3 chords in root position, found on the "function" line.

String:	⑥	④	③	②
Function:	Root	7	3	5

The fretboard graphic in figure 20.5 should help you to relate the various chord colors to the G7 shape that we've been using. Here they are with a ⑥ as the bottom note for these five shapes.

132

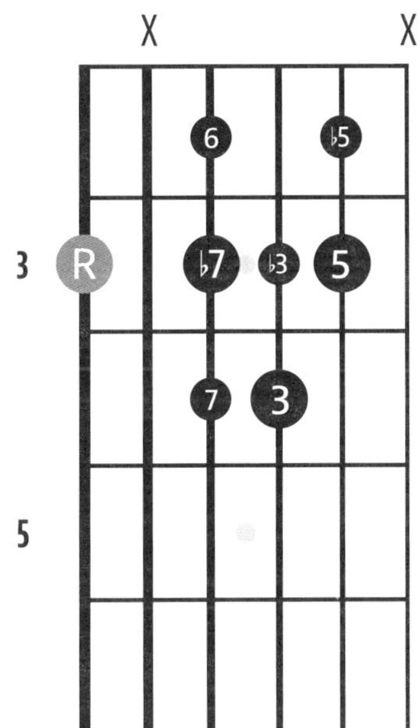

Drop 3 Chord Qualities ⑥④③②				
	⑥	④	③	②
Function:	Root	7	3	5
G7	G	F (♭7)	B	D
Gmaj7	G	F♯	B	D
Gmin7	G	F (♭7)	B♭ (♭3)	D
Gmin7♭5	G	F (♭7)	B♭ (♭3)	D♭ (♭5)
Gdim7	G	E (dim7, same as ♮6)	B♭ (♭3)	D♭ (♭5)

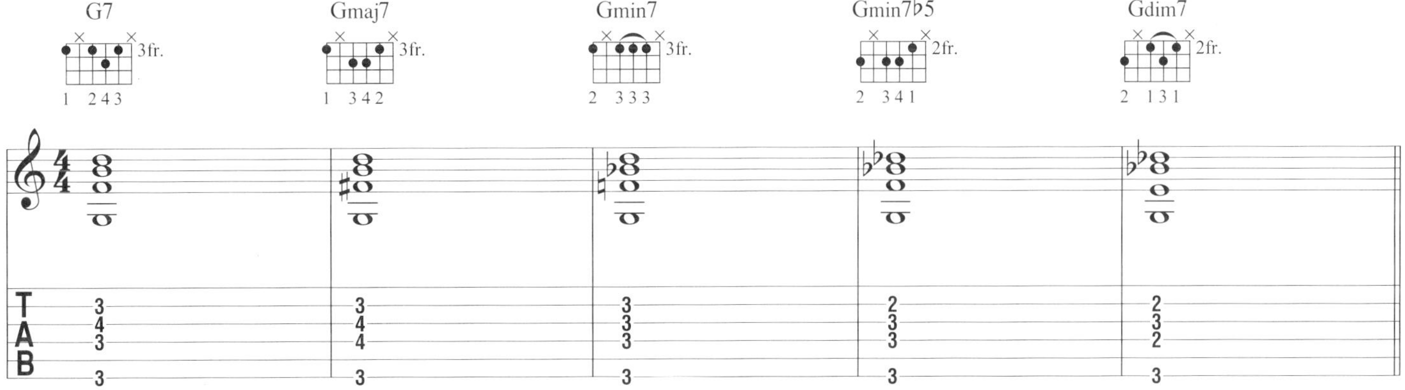

FIG. 19.5. Drop 3 Fretboard Diagram, Function Chart, and Chord Notation on ⑥④③②

Using ⑤ as the chord-root's home base for these five shapes, here are the same qualities with a ⑤ root.

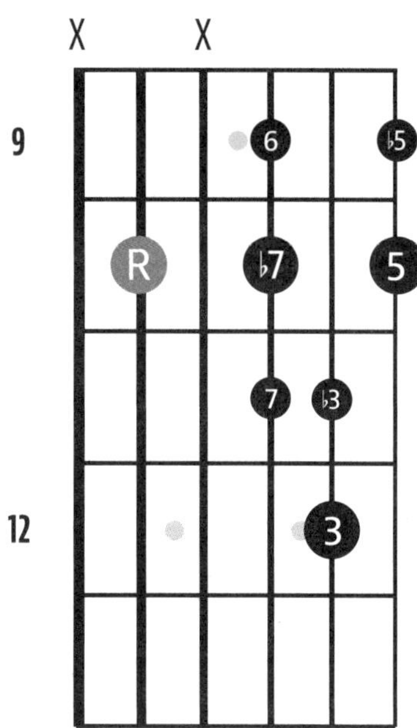

Drop 3 Chord Qualities ⑤③②①				
	⑤	③	②	①
Function:	Root	7	3	5
G7	G	F (♭7)	B	D
Gmaj7	G	F♯	B	D
Gmin7	G	F (♭7)	B♭ (♭3)	D
Gmin7♭5	G	F (♭7)	B♭ (♭3)	D♭(♭5)
Gdim7	G	E (dim7, same as ♮6)	B♭ (♭3)	D♭(♭5)

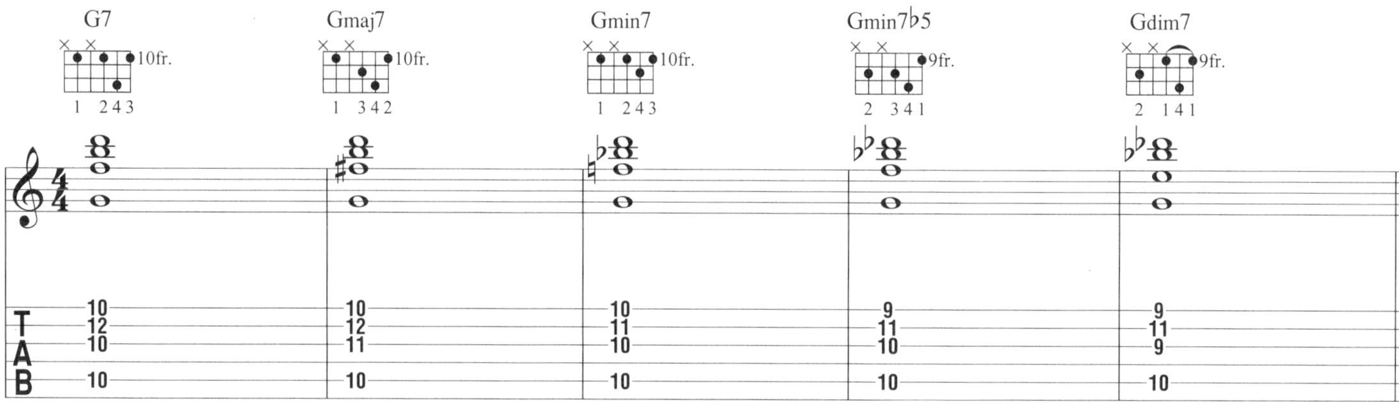

FIG. 19.6. Drop 3 Fretboard Diagram, Function Chart, and Chord Notation ⑤③②①

Remember, keeping track of the quality of the 3, 5, and 7—that is, knowing whether they are major, minor, or diminished—allows you to gain control of all of these chord qualities. The ⑤ orientation of the drop 3 shape may help you to gain control of the various colors.

Exercise 19.1. Drop 3 Min7 and Dom7 through Twelve Keys

This exercise will help you learn drop 3 shape for two chord qualities: min7 and dom7 through twelve keys.

Let's gain control of these new drop 3 shapes beginning with two chord qualities. This exercise moves min7 and dom7 chords through twelve keys on ⑥④③② and ⑤③②①. Pay particular attention to muting the strings where the × appears in each. Dominant 7 voicings on ⑤③②① are among the most challenging shapes (and least popular) in the *Chords 101* course, so be patient, but keep trying! Use the min7 voicing as a means of preparing the more difficult dom7 voicing. Play with good time, but think ahead to the next shape. Work toward planting the fingers in place a bit earlier for a cleaner, fuller sound at the point of chord change.

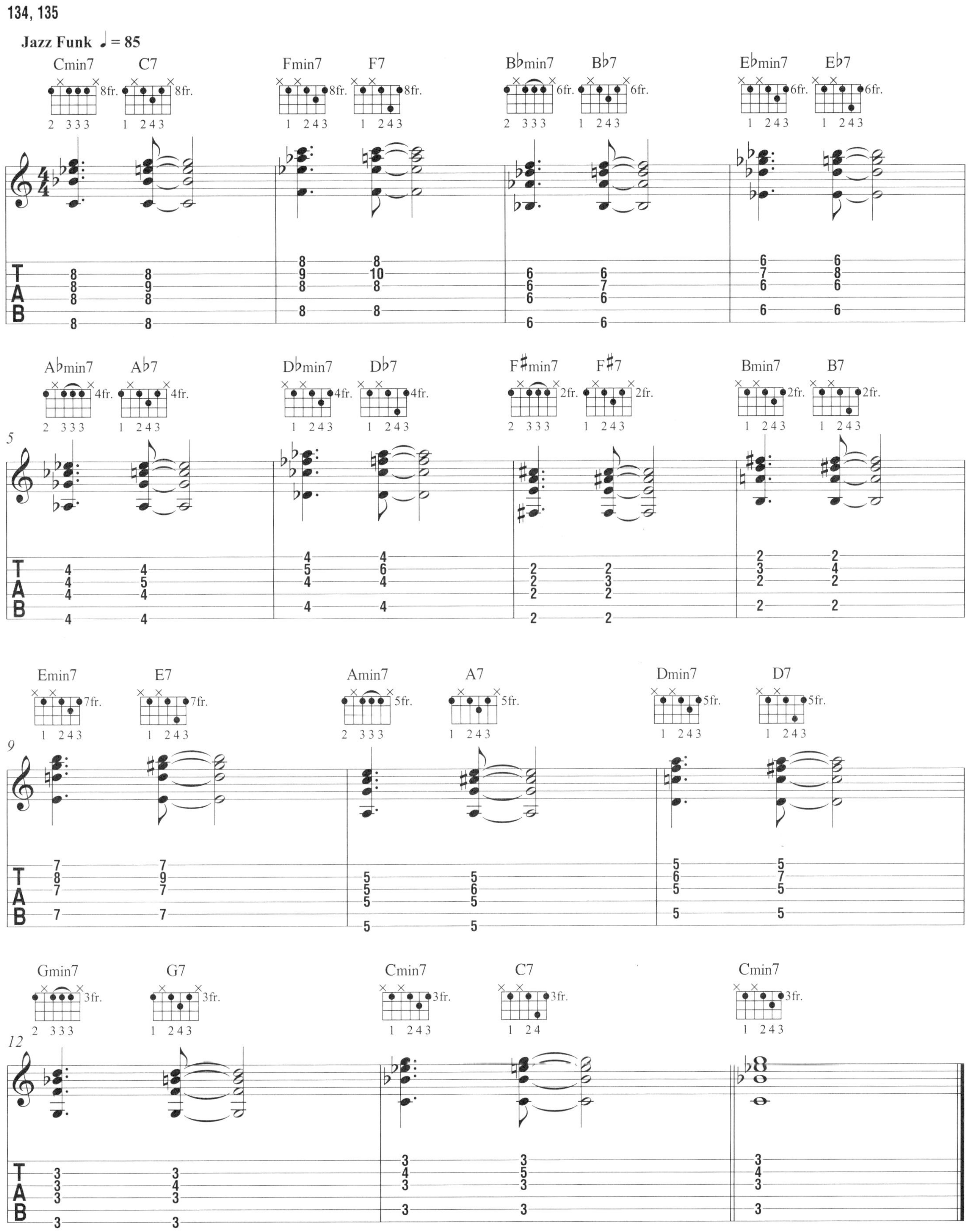

FIG. 19.7. Exercise 19.1. Drop 3 Min7 and Dom7 through Twelve Keys

Exercise 19.2. Drop 3 Diatonic Chords in F and B♭

136, 137

Here is an exercise with a focus on the diatonic chords of F major and B♭ major. The most common problem with drop 3 voicings involves the strings that are necessarily muted. You need to integrate a slight arch in your first finger of your fretting hand to allow essential chord tones to sound while muting the "skipped" string.

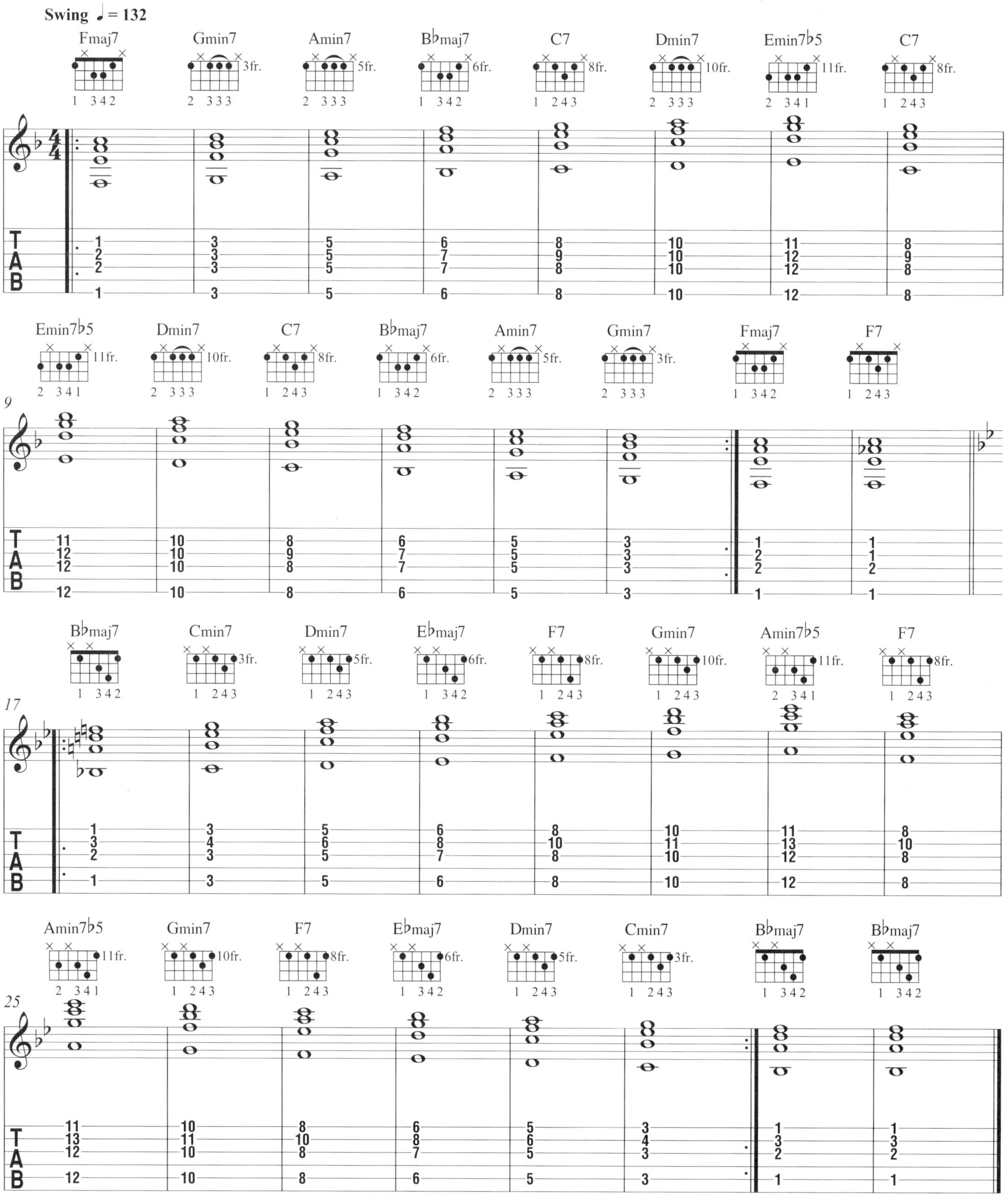

Swing ♩ = 132

Fmaj7 Gmin7 Amin7 B♭maj7 C7 Dmin7 Emin7♭5 C7

Emin7♭5 Dmin7 C7 B♭maj7 Amin7 Gmin7 Fmaj7 F7

B♭maj7 Cmin7 Dmin7 E♭maj7 F7 Gmin7 Amin7♭5 F7

Amin7♭5 Gmin7 F7 E♭maj7 Dmin7 Cmin7 B♭maj7 B♭maj7

FIG. 19.8. Exercise 19.2. Drop 3 Diatonic Chords in F and B♭

LESSON 20

Major 6 and Minor 6 Voicings

Classic standard songs from the twentieth century frequently used very basic chord sounds when establishing the home key or resolving to the home key at the song's ending. Major 6 or minor 6 chords are part of what every guitarist should know if they want to sound idiomatic in these earlier styles.

Major 6 and minor 6 chords are less common in contemporary lead sheets and chord charts than they were in fakebooks produced in the 1950s and 1960s.

Although it's pretty much common practice to substitute major 7 chords for major 6 and minor 7 chords for minor 6, it is still necessary to have these voicings under control so that you know what to do when you encounter them. Country swing, Django Reinhardt–style jazz, and pre-modal jazz are better served by min6 and maj6 than their more contemporary substitutes.

Major 6 and minor 6 chords add a voice at the interval of a major sixth to the basic triad.

MAJOR 6

Major 6 chords consist of root, 3, 5, and ♮6. Here is the root position drop 2 Cmaj6 voicing on ⑤ and the root position drop 3 on ⑥. The ⑤ voicing is particularly difficult for many guitarists, but consistent effort will allow this somewhat awkward shape to become part of your vocabulary.

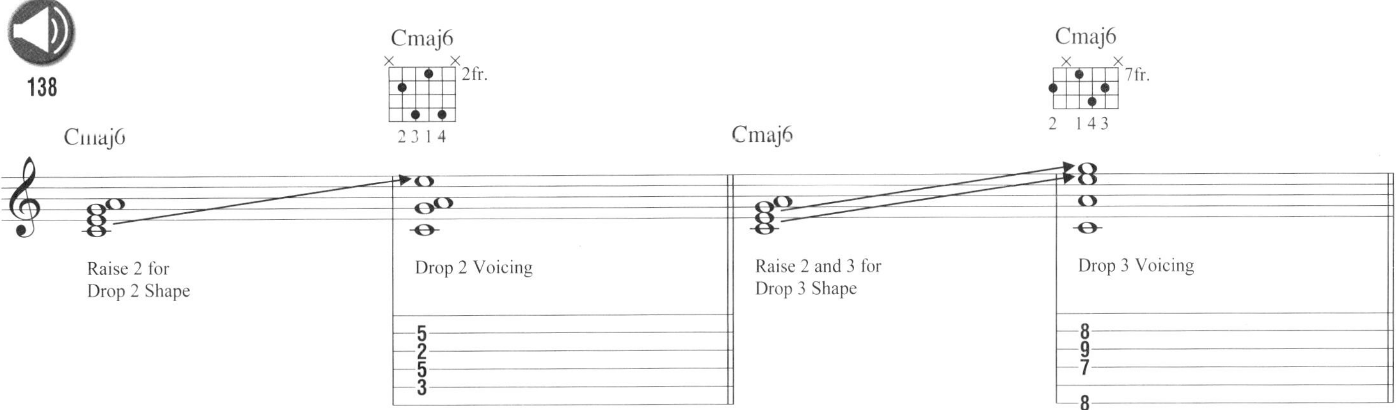

FIG. 20.1. Building Drop 2 and Drop 3 Voicings for Cmaj6

MINOR 6

Minor 6 chords consist of root, ♭3, 5, and ♮6. Here is the root position drop 2 Cmin6 voicing on ⑤ and the root position drop 3 on ⑥.

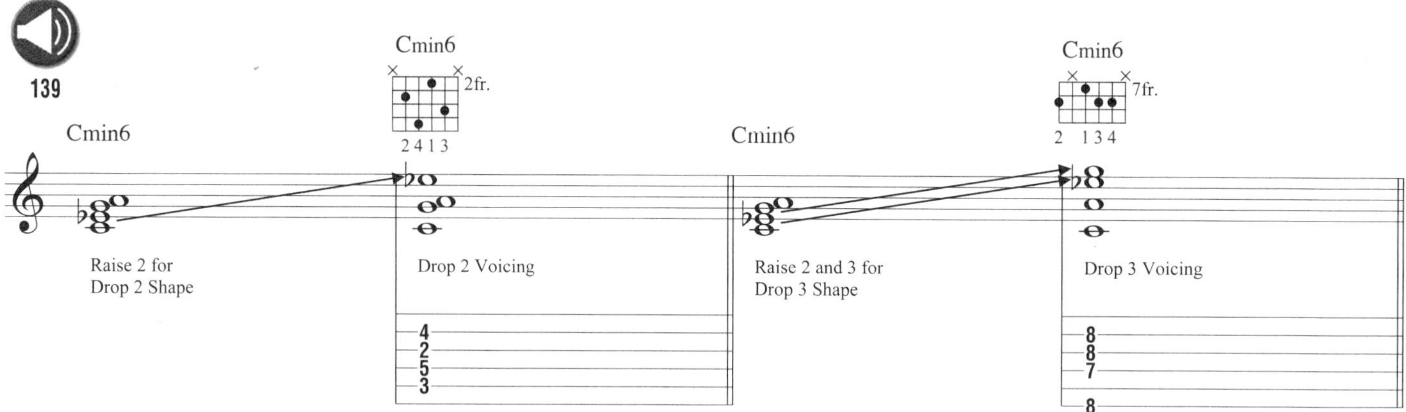

FIG. 20.2. Building Drop 2 and Drop 3 Voicings for Cmin6

MAJOR 6 AND MINOR 6 CHORDS: SHARING CHORD TONES WITH MIN7 AND MIN7♭5

Major 6 voicings can be seen as inversions of minor 7 chords. There are several unique characteristics found in major 6 and minor 6 chords. Major or minor 6 chords are made up of triads with added sixths, but no seventh. Major or minor 6 chords, since they don't have sevenths, provide a more stable sound, helpful in defining the home base of key. These two harmonic shapes have a unique, dual-identity secret, however.

In fact, if you think "C major, over its ♮6," you'll see an Amin7 appear. Similarly, for Cmin6, if you think "C minor over its ♮6, you'll see Amin7♭5."

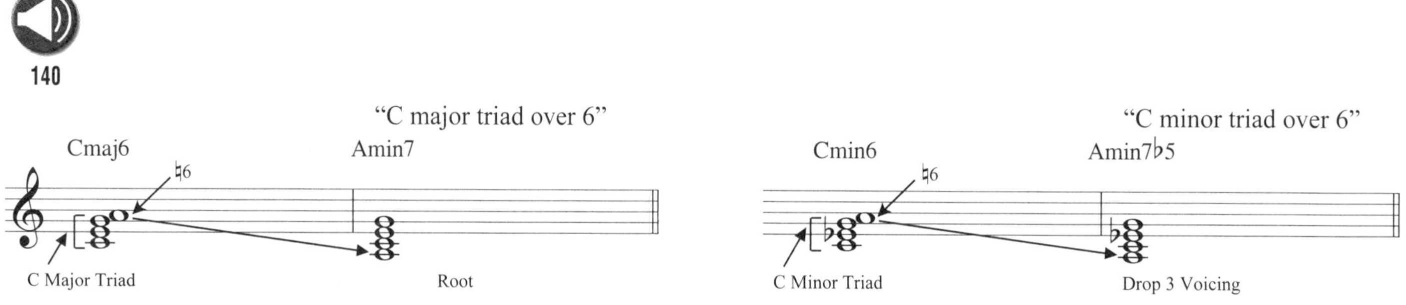

FIG. 20.3. Cmaj6 in Relation to Amin7; Cmin6 in Relation to Amin7♭5

Major or minor 6 chords can be seen as specific inversions of specific minor 7 or minor 7♭5 chords. *Or,* minor 7 and minor 7♭5 can be seen as specific inversions of major 6 or minor 6 chords.

Here are the inversions of a drop 3 Gmaj6 on ⑥④③②, where you'll see an appearance of Emin7 when the chord has an E bass.

141

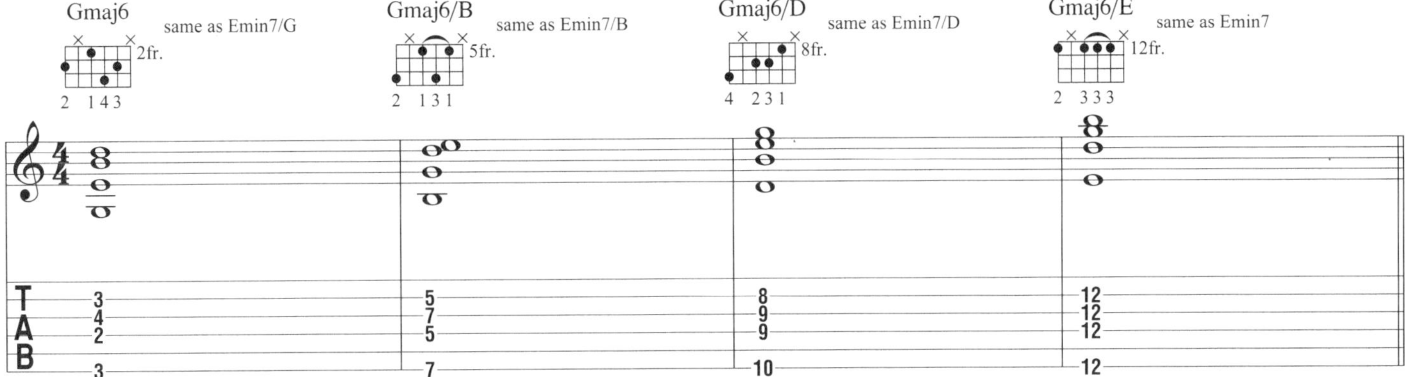

FIG. 20.4. Gmaj6 ⑥ Drop 3 in All Inversions with Related min7 Chord Names

Here is the drop 2 version of Gmaj6 on ⑤④③②, shown in all inversions. The root position Gmaj6 is in ninth position, and the Emin7 appears when G major is over its ♮6, in seventh position.

142

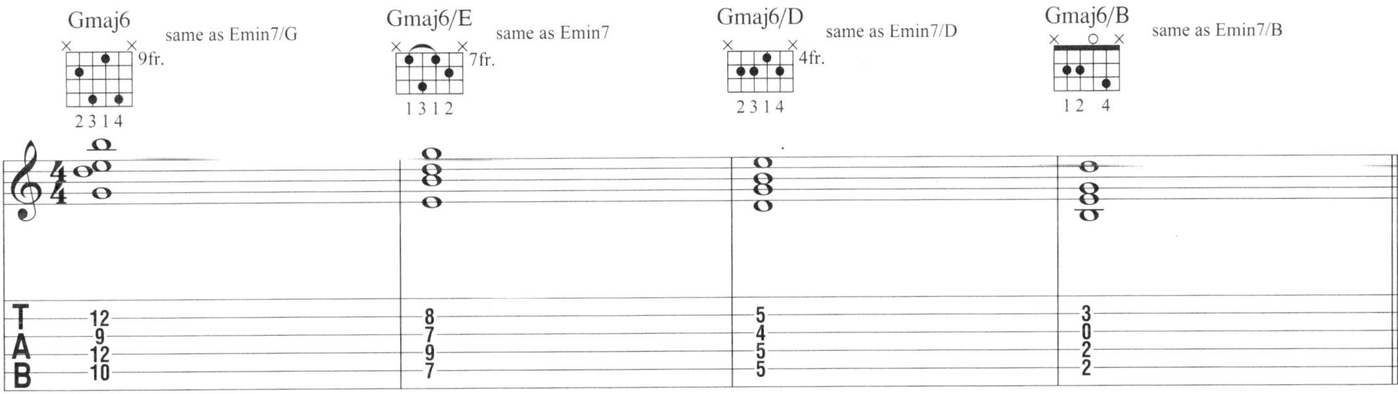

FIG. 20.5. Gmaj6 on ⑤: Drop 3 in All Inversions with Related min7 Chord Names

SOLID TAKE: FREDDIE GREEN STYLE FOR RHYTHM GUITAR

Use all down strokes with your pick and release the pressure with your fretting fingers to punctuate each quarter note—not too long and not too short. Freddie Green is acknowledged as the master of quarter-note style chordal playing, coming to prominence with the Count Basie Orchestra.

Exercise 20.1. Chord Voicings for "Whispering"

Play through the chord changes (figure 20.6) of the standard-progression style song "Whispering" (figure 20.7). Although notated with whole-notes and half-notes throughout, it's appropriate to play "four-to-the-bar" in Freddie Green style (see the Solid Take).

143

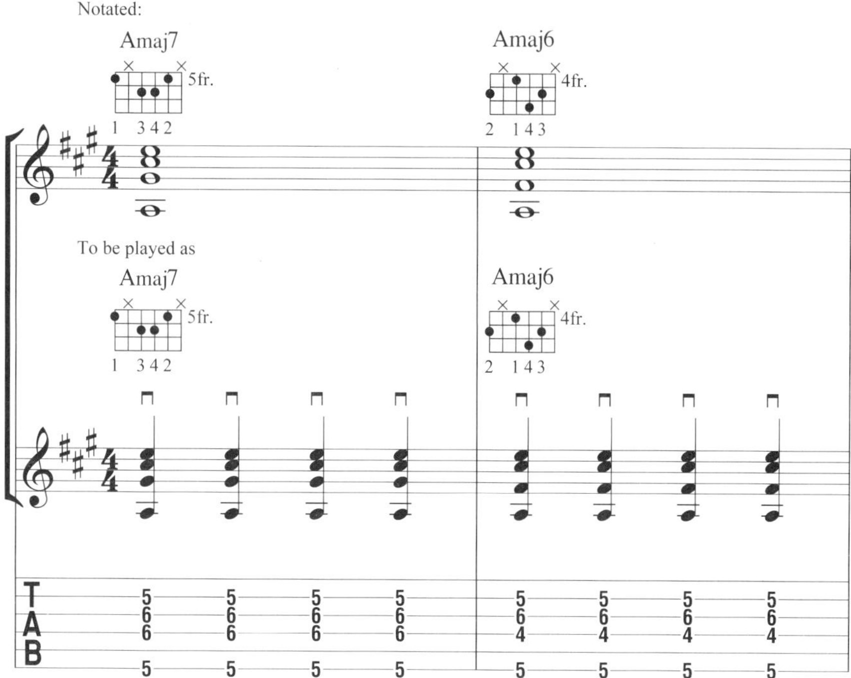

FIG. 20.6. Swing Style: "Four to the Bar"

Here's the entire song progression for "Whispering" in a key that is convenient to put major 6 and minor 6 shapes under your fingers:

FIG. 20.7. Exercise 20.1. Chord Voicings for "Whispering"

LESSON 21

Dom7(9) and Dom7(13)

Our next batch of voicings will introduce you to the world of 9, 11, and 13 chords—and the exercises will show you how to develop fluency with these sounds with manageable fingerings.

ROOT, 3/7, TENSION VOICINGS

I remember the first time that I saw a chord voicing for a dominant-seventh chord with all of the tensions written out. It looked something like this:

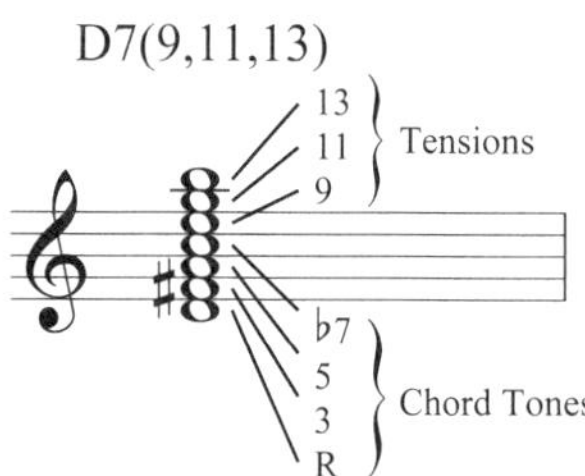

FIG. 21.1. D7 with Chord Tensions

Q: How did guitarists accomplish this skyscraper of chord tones? How was I going to do this?

A: If we're going to imply a five- or seven-note chord structure with only four notes, we have to choose the notes wisely. Instead of using drop 2 or drop 3 voicing strategies, we start with the essential tones and then add a chord tension.

First, let's look at the relationship of the D Mixolydian scale with chord tones and tensions identified.

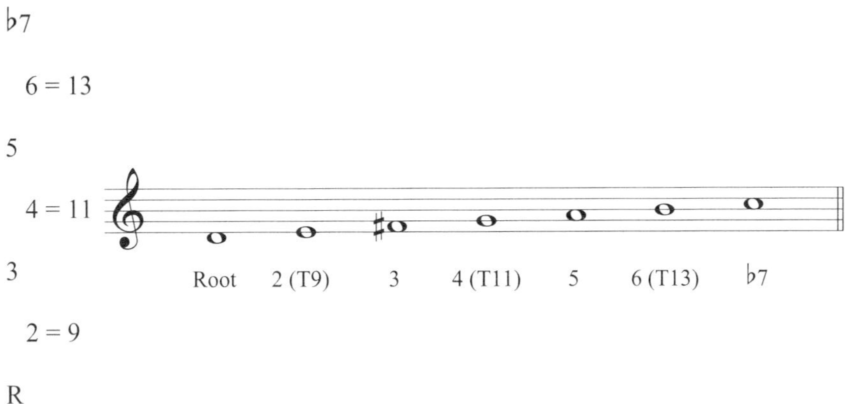

FIG. 21.2. Comparing Chord Tone Stack with D Mixolydian Scale

Chords can be seen as stacks of scale notes, like children's building blocks. Knock the stack of blocks over and put them in musical alphabetical/scalar order, starting from the root, and you can end up with a familiar chord scale.

The key to implying a big chordal sound is careful selection of chord tones. What are the most important elements?

I like to call the 3 and the 7 of the chord the "harmonic molecules" of four-part chords. A "molecule" is the smallest part of a substance that acts like that substance. The 3 and 7 of any four-part chord imply the whole sound with only two tones. To build these big sounds with concise voicings, we need to use root, 3, 7, and a tension. (From here on, we'll use **T** for tension.)

The 3 and 7 (called the "guide tones," and discussed in more detail in lesson 24) are the two most important tones of any four-part chord, in terms of defining that chord's character. When building chords with tensions (9, 11, 13), we have to prioritize the most important tones and fill in from there.

Dominant 7(9) Chords with R3/7T (R379)

Since tensions are involved, drop 2 and drop 3 voicing strategies aren't as helpful as the R3/7T approach when building a dominant 7(9). As a rule, 3/7 or 7/3 combinations fit very well on ④③, and we've already been using this central positioning of these essential voices in many of the voicings that we've accumulated so far. For example, here's a voicing that functions well for a D7(9). The root is on ⑤, 3/7 on ④③, and tension on ②. This structure is often called R379.

146

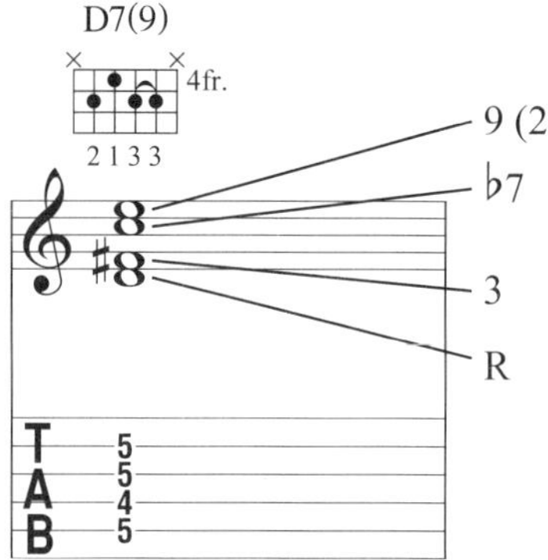

FIG. 21.3. D7(9) as an R379 Voicing

Dominant 13 Chords with Root, 7/3, T13 (R736)

R736 voicings are also effective in playing dominant voicings. (Again, the 13 and 6 are enharmonically the same, and R736 is the commonly used term.) The most important tones, the 3 and 7, are included, and the 6 (i.e., 13) is easily added.

147

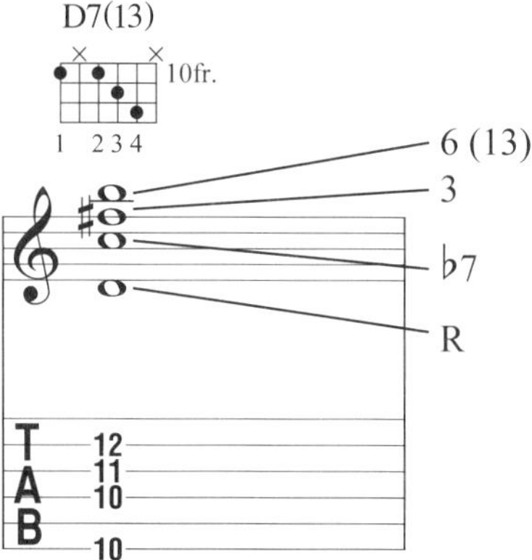

FIG. 21.4. D7(13) as a R736 Voicing

Exercise 21.1. R379 and R736 Shapes

Play through the following to gain control of these all-important chordal shapes. Remember, R379 voicings imply dominant 7(9) chords, and R736 chords imply dominant 7(13) chords.

148, 149

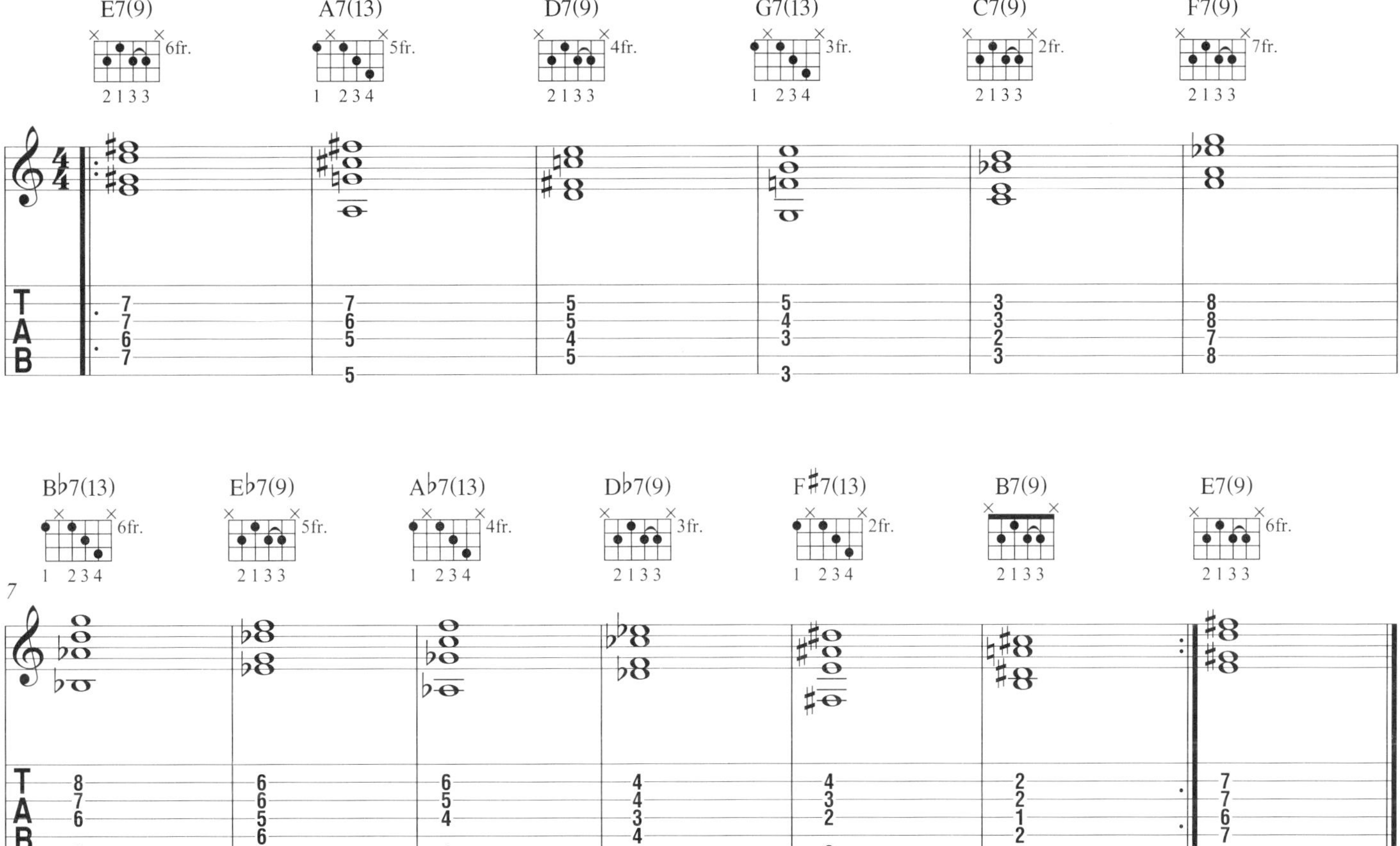

FIG. 21.5. Exercise 21.1. R379 and R736 Shapes

Exercise 21.2. Dominant 7 and Dominant 9 Chord Practice

Let's practice our dominant 7(9) and dominant 7(13) chords by working the following exercise up to speed. I encourage you to do exercise 21.2 (figure 21.6) repeatedly until you have mastered the chords. Use the half-note rests as an opportunity to "fill" with ad lib eighth notes if you wish. Take care with accuracy on the first beat with each chord. Don't make the listener wait for the new harmonic sound!

150, 151

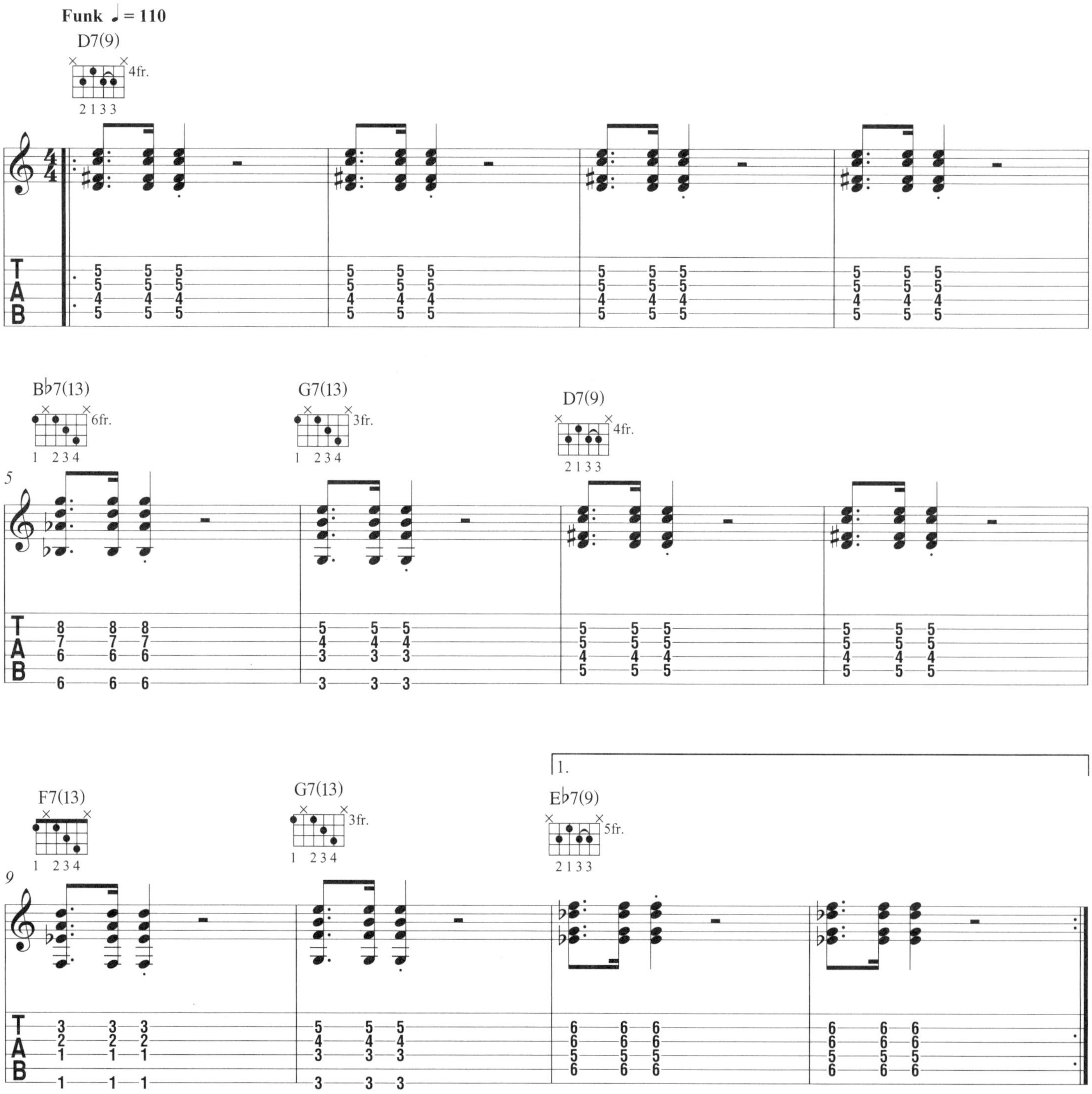

Funk ♩ = 110

D7(9) 4fr. 2 1 3 3

5

B♭7(13) 6fr. 1 2 3 4 — G7(13) 3fr. 1 2 3 4 — D7(9) 4fr. 2 1 3 3

9

F7(13) 1 2 3 4 — G7(13) 3fr. 1 2 3 4 — 1. E♭7(9) 5fr. 2 1 3 3

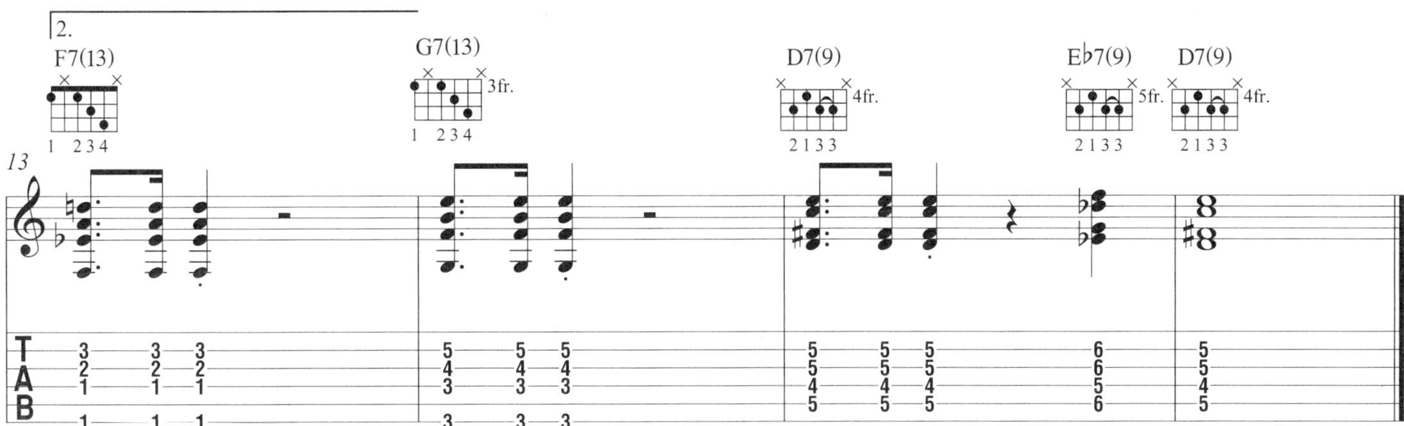

FIG. 21.6. Exercise 21.2. Dominant 7 and Dominant 9 Chord Practice

I hope that you're seeing many practical applications for the skills you've developed with all of the exercises you've been playing. If you've stuck with the material so far, there's no doubt that you have seen an improvement in your vocabulary, agility and sound produced. Developing chordal technique is great for your hands, and therefore, your tone. Perseverance pays off in many ways.

LESSON 22

Dominant 7 Voicings with Altered Tensions

If you're aware of the root, chord tones, and tensions of a chord, it's easy to come up with *alterations* (notes raised or lowered by a half step) on the spot. It's not easy to gain this type of awareness, but you're on your way.

1. Know where the nearest root, or implied root, of the chord is on the fretboard.
2. Know where the 3 and 7 of the chord are on the fretboard.
3. Alter the 5, 9, 11, or 13 of the chord at will.

We are continuing with building voicings with R3/7T structures. Beginning with a C9 chord on ⑤④③②, let's look at the function of each chord tone in the voicing.

From the fifth string up:

	⑤	④	③	②
Note:	C	E	B♭	D
Function:	Root	3	♭7	9

152

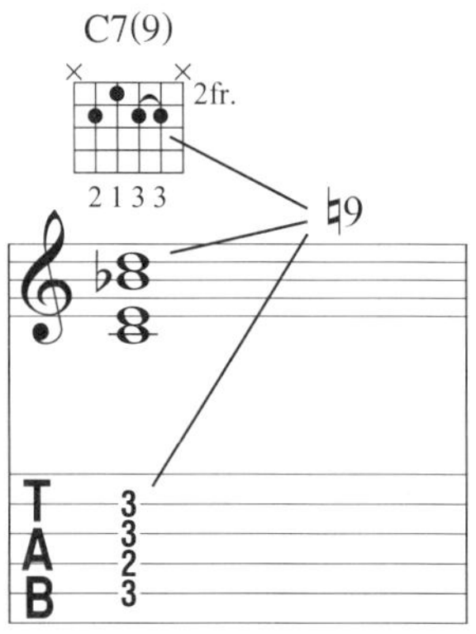

FIG. 22.1. C7(9)

ALTERATIONS INVOLVING ♯9 AND ♭9

Please note that there is no 5 in this voicing. As we learned, the 3 and 7 are the most defining voices in a chord, and the 5 of a chord isn't essential to the chord sound unless it's chromatically altered in some way. Since the 5 isn't altered in C7(9), it doesn't have to be included. For a C7(♯9) voicing, take the ♮9 found on the second string and raise it one half step (one fret), making it D♯. There is a beautifully dissonant interval to be found between the E on the fourth string and the D♯ on the second string. Notice how this dissonance makes the dominant chord more interesting; it gives it "color." Next, try the ♭9, found right underneath the ♮9.

153

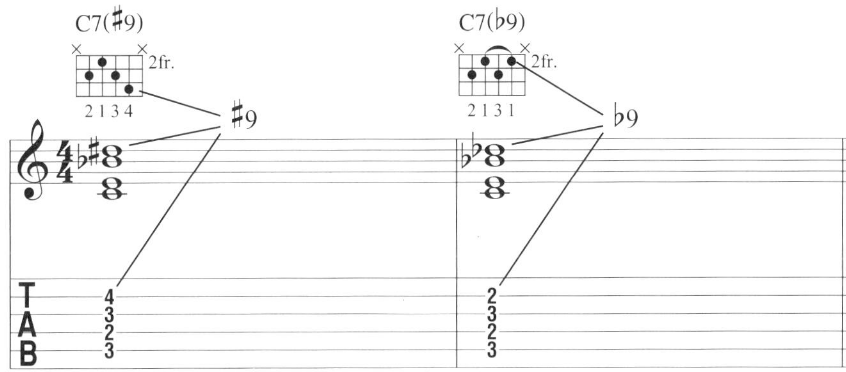

FIG. 22.2. C7(♯9 and ♭9)

MORE DOMINANT ALTERATIONS: ♭5, ♯5, ♭13, ♮13, AND COMBINATIONS

Expanding to ⑤④③②①, let's add the 5 to the mix. Here is C7(9) with the 5 added on the ①. The third finger barre is a challenge, but it's common practice. The 5 can be replaced by the 6, properly identified as the 13, since the 7 is present.

154

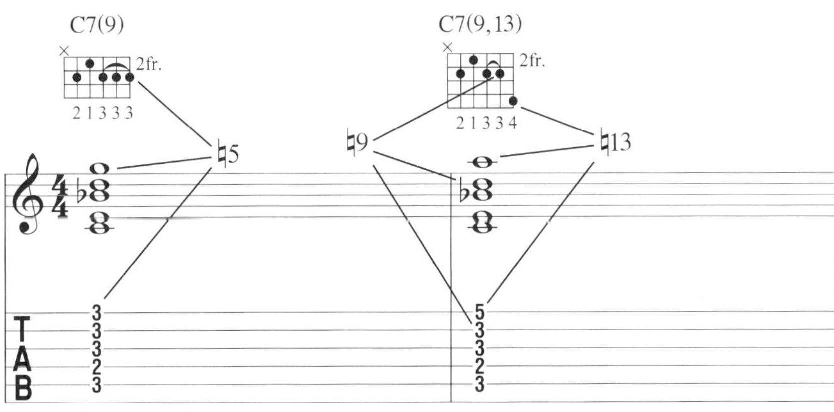

FIG. 22.3. C7(9) and C7(9,13)

SOLID TAKE: DON'T MUTE THE 3 ON ④!

Many students have problems with sounding the 3 in the figure 22.3 voicings, found here on the second fret of ④. Arch the second finger on the lowest string to allow the all-important 3 of the chord to ring clearly. It takes a lot of effort to get this ability together, but stay vigilant and it will happen.

Here is a graphic map of the tensions that we are bringing to the level of fluency.

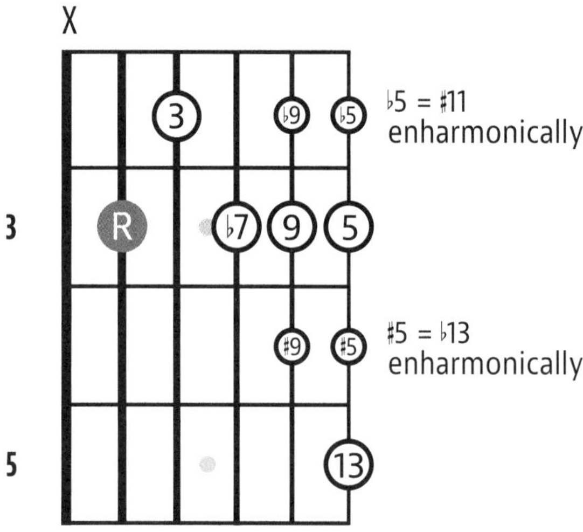

FIG. 22.4. ⑤ C7 Interval Graph for R37T Voicings

Exercise 22.1. Finding Altered Tensions

Seeing the relationship of the notes to the root of the moment rather than memorizing specific "grips" on the neck allows you to alter the chords much more freely. Run through the following exercise to explore various combinations of dominant chords with tensions. Relate the shapes, rather than building each from scratch. To get the most out of this drill, play through the exercise three times with the recorded track, as follows:

1. as whole notes
2. as arpeggiated chords
3. with improvised rhythmic material

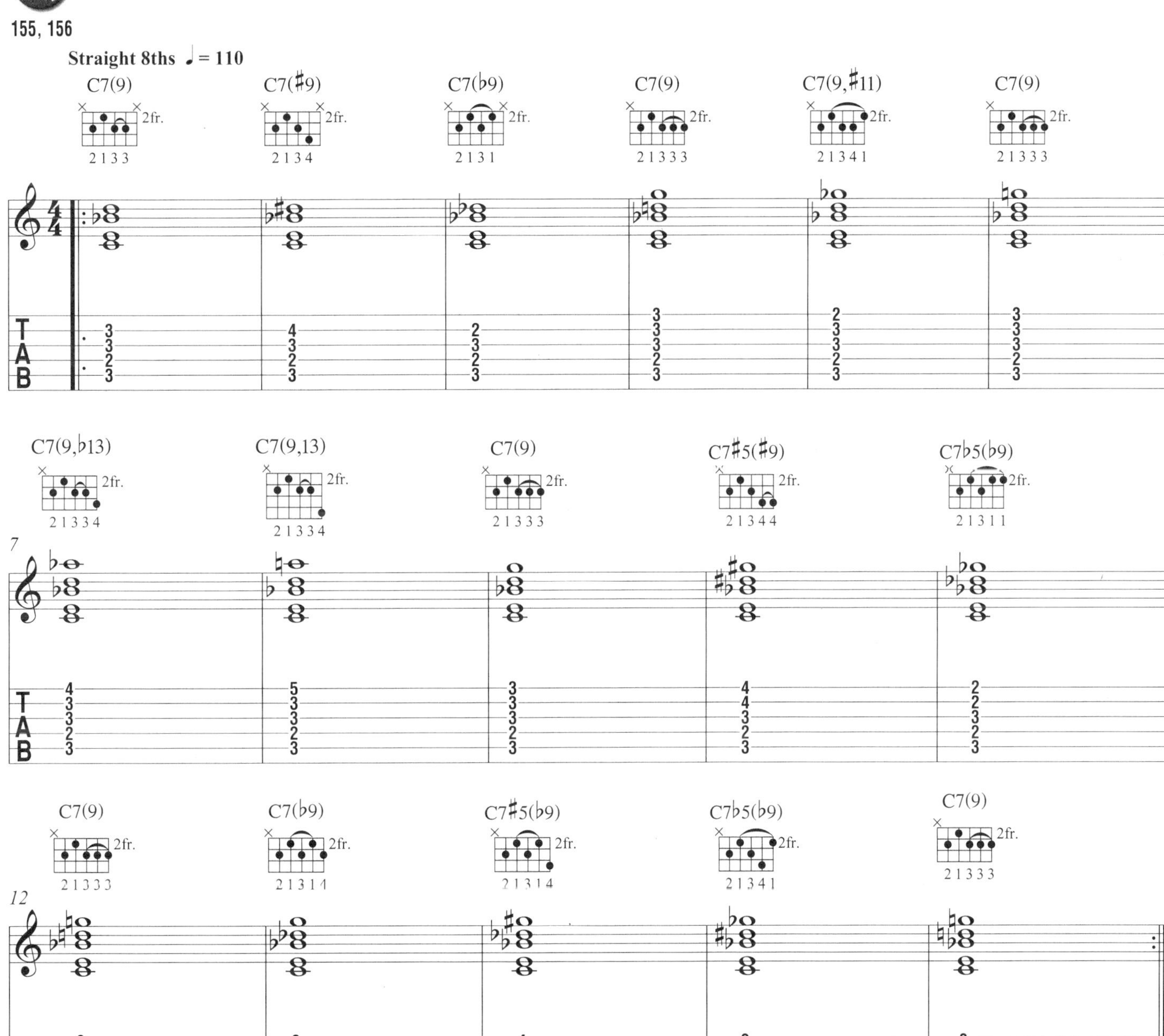

FIG. 22.5. Exercise 22.1. Finding Altered Tensions

SOLID TAKE: FULL SERVICE, ON-TIME DELIVERY!

When I listen to people playing this type of exercise, a reminder to give the full chord sound right at the point of chord change is often necessary. We love on-time delivery from internet retailers, with everything we've ordered, all in the same package! Give the same all-inclusive, on-time delivery to your listeners. The most challenging part of playing chord changes is at the precise moment that the chord changes.

BASIC TENSIONS AND ENHARMONIC EQUIVALENTS WITH IMPLIED ROOT ON ⑥

Let's look at some of the various alterations of R37T voicings with G7. A basic drop 3 voicing can be seen as a R73T voicing when we choose various options on ②.

In G7 as a basic R♭735 voicing, the 5 is the highest tone of the chord. You simply make the choice of tension on ②. The ♯5 is one fret higher; ♭5 is one fret lower, and the 13 is two frets higher. Similarly, the ♭13 is one fret higher, and the ♯11 is one fret lower.

The ♯11 and ♭5 are enharmonic equivalents. That means that they are the same pitch, only with different note names, as shown in figure 23.6. On a G7 chord, the ♯11 is C♯, and the ♭5 is D♭. C♯ and D♭ are, for our purposes, the same note. Berklee's Harmony Department considers the ♭5 a chord tone but the ♯11 a tension. It's easier for most guitarists to think of these voicings as the same thing—but it's easy to get confused about it!

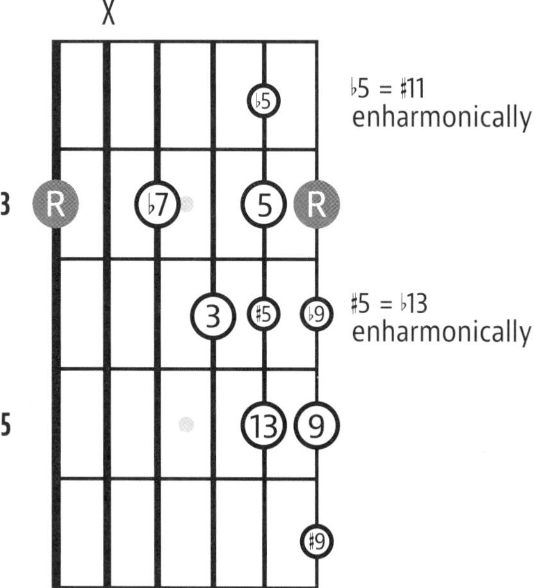

FIG. 22.6. ⑥ G7 Interval Graph for R3/7T Voicings

Play through the following voicings, and see how closely related they are, but how different they sound from each other.

157

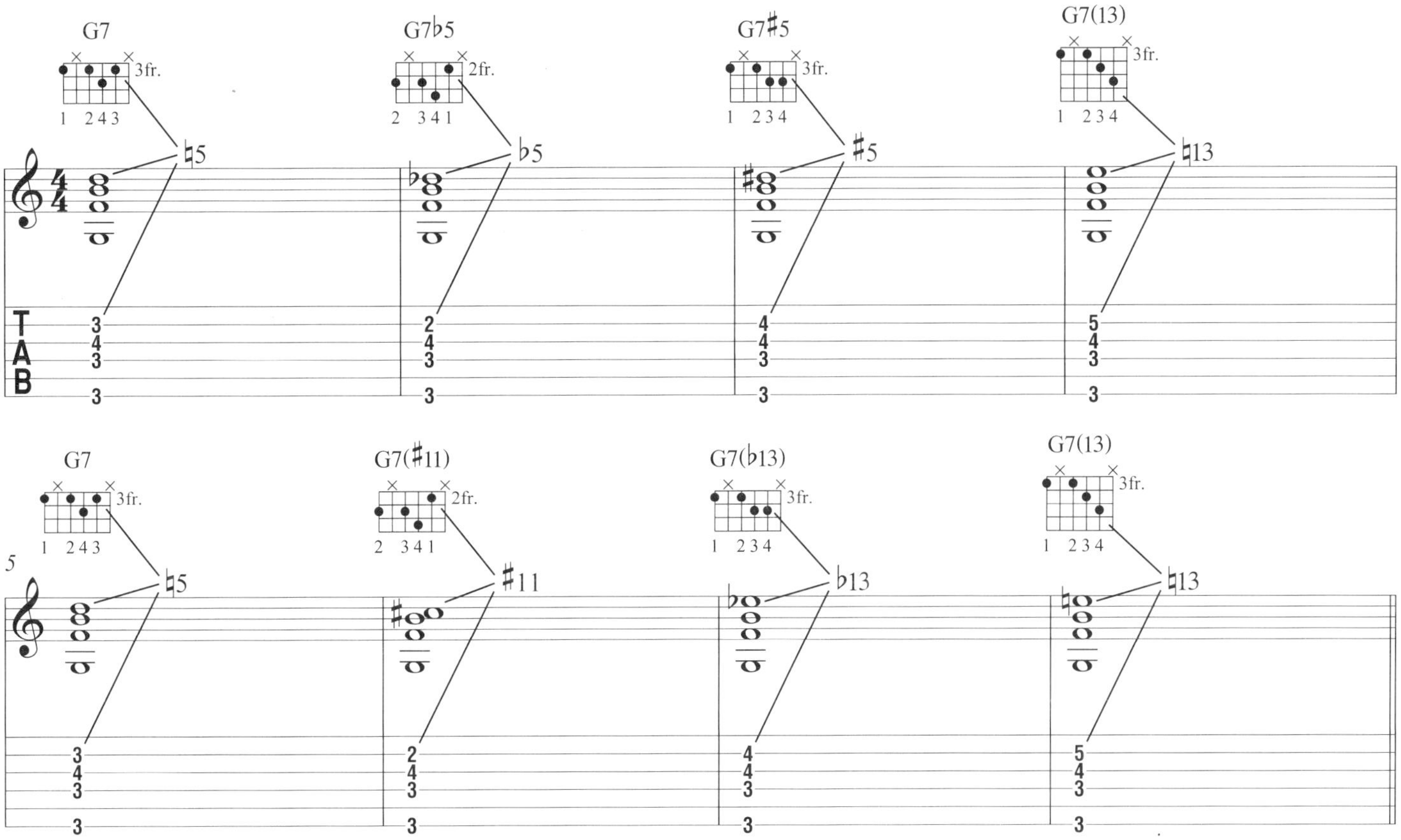

G7 | G7♭5 | G7♯5 | G7(13)

G7 | G7(♯11) | G7(♭13) | G7(13)

FIG. 22.7. G7 Drop 3 ② Tension Variations Near Fifth

G7 WITH MORE TENSIONS AND ALTERATIONS: ROOT/3/7 WITH TENSIONS

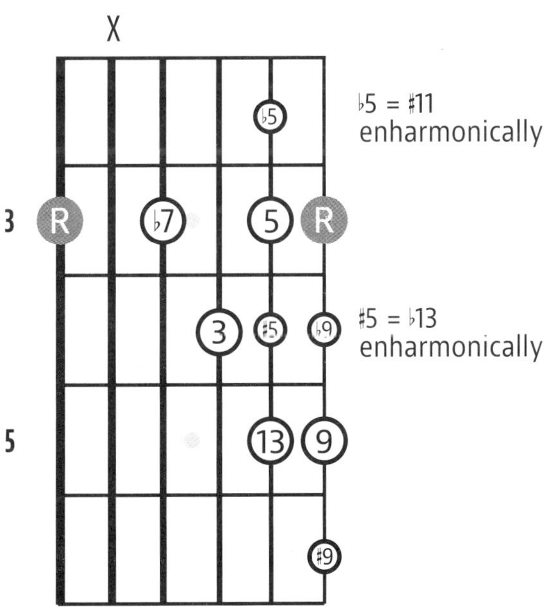

FIG. 22.8. G7 Interval Map Third Position

158

Here are some combinations of alterations of G7 with two alterations.

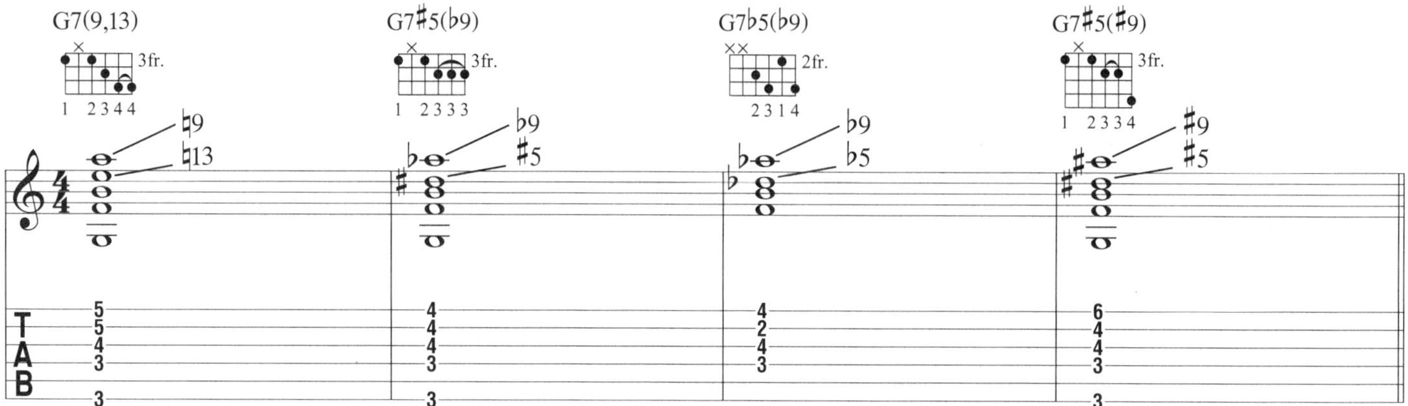

FIG. 22.9. G7 with Two Tensions

Solid Take: Choosing Alterations Wisely and Jazz Players' Secret Harmonic Handshake

If you were reading a book out loud and saw the following words, how would you pronounce them? Try saying each one, speaking clearly:

"Wind" "Live" "Record"

Now, look at the following phrases and observe your pronunciation of each:

Wind, blowing from the west.
Wind your antique watch carefully.

Live music onstage tonight!
Live every day as if it's your last!

Record album on a turntable in a music store.
Record your performances and submit them as an MP3.

Heteronyms are words that are spelled the same way but spoken differently. The reader does not know how to say the first word until they see where the phrase is heading. Context is the key to pronouncing these special words properly.

When I found out how to play dom7♯5(♯9), I would play every dominant chord with those alterations. The chords sounded modern, radical, and exciting. As much as I loved them, I could tell that they didn't always fit with the standard songs, or rock, or blues country songs, either. Some of the notes sounded wrong. The chords sounded good on their own, but they didn't sound right in the progression. Eventually, I learned that it's helpful to look at the chord of resolution to find a smooth, logical choice.

Alteration (or lack thereof) of dominant seventh chords can be informed in the same way. Guitarists often feel that they can alter dominants at will, and they can, but quality of the results can vary. See where you're going to inform your choice of chord tones.

The word "heteronym" isn't typically used as a musical term, but the concept helps me to sort things out. These particular tensions reflect the key of the moment, and they allow the progression to flow smoothly, often reflecting the key of the song.

If you're resolving from a dominant 7 up a perfect fourth (same as down a perfect fifth) to a minor chord, dom7(♭9,♭13) often sounds best. If you see C7, look at the next chord. If the chord is resolving up a perfect fourth to a minor chord, try C7(♭9,♭13).

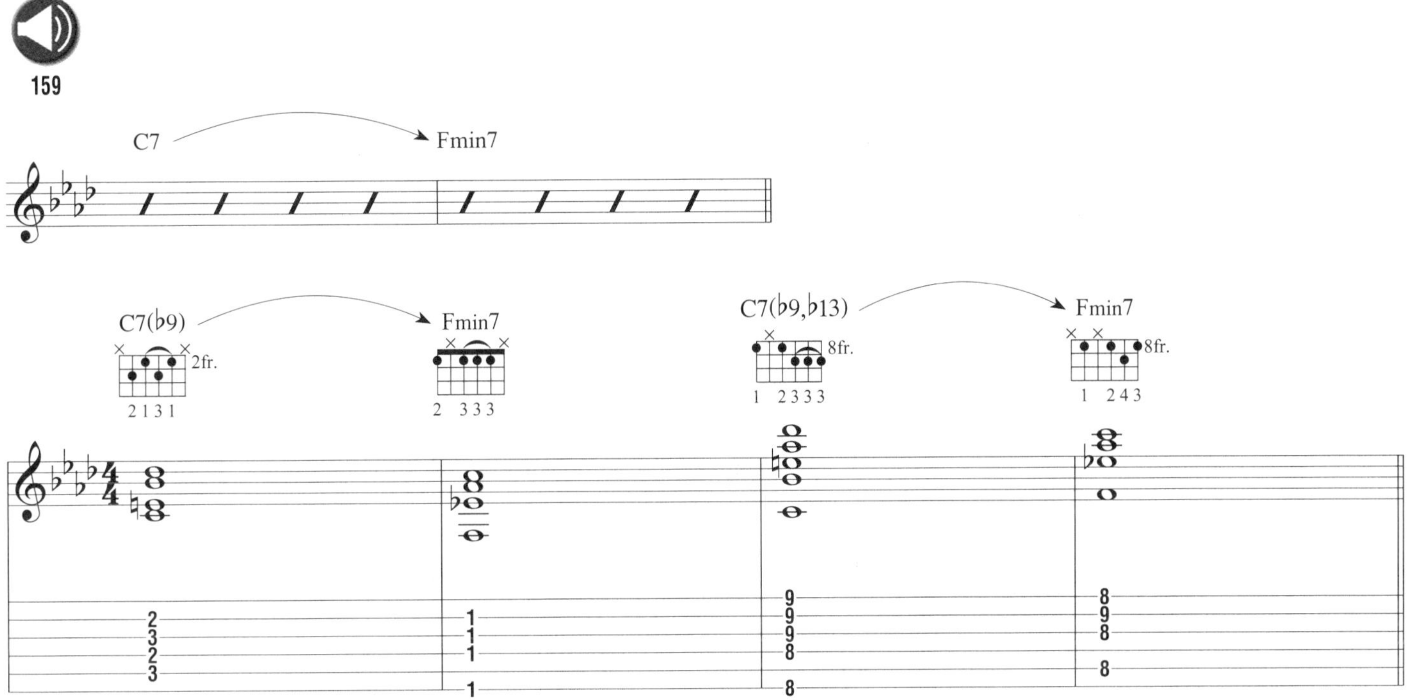

FIG. 22.10. V7 to Imin

If you're resolving a C7 up a perfect fourth to a major chord, like maj6, maj7, or dom7, use natural tensions, as found in C7(♮9,♮13).

FIG. 22.11. V7 Resolving to Dominant 7

When resolving a dominant seventh chord down a minor second, Berklee treats this chord as a dominant substitute, or a "sub five" or "subV." Try dom7(♯11), enharmonically the same as dom7♭5. The subV function dom7 chord works extremely well with this type of voicing.

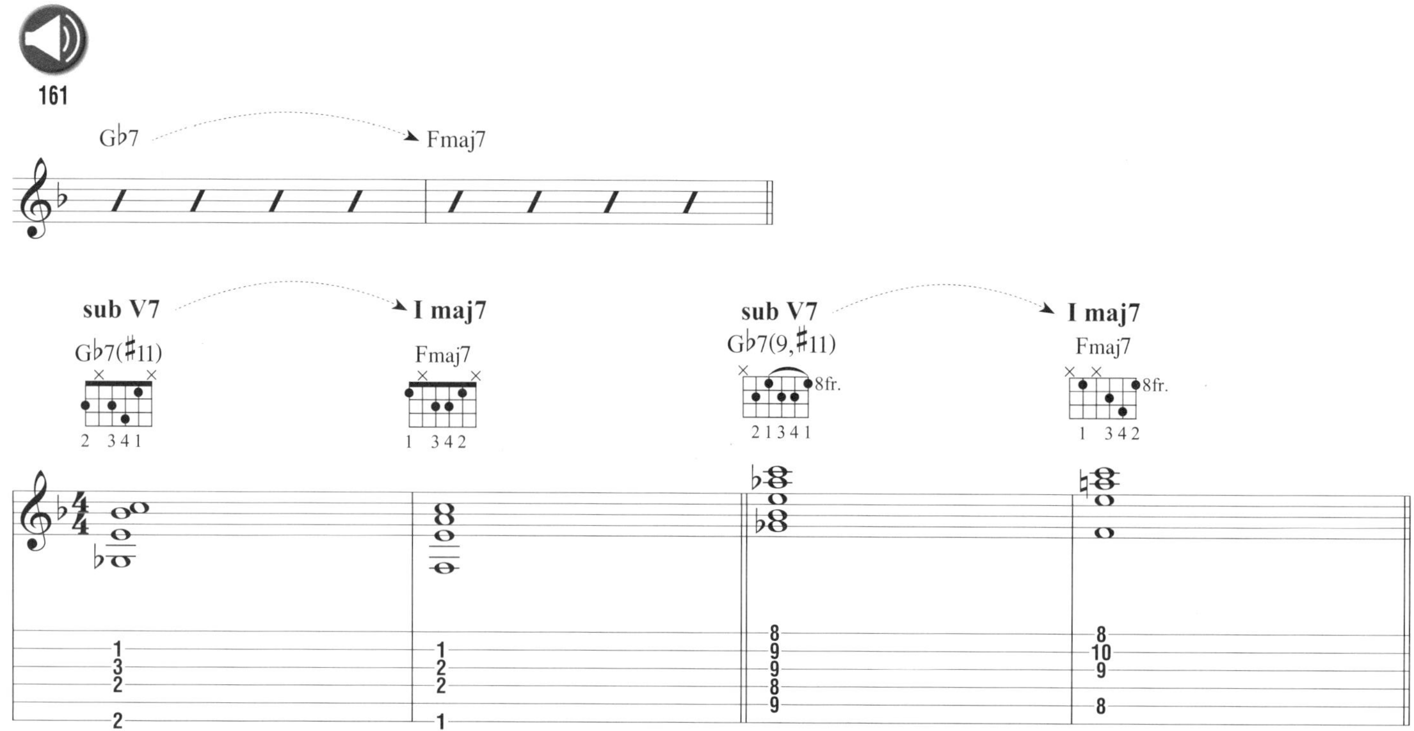

FIG. 22.12. SubV Half-Step Down Resolution

These resolutions tend to be smooth and consonant sounding.

Lead sheets are shorthand outlines of a song's harmony, and fakebooks often omit alterations on dominant seventh chords, leaving the player to figure things out. When you see a dominant seventh chord, look to see where the progression moves. Listen to the results, and see for yourself.

Standard lead sheets often simply list dominant seventh chords without specifying the appropriate tensions. It's incumbent upon the guitarist to understand and play proper voicings. Looking at the way that the dominant chord resolves is the best way to figure out the right tensions/alterations. Jazz standards and jazz-influenced music (including R&B, Chicago blues, and neo soul) require players to be informed. This is why I call it the "Secret Harmonic Handshake." For example, the chart may say C7, but if the song is in F minor, an informed player would play C7(♭9,♭13).

Secret Harmonic Handshake Formula	
Chord Following Dominant 7 Chord	**Implied Dominant 7 Chord Quality**
Major (Root P4 above or P5 below dominant chord)	Dominant 7(9,13)
Minor (Root P4 above or P5 below dominant chord)	Dominant 7(♭9,♭13)
Major or minor (half step below or a whole step above dominant chord)	Dominant

If you're interested in exploring this subject more, research the topic "secondary dominants," as found in Berklee harmony textbooks (such as *The Berklee Book of Jazz Harmony* by Joe Mulholland and Tom Hojnacki, and *Modern Jazz Theory and Practice* by Steve Rochinski). Whenever possible, listen to great performances, try to play along, and work to make informed additions to your vocabulary. A primary key to develop these skills is to learn from great musicians who dedicated their musical lives to leaving a legacy of elegant clues to inform all who have followed. Work to figure things out by playing along with great recordings.

Exercise 22.2. Using Tensions

The "Using Tensions" exercise is a neo-soul piece that uses drop 2, drop 3, and R3/7T voicings.

162, 163

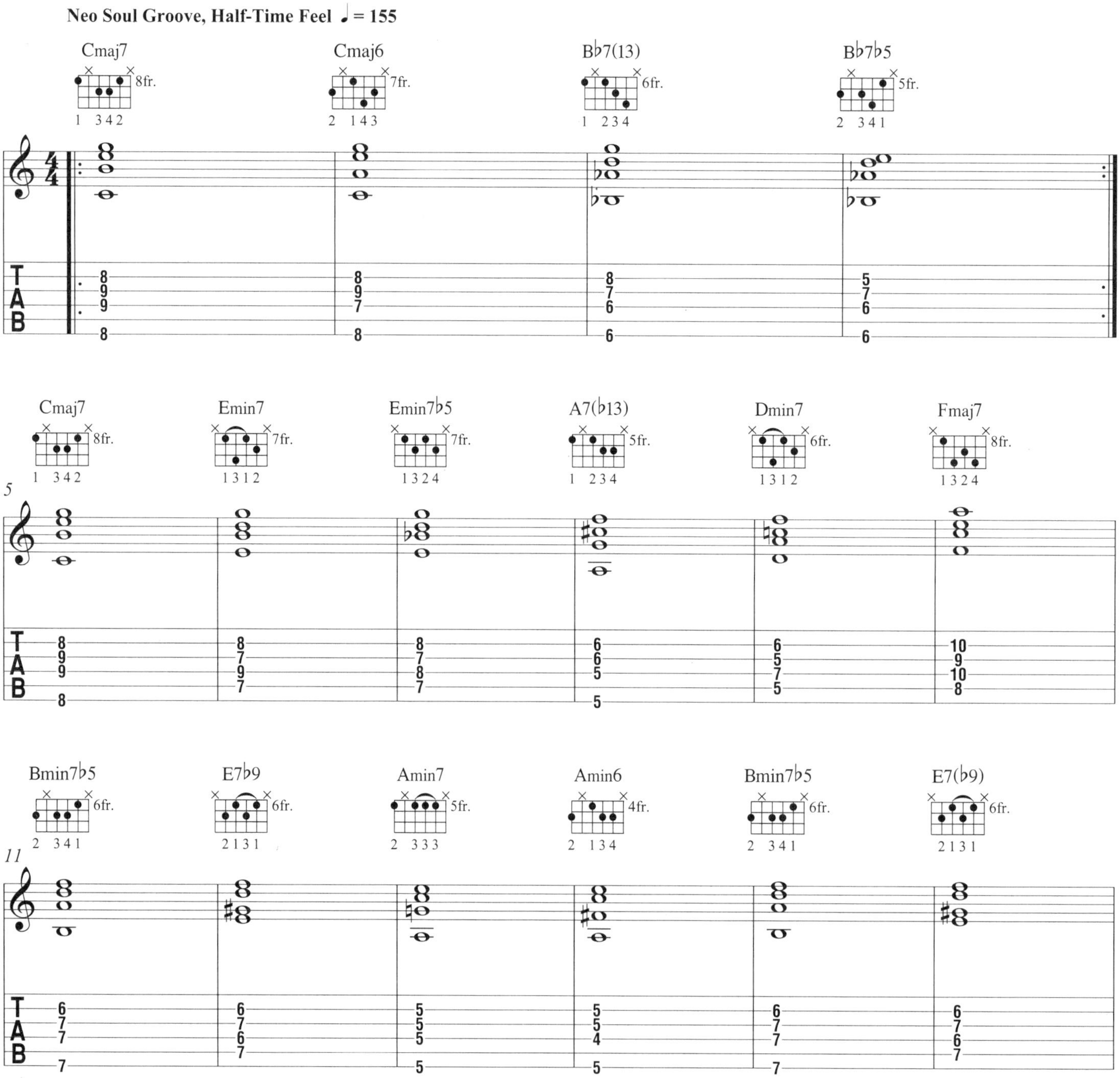

Neo Soul Groove, Half-Time Feel ♩ = 155

Cmaj7 | Cmaj6 | B♭7(13) | B♭7♭5

Cmaj7 | Emin7 | Emin7♭5 | A7(♭13) | Dmin7 | Fmaj7

Bmin7♭5 | E7♭9 | Amin7 | Amin6 | Bmin7♭5 | E7(♭9)

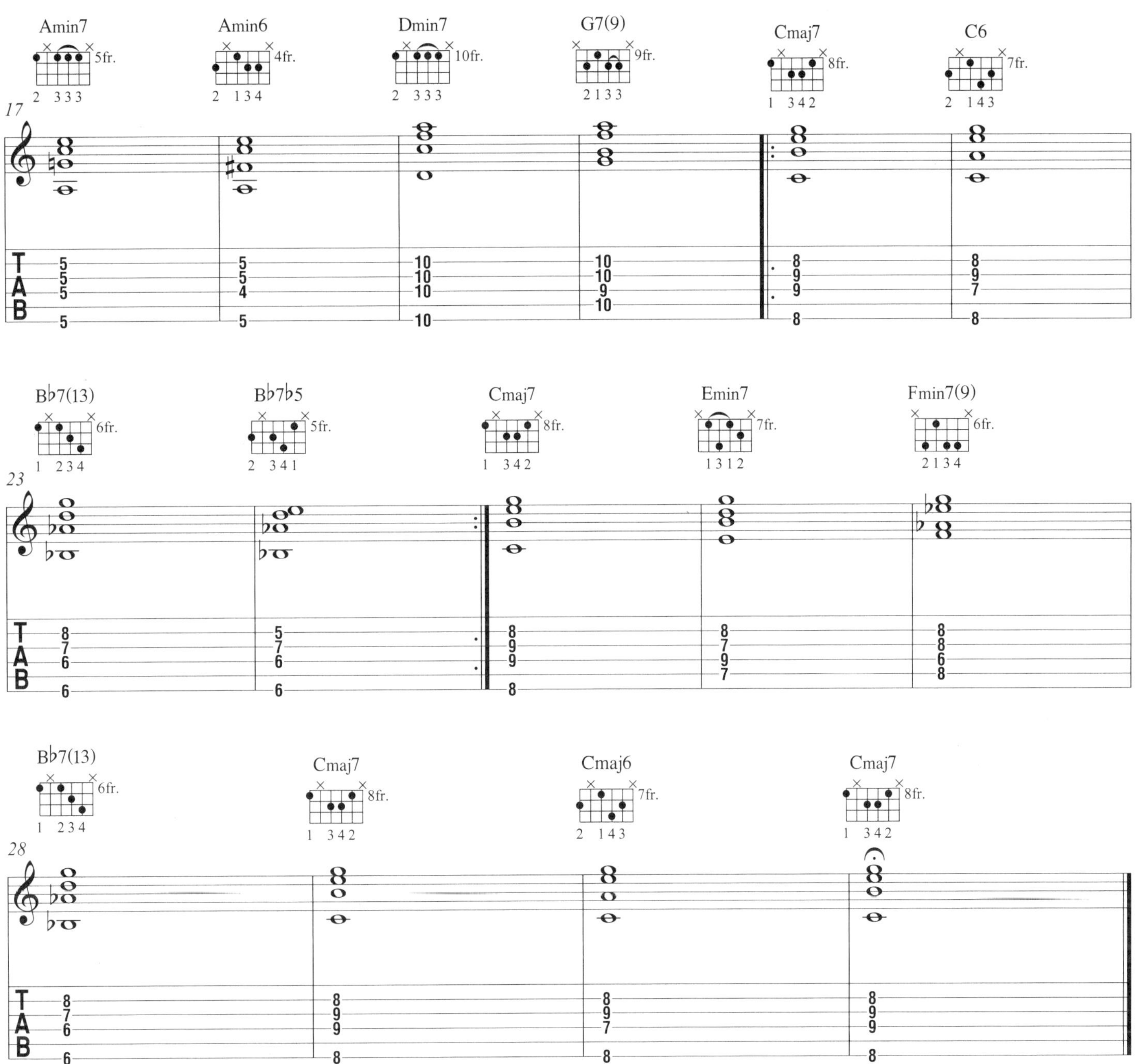

FIG. 22.13. Exercise 22.2. Using Tensions

Our toolkit of standard guitar chords is now effectively complete. Basic four-part chords are available to us in drop 2 and drop 3 configurations and R3/7T voicings broaden the spectrum of harmonic possibilities. With the voicings introduced in this lesson, we're equipped for nearly any harmonic situation.

By now, you can feel proud that you have done an amazing amount of work. Coming up, you'll see lots of applications for the material we've learned and, as always, some new concepts to integrate in your chordal approach.

LESSON 23

Guide Tone Voicings

Four-part chords usually consist of the root, 3, 5, and 7. As we saw earlier, the 3 and 7 are the most essential, defining elements of any seventh chord—the harmonic molecules. Guide tone voicings provide the most concise structures for chordal accompaniment in many styles. Using these two tones, we're able to imply a sound that implies much more than two notes. When they're the right two notes, played with great time and a full tone, the music produced can approach absolute perfection.

It's a great way to find simplicity on the other side of complexity.

GUIDE TONE, NO ROOT VOICINGS

The 3 and 7 are critical in communicating the sound of a chord. To play these effectively, you need to have a clear idea of the root of the chord as an anchor point for these small voicings. In fact, the easiest way to think of them is to include the root at first, but in actual practice, it often sounds best to omit the root to boil your chordal performance down to the essential elements.

There is always a lot to be learned by watching live performances or videos of great guitarists playing. Often, the best players not only sound terrific, but they also make it look easy. They make a couple of notes on the fretboard into an elegant way of making a huge harmonic sound.

One way they do this is by using *guide tones*, those chord tones that most define a chord's particular sound: the 3, 7, and altered tones of the chord. After you've worked with guide tone shapes, you'll see that finding shapes with fewer notes that imply larger sounds isn't only easier; it often sounds better within the context of a band. We'll start with root, 7, and 3 shapes.

The 3 and 7, or the 7 and the 3 on ④ and ③, are the foundation of guide-tone voicings. Let's look at G7 as a root/guide-tone voicing in two positions. (We can abbreviate these as **R37**.)

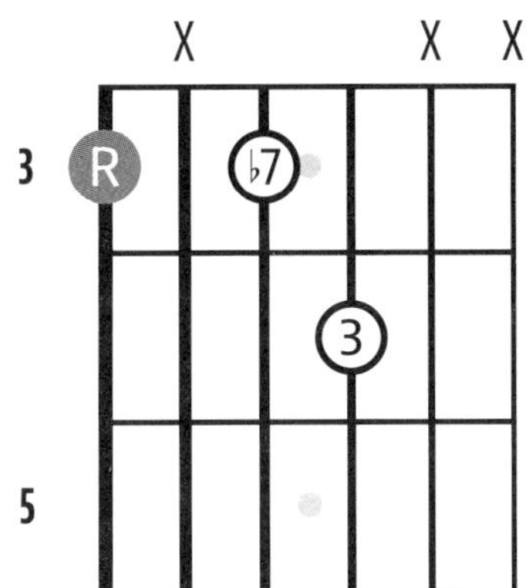

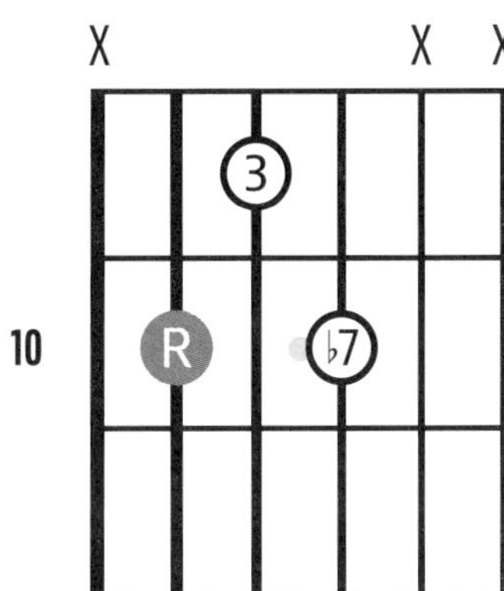

FIG. 23.1. R37 Voicings with Roots on ⑥ and ⑤

Strings ④ and ③ are an excellent home for the 3 and 7 of any chord in any key, due to the range considerations, and as used by orchestrators and arrangers.

Figure 23.2 is a general set of guidelines with regard to range of chord tones for your reference. Strings ④ and ③ are the ideal range for 3/7 or 7/3 voicings.

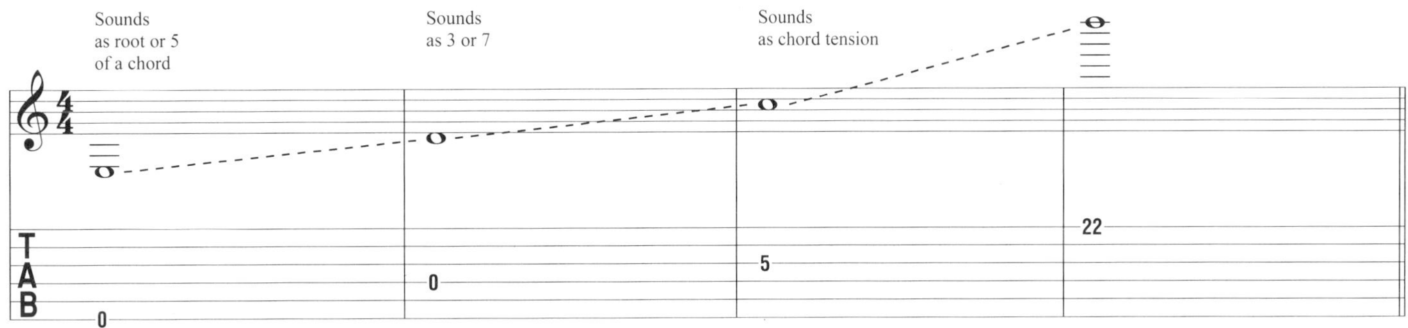

FIG. 23.2. Range for Chord Tones

The central challenge with this type of voicing is developing fluency with the all of the combinations of chord tones. These voicings are effective, but it takes persistent, conscious practice to gain control of these shapes, so that you're playing these compact voicings with accuracy.

Instead of adding notes to the voicings, we've taken notes away. In the right circumstances, two or three notes can be just what the doctor ordered. When the number of players in a band is large, a couple of notes—placed exactly where they should be range-wise and rhythmically—can be the best texture you can provide. The smaller voicings take just as much concentration as the larger models.

164

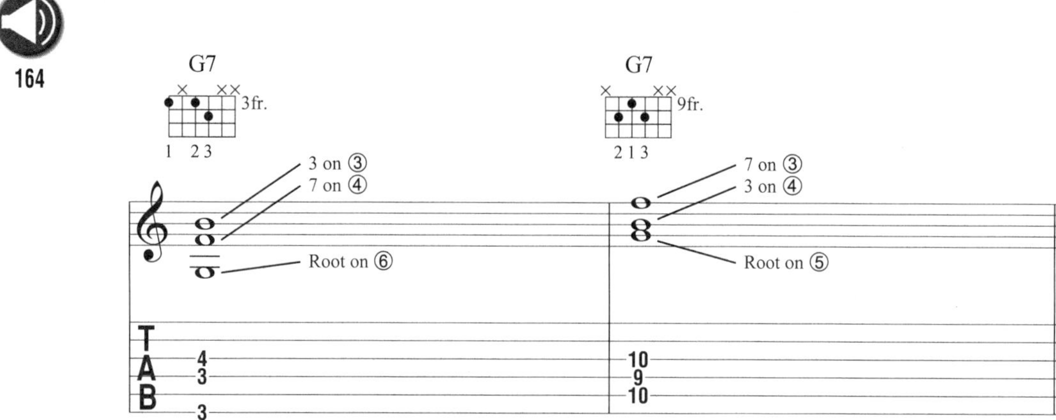

FIG. 23.3. R73 and R37 Voicings for G7

Play through the following voicings, taking note of the position of the chord tones and taking care with muting the unneeded string sounds.

165

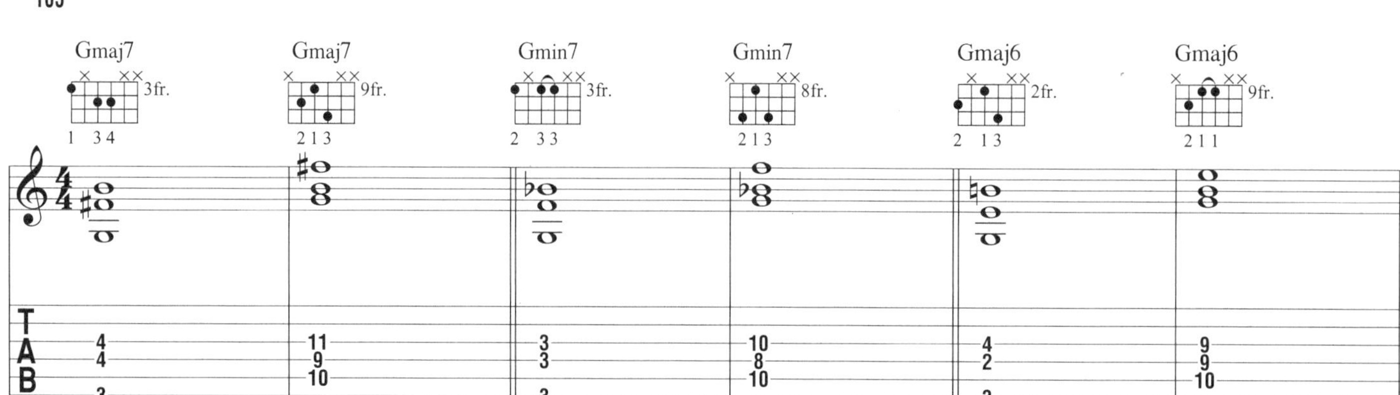

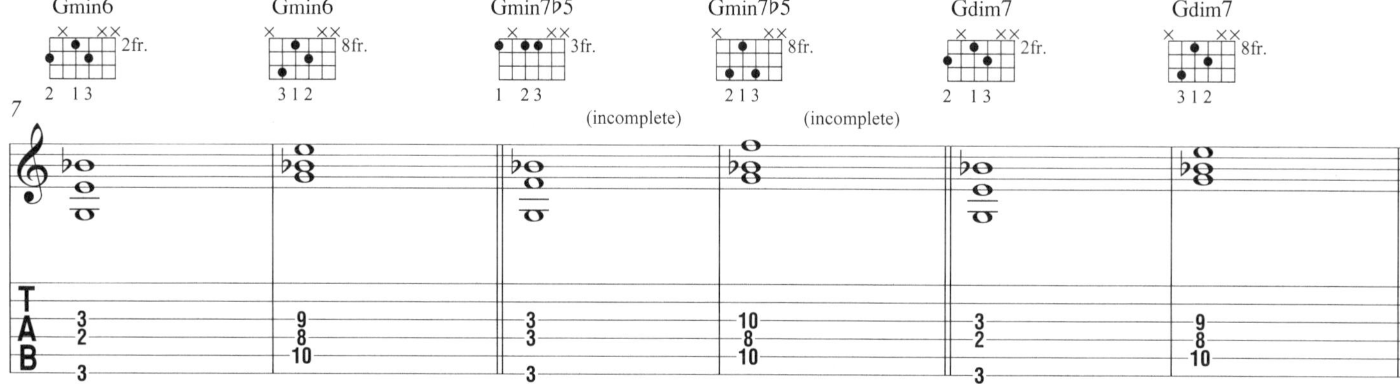

FIG. 23.4. R73 and R37 Voicings for Essential Chord Qualities

The best way to develop and use guide tone voicings is the following:

1. Start with R3/7 (root/guide-tone) voicings with root on ⑥ or ⑤.
2. Omit the root and play guide tones only.

Exercise 23.1. Guide Tone Blues with Three-Note and Two-Note Voicings

166, 167

Play through this blues progression, featuring voicings with root and guide tones, and then guide tones only.

FIG. 23.5. Exercise 23.1. Guide Tone Blues with Three-Note and Two-Note Voicings

Exercise 23.2. Standard Progression Guide Tone Practice

The R37 and R73 voicings offer big sound on a standard progression. The form of this progression is the common AABA structure with each section lasting eight bars. You may play the root/guide tones voicings as written, or as guide tones only, with the root omitted. The B section features four-note voicings, to outline the more complex section in G minor.

168, 169

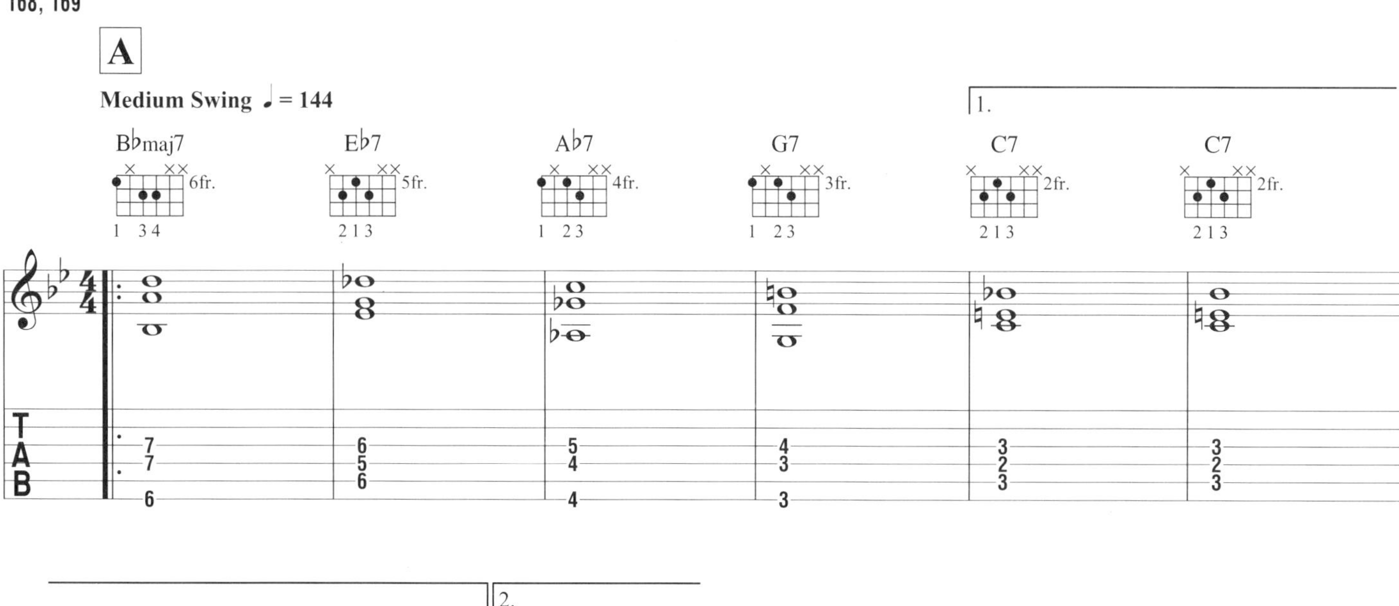

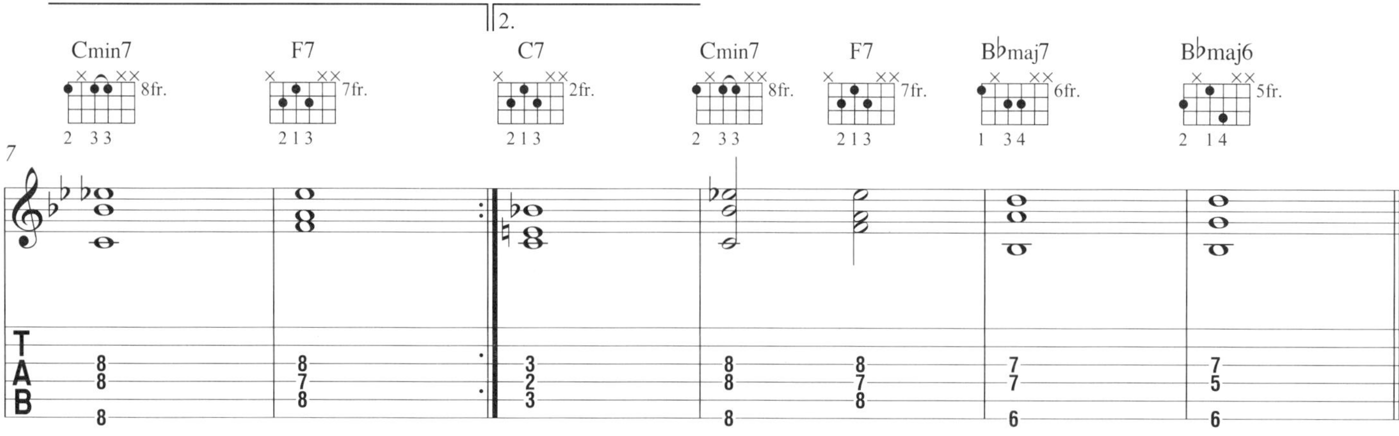

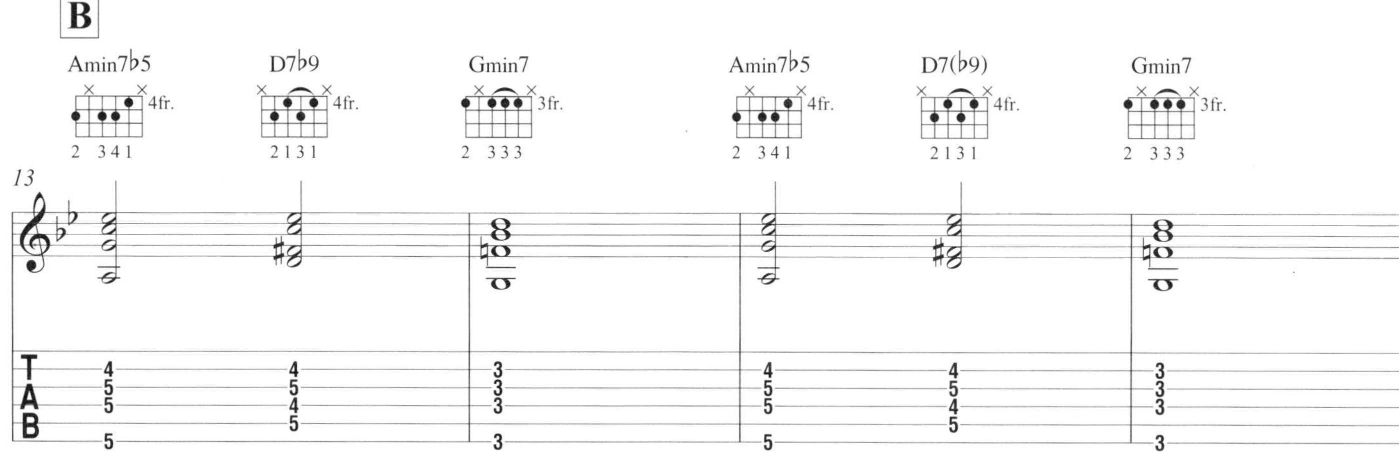

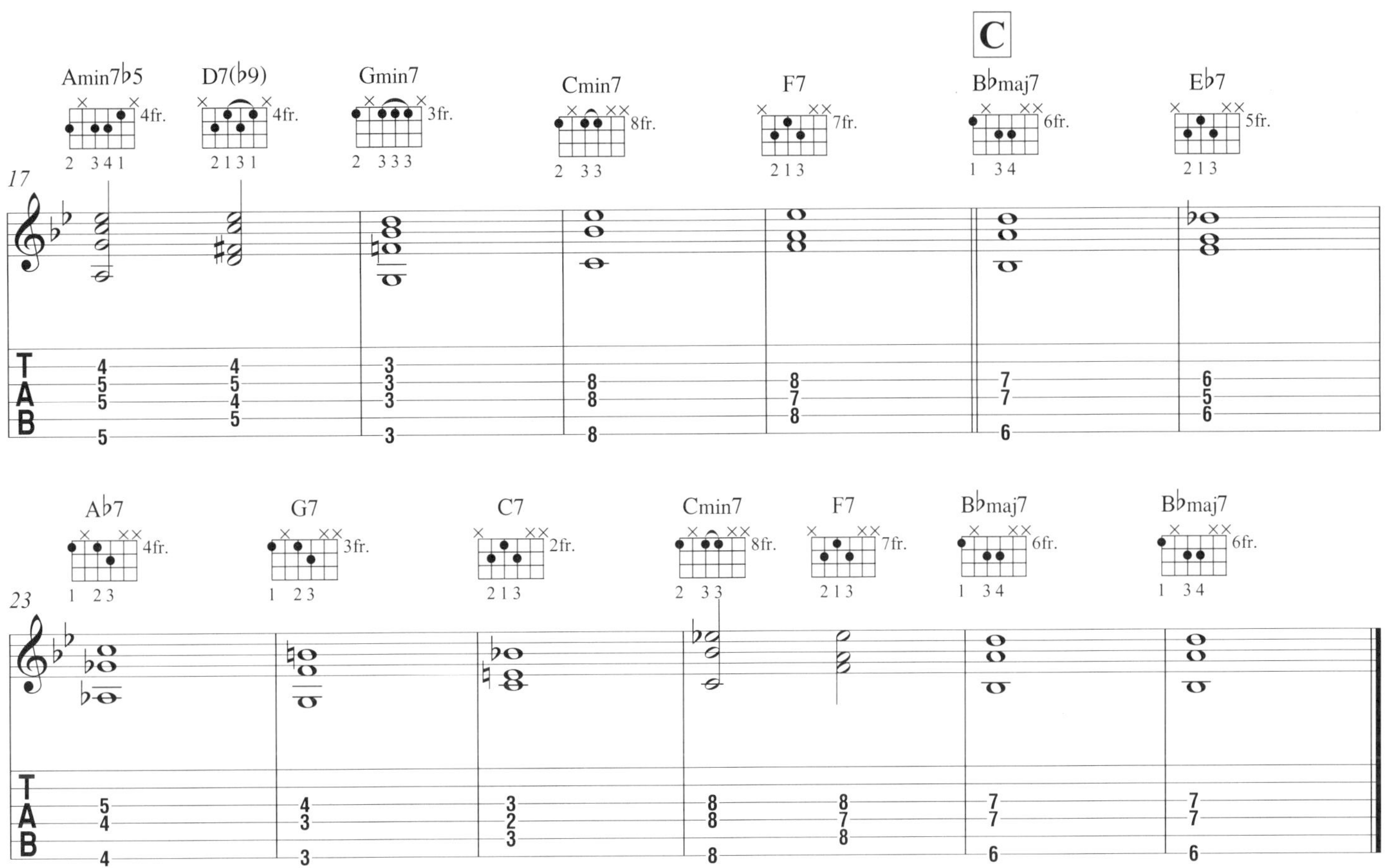

FIG. 23.6. Exercise 23.2. Standard Progression Guide Tone Practice

LESSON 24

Hybrid Chords (Triads Over Bass Notes)

It's time to delve into the world of triads over bass notes, allowing us to use the mighty triad in a new way.

A hybrid chord or, a "triad over bass note," refers to a four-voice chord made up of a triad played above a note that is not found in that triad. The note in the bass has to be different than any of the triad's chord tones. The bass note does not serve as the root of the chord, but it helps to define the way the chord is heard.

In notation, we use a slash between the chord and the bass note, as we did with inversions (see chapter 7). This is a fast way to notate relatively complex sounds simply. It's also an excellent way for guitarists to imply complex sounds with very few notes. The open, somewhat vague quality of these structures is attractive to many performers and composers.

SOLID TAKE: INVERT THE TRIAD, KEEP THE BASS NOTE THE SAME!

The given triad can be in any inversion, but the bass note stays unchanged. This is central to the understanding and use of these voicings. Although it is possible to generate inversions with the bass note added to the mix, the real flavor of these chords is found with static bass.

Also, play the triad *and* the bass note! Guitarists are sometimes encouraged to play the three notes of the triad and to let a bassist play the bass note. To get the most out of these sounds, you have to play all four notes. It takes a bit of work and some uncomfortable stretches, but the results are worth the effort.

Here are some of the many of the possibilities for hybrid chords. Some are more common than others (inversions with redundant notes are weaker choices).

	Hybrid Chord Formula	Useful as Hybrid?	Equivalent 4-Voice Chord	Alternate 4-Voice Chord
C/C	I/I	No (triad)	C triad root	
D♭/C	♭II/I	Yes	Cmin7(♭9) C Phrygian Same as D♭maj7(♯11) D♭ Lydian	
D/C	II/I	Yes	Cmaj7(♯11) C Lydian	C7(9,♯11,♮13) C Lydian ♭7 For use as subV
E♭/C	♭III/I	Yes	Cmin7 (Dorian Cmin7 ♮13, Phrygian Cmin7 ♭9, ♭13 Aeolian Cmin7 ♭13	
E/C	III/I	Yes	Cmaj7 ♯5 C Lydian augmented Cmaj7(♭13) C harmonic major	A♭7alt/C A melodic minor Also D7(9,♯11,♮13)/C A melodic minor
F/C	IV/I	No (triad inversion)	Inversion of F triad	
G♭/C	♭V/I	Yes	C7(alt) D♭ melodic minor	G♭maj7(♯11) G ♭ Lydian
G/C	V/I	Yes	C maj7(9) C diatonic major	Cmaj7(9,♯11) C Lydian Since no 3 is specified, Cmin(maj7) is a possible interpretation
A♭/C	♭VI/I	No (triad inversion)	Inversion of A♭ triad	
A/C	VI/I	Yes	C7(♭9,♯11,♮13) also A7(♭9,♯11,♮13) E♭7(♭9,♯11,♮13) G♭7(♭9,♯11,♮13) C half-whole symmetrical diminished	
B♭/C	♭VII/I	Yes	C7(9)sus4	C7(9,♯11,♮13)
B/C	VII/I	Yes	Cdim(maj7) Note: Inversions of dim(maj7) are not symmetrically identical.	B7(♭9,♯11,♮13) also D7(♭9,♯11,♮13) F7(♭9,♯11,♮13) A♭7(♭9,♯11,♮13) C half-whole symmetrical diminished

Our focus involves the following, most commonly used hybrid chords. Although transposable to all keys, we will look at all voicings with a C bass.

♭VII/I V/I II/I VII/I ♭II/I

♭VII/I IMPLIES DOMINANT 7(9)SUS4

B♭/C can be seen as an incomplete C9sus4 chord (the 5 is omitted).

Note	C	B♭	D	F
Function	bass note	♭7	9	4 (or 11)

Here are some of the places that this chord can be played on the fretboard. Note that the bass note is not the root of the triad. The notes of the triads are identified in relation to the bass notes.

170

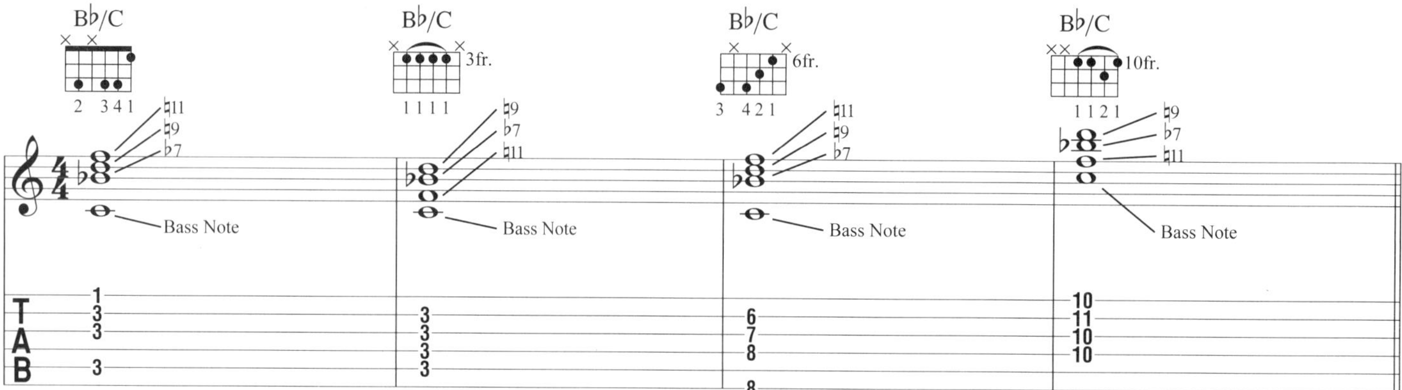

FIG. 24.1. Voicings for ♭VII/I as B♭/C

V/I IMPLIES MAJ7(9)

G/C can be seen as an incomplete Cmaj7(add9). The 3 is not specified, so it could also be interpreted as Cmin(maj7), but the use of this chord is most frequently as a major sound. Part of the beauty of these voicings is the vague, undefined nature of their sound.

Note:	C	G	B	D
Function:	Bass Note	5	major 7	9

Try playing these voicings to get a feel for this chord.

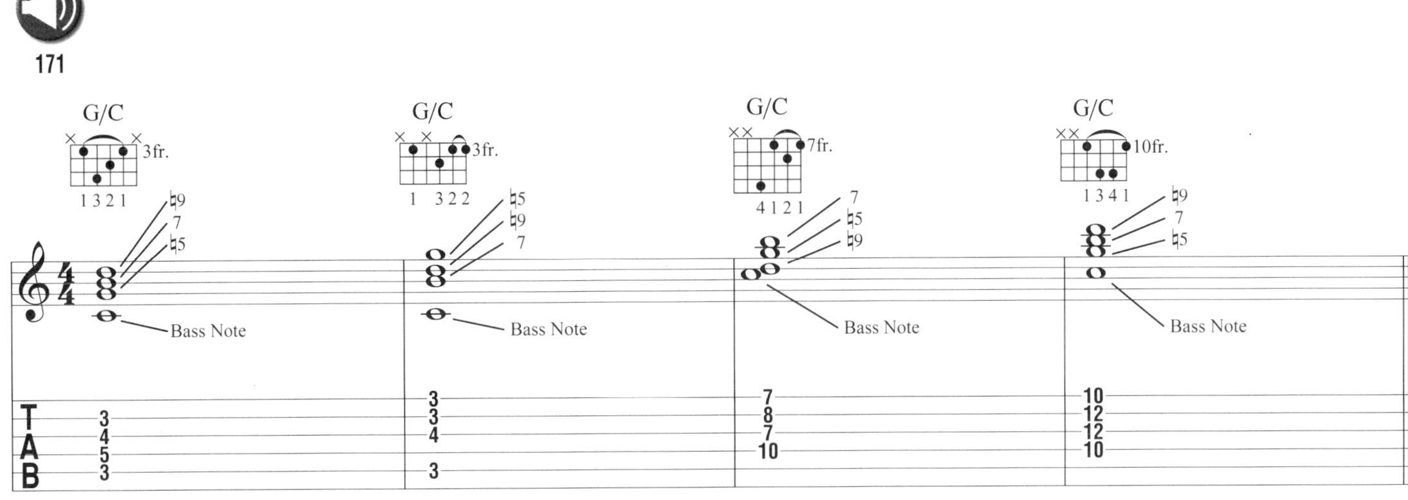

FIG. 24.2. Voicings for V/I as G/C

II/I IMPLIES MAJ7(♯11)

D/C can be seen as an incomplete C9sus4 chord (the 5 is omitted).

Note:	C	D	F♯	A
Function:	Bass Note	9	♯4 or ♯11	6 or 13

Here are some of the places that this chord can be played on the fretboard. Note that the bass note is not the root of the triad. The notes of the triads are identified in relation to the bass notes.

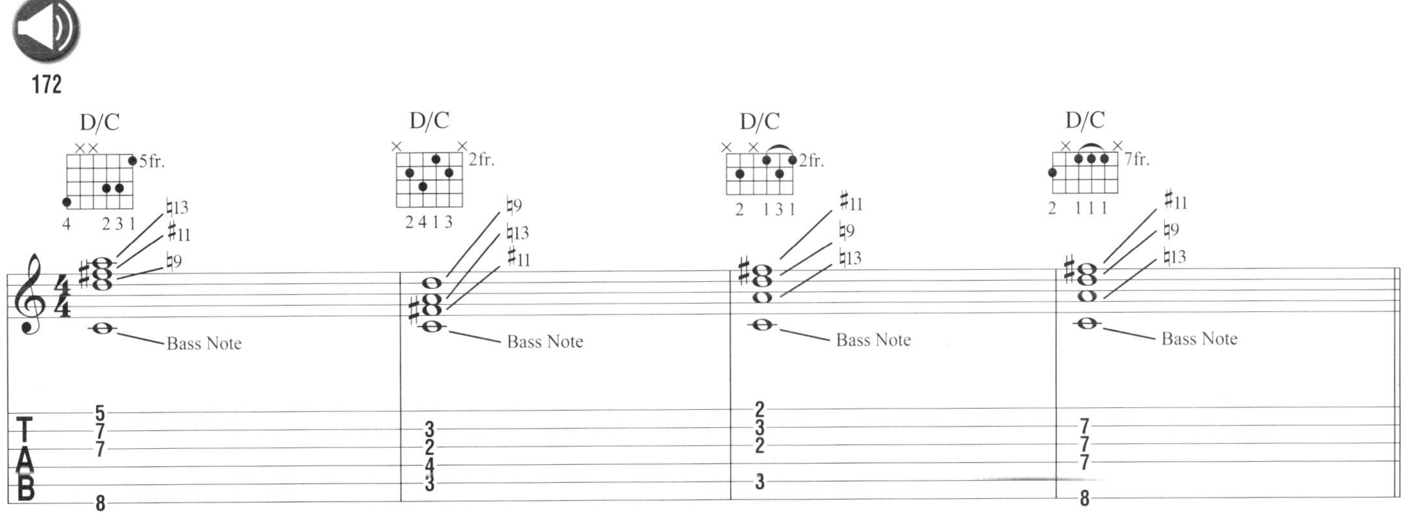

FIG. 24.3. Voicings for II/I as D/C

VII/I IMPLIES DIM(MAJ7)

B/C can be seen as a voicing for diminished(maj7) chord, although it is easy to be confused by the enharmonic chord tones.

Note:	C	B	D♯	F♯
Function:	Bass Note	7	♭3 (enharmonically)	♭5 (enharmonically)

Here are some of the places that this chord can be played on the fretboard. Note that the bass note is not the root of the triad. The notes of the triads are identified in relation to the bass notes.

173

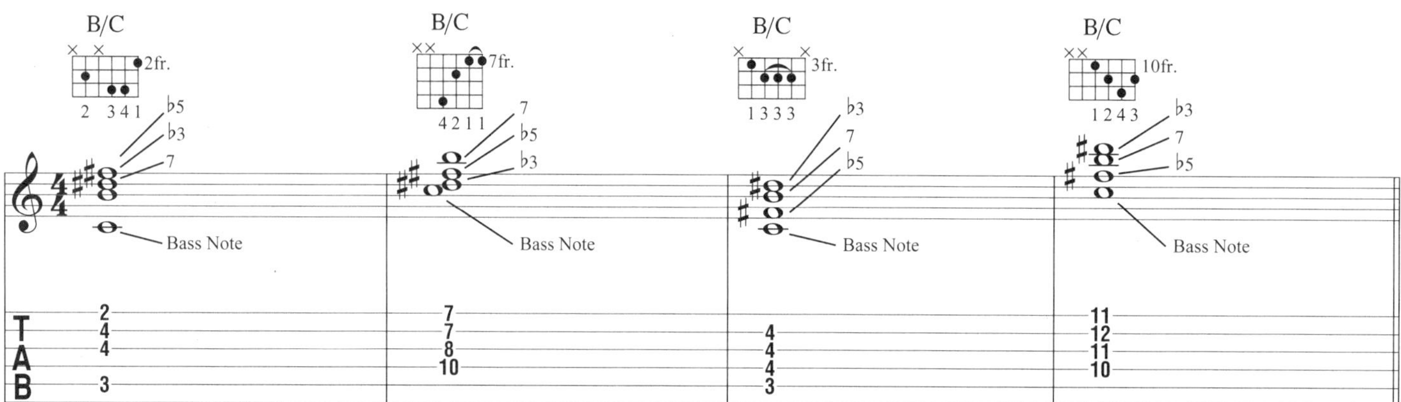

FIG. 24.4. Voicings for VII/I as B/C

♭II/I IMPLIES MIN7(♭2,♭6) PHRYGIAN MODAL SOUND

D♭/C can be seen as a voicing for the colorful shade of min7 that features a ♭2 degree, found in the Phrygian mode of the diatonic major scale.

Note:	C	D♭	F	A♭
Function:	Bass Note	♭2	4	♭6

174

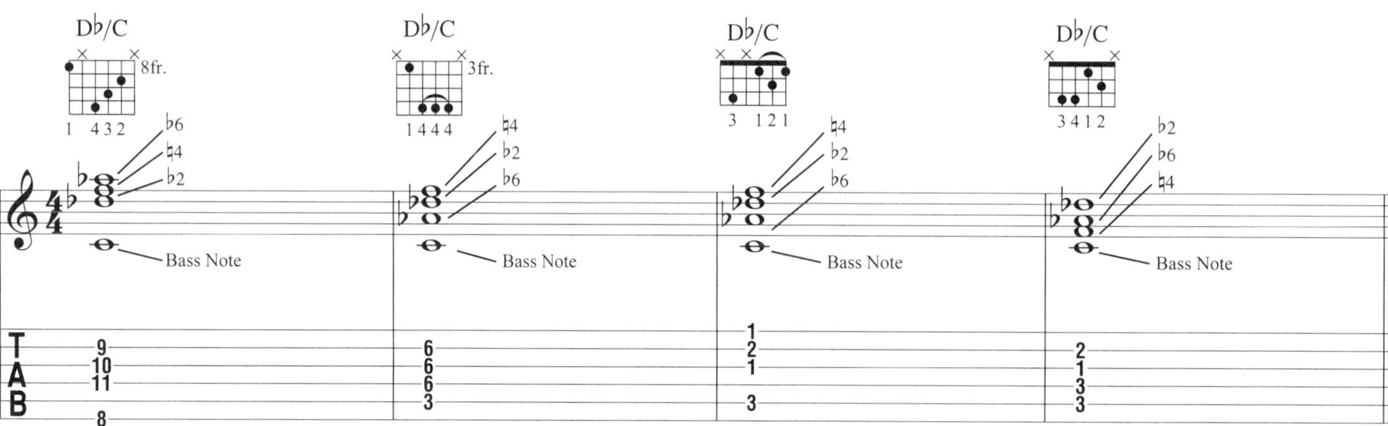

FIG. 24.5. Voicings for ♭II/I as D♭/C

Another way of looking at the ♭II/I chord, here as D♭/C, is to see it as a third inversion of D♭maj7. C Phrygian and D♭ Lydian are modes that share A♭ major as a parent scale. Triads over bass notes can be interpreted in various ways. Looking at the previous example as D♭maj7/C, the tones can be seen as follows.

175

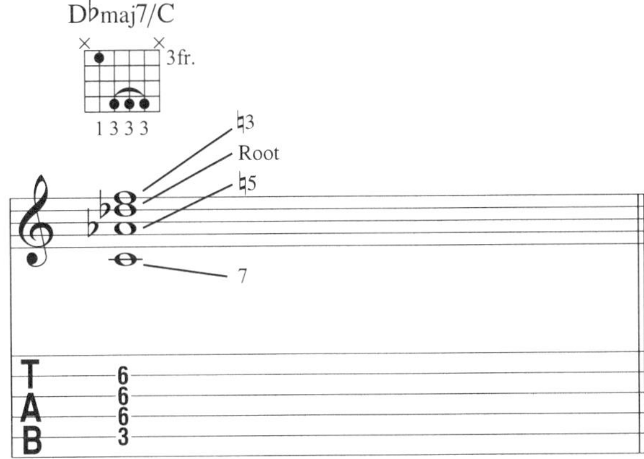

FIG. 24.6. Voicing for D♭maj7/C

Exercise 24.1. Triads Over Bass Note Chord Practice

Let's practice our triads over bass note voicings by playing through this exercise. The only way to gain fluency with them is consistent, methodical practice.

As mentioned, guitarists are often told to leave the bass note out of hybrid voicings for ease of playing and convenience. This approach is definitely easier, but it's leaving the complexity and interest out of the voicing. The dissonance that occurs in every interesting hybrid voicing is only possible when you play all four voices. Leave all of the ingredients in the hybrid recipe!

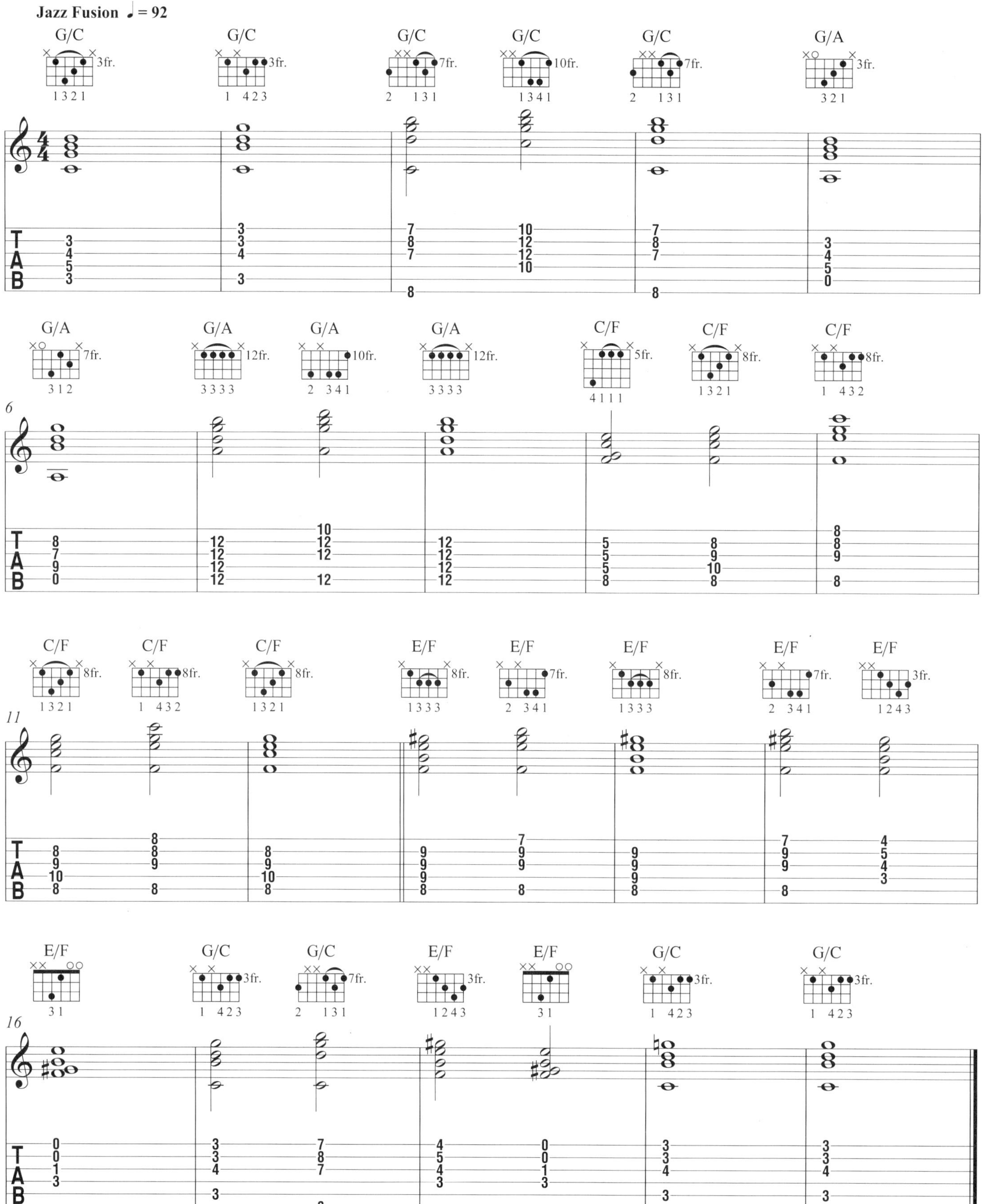

FIG. 24.7. Exercise 24.1. Triads Over Bass Note Chord Practice

LESSON 25

Inverting Drop 2 and Drop 3 Voicings

One of the goals of *Berklee Guitar Chords 101* is for guitarists to think of chord tones and voicings rather than "grips" on the fretboard. Inverting chords involves a lot of practice on the guitar, but doing some brainwork to figure out the voicings is "job 1" when you're getting serious about it.

In elementary school, we're taught to memorize multiplication tables (2 x 2 = 4, 4 x 4 = 16, 12 x 12 = 144, etc.). It's relatively easy to get that basic information together and "remember" the answer. With a math problem that's more complicated, like 123 x 561, students need to "do the math" to get the right answer.

On the guitar, it's relatively easy to memorize basic chord grips, but fluency with inversions can be elusive—and it can be nearly impossible without some theory work. It's not easy, but it's worth the effort. Let's revisit the basics of inversions.

DROP 2 THROUGH USE OF THE RAISE 2 PROCESS

Reviewing the inversion generator tables, let's look at a Dmin7 as a drop 2, using the raise 2 process.

Step 1: Spell the chord in close position and put the chord tones on the bottom line. Alternate Step 1: If you know the initial voicing, put the stack of tones in the first column.

Chord Voicing in Raise 2	Dmin7 Raise 2				
	Root Position	**First Inversion**	**Second Inversion**	**Third Inversion**	
					Lead
	D	F	A	C	Bottom Note
	Chord Tones in Close Position Order				

Chord Voicing in Raise 2	Dmin7 Raise 2				
	Root Position	**First Inversion**	**Second Inversion**	**Third Inversion**	
	F				Lead
	C				
	A				
	D				Bottom Note
	Chord Tones in Close Position Order				

FIG. 25.1. Inversion Generator for Dmin7 Step 1

Step 2: Fill in the open squares, using musical alphabetical order from left to right.

Dmin7 Raise 2				
Root Position	**First Inversion**	**Second Inversion**	**Third Inversion**	
F				Lead
C				
A				
D	F	A	C	Bottom Note

Chord Voicing in Raise 2 (left label) · Chord Tones in Close Position Order (bottom label)

Dmin7 Raise 2				
Root Position	**First Inversion**	**Second Inversion**	**Third Inversion**	
F	A	C	D	Lead
C	D	F	A	
A	C	D	F	
D	F	A	C	Bottom Note

Chord Voicing in Raise 2 (left label) · Chord Tones in Close Position Order (bottom label)

FIG. 25.2. Inversion Generator for Dmin7 Step 2

Step 3: Find the chord voicing shapes on the guitar fretboard. This particular set of voicings works well on ⑤④③② or ④③②①.

178

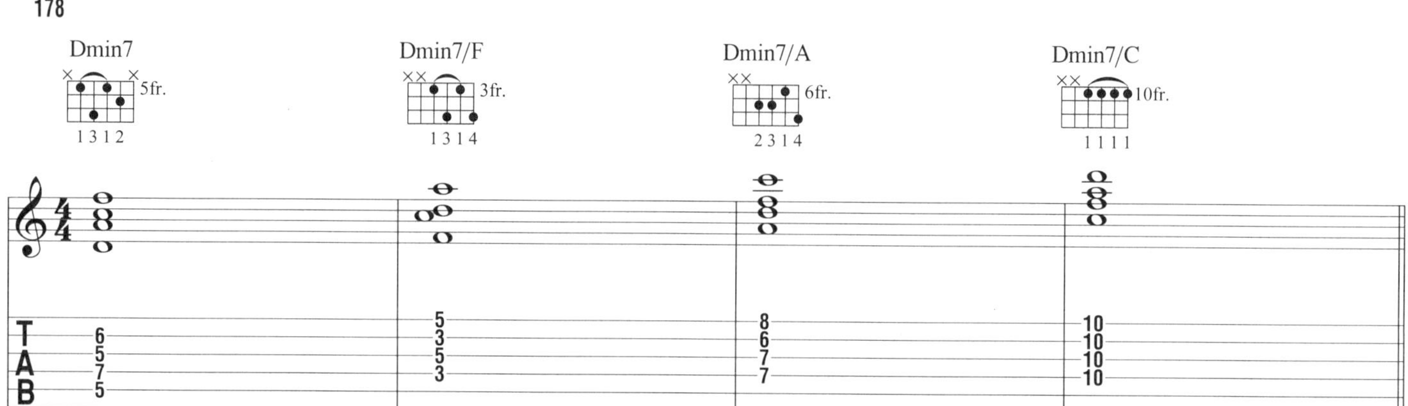

FIG. 25.3. Options for Dmin7 in All Inversions

DROP 3 THROUGH USE OF THE RAISE 2 AND 3 PROCESS

Inversion generator tables work for drop 3 shapes too. Let's look at a G7 as a drop 3, using the raise 2 and 3 process.

Step 1: Spell the chord in close position in the bottom row. Alternate Step 1: If you know the root position raise 2 and 3 voicing, put the stack of tones in the first column.

Chord Voicing in Raise 2 and 3

G7 Drop 3				
Root Position	First Inversion	Second Inversion	Third Inversion	
				Lead
G	B	D	F	Bottom Note

Chord Tones in Close Position Order

Chord Voicing in Raise 2 and 3

G7 Drop 3				
Root Position	First Inversion	Second Inversion	Third Inversion	
D				Lead
B				
F				
G				Bottom Note

Chord Tones in Close Position Order

FIG. 25.4. Inversion Generator for G7 Drop 3 Step 1

Step 2: Fill in the open squares, using close position order from left to right.

Chord Voicing in Raise 2 and 3

G7 Drop 3				
Root Position	First Inversion	Second Inversion	Third Inversion	
D				Lead
B				
F				
G	B	D	F	Bottom Note

Chord Tones in Close Position Order

Chord Voicing in Raise 2 and 3

G7 Drop 3				
Root Position	First Inversion	Second Inversion	Third Inversion	
D	F	G	B	Lead
B	D	F	G	
F	G	B	D	
G	B	D	F	Bottom Note

Chord Tones in Close Position Order

FIG. 25.5. Inversion Generator for G7 Drop 3 Step 2

Step 3: Find the chord voicing shapes on the guitar fretboard. Drop 3 voicings work best with ⑥④③② or ⑤③②①.

179

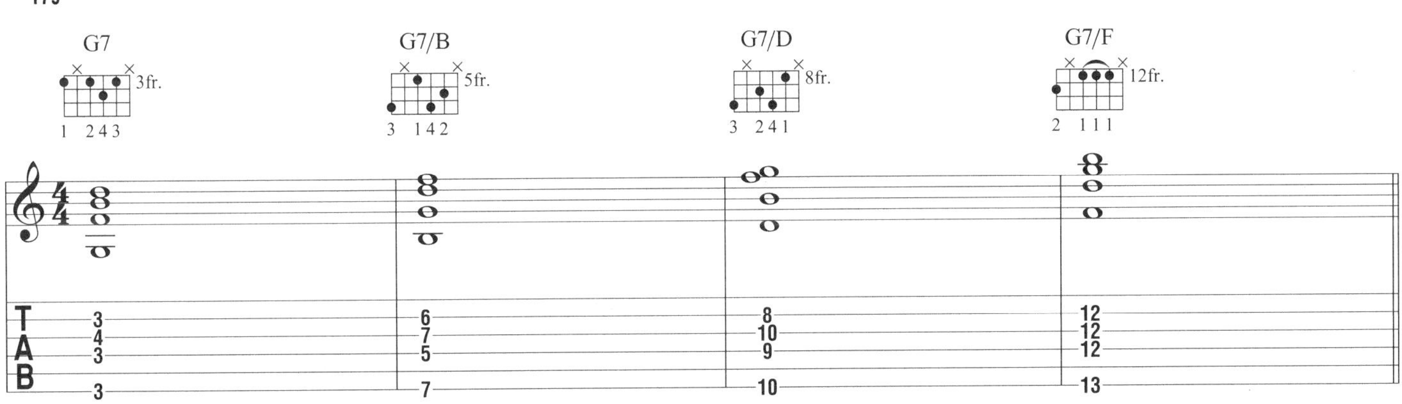

FIG. 25.6. Options for G7 in All Inversions

Work on chordal inversions pays off in more than a few ways. With control of inversions, a guitarist has many more options for chordal playing, allowing smoother voice leading from chord to chord. The resultant understanding of the fretboard will inform your accompaniment, improvisation, and compositional choices.

Exercise 25.1. Inversions of Dominant 7, Minor 7, and Maj7

Let's get some experience with three chord qualities, using drop 3 and drop 2 configurations in two keys. Simple alteration of the third or the seventh yields the various chord qualities.

The following exercise features three chord qualities in all inversions. The drop 3 voicings are on ⑥④③② and the drop 2 voicings involve ⑤④③② and ④③②① for ease of fingering. Play with good time, while thinking ahead to the next shape. Work to plant the fingers in place a bit earlier for a cleaner, fuller sound at the point of chord change.

180, 181

Straight 8ths ♩ = 82

Drop 3

G7 (3fr., 1 243) | G7/B (5fr., 3 142) | G7/D (8fr., 3 241) | G7/F (12fr., 2 111) | G7/D (8fr., 3 241) | G7/B (5fr., 3 142) | G7 (3fr., 1 243)

TAB: 3-4-3-3 | 6-7-5-7 | 8-10-9-10 | 12-12-12-13 | 8-10-9-10 | 6-7-5-7 | 3-4-3-3

Drop 2

C7 (3fr., 1314) | C7/E (2314) | C7/G (5fr., 1112) | C7/B♭ (8fr., 1211) | C7/G (5fr., 1112) | C7/E (2314) | C7 (3fr., 1314)

5

TAB: 5-3-5-3 | 3-1-3-2 | 6-5-5-5 | 8-8-9-8 | 6-5-5-5 | 3-1-3-2 | 5-3-5-3

Drop 3

Gmin7 (3fr., 2 333) | Gmin7/B♭ (5fr., 2 143) | Gmin7/D (8fr., 2 131) | Gmin7/F (11fr., 4 231) | Gmin7/D (8fr., 2 131) | Gmin7/B♭ (5fr., 2 143) | Gmin7 (3fr., 2 333)

9

TAB: 3-3-3-3 | 6-7-5-6 | 8-10-8-10 | 11-12-12-13 | 8-10-8-10 | 6-7-5-6 | 3-3-3-3

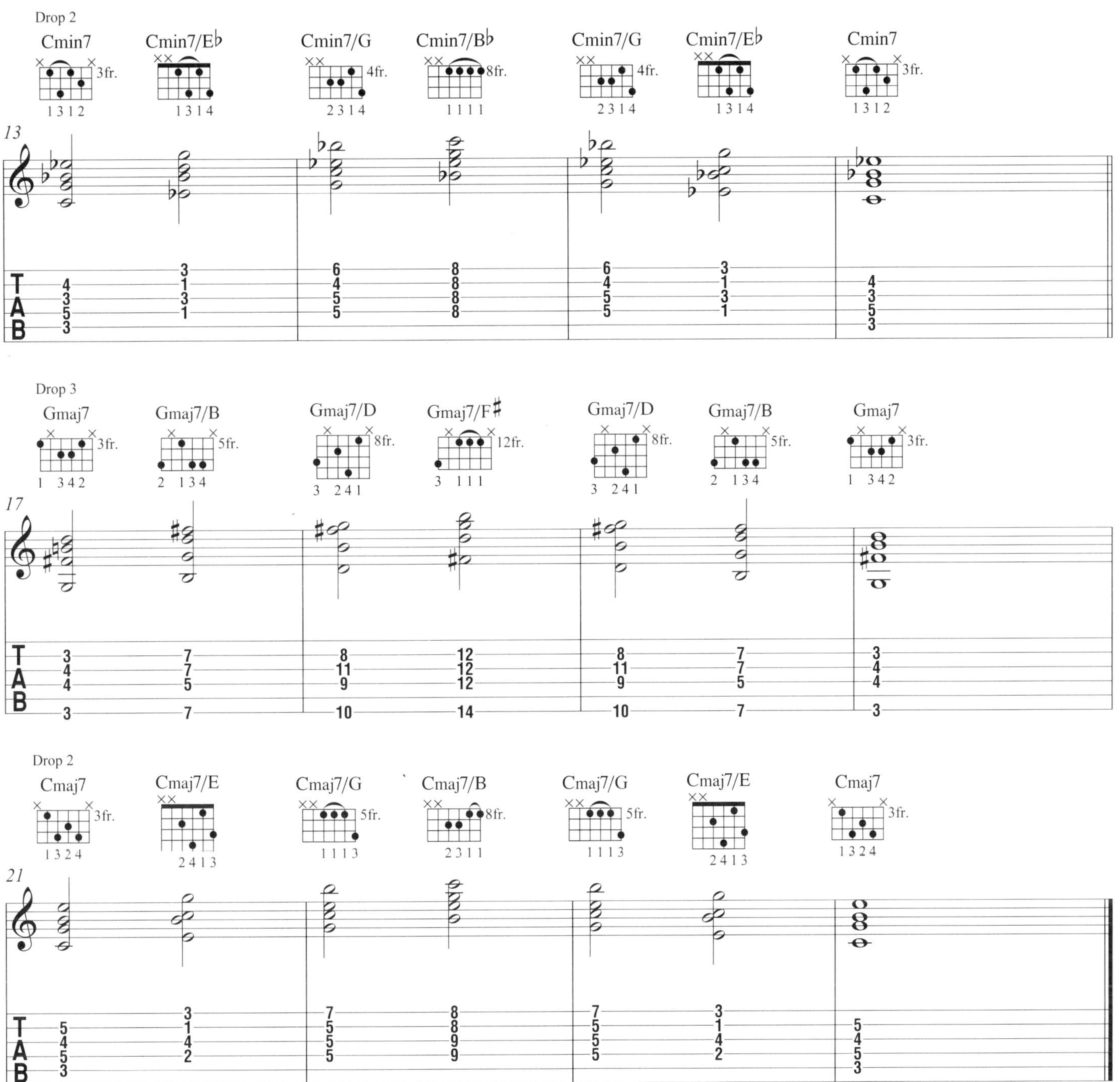

FIG. 25.7. Exercise 25.1. Inversions of Dominant 7, Minor 7, and Major 7

APPENDIX A

Chord Tones and Tensions on the Fretboard

Root ⑤ Drop 2 (Same as Raise 2)	Dominant 7 Configuration: D7 D7 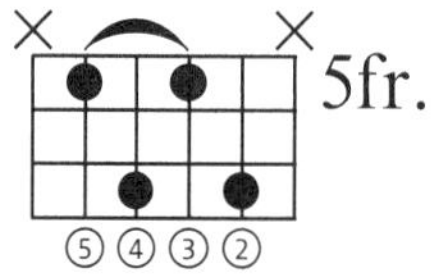 5fr. ⑤④③② R 5 7 3	Root is on ⑤ 5 is on ④ 7 is on ③ 3 is on ② **Tensions Nearby:** ♮13 or ♭13 on ①
Root ④ Drop 2 (Same as Raise 2)	Dominant 7 Configuration: G7 G7 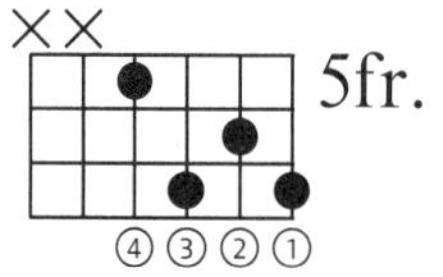 5fr. ④③②① R 5 7 3	Root is on ④ 5 is on ③ 7 is on ② 3 is on ①
Root ⑥ Drop 3 (Same as Raise 2 and 3)	Dominant 7 Configuration: D7 D7 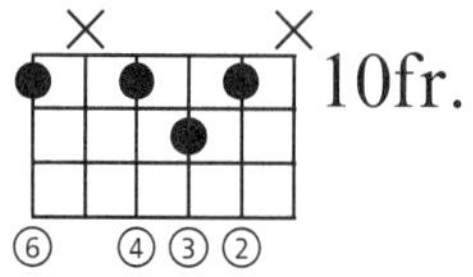 10fr. ⑥ ④③② R 7 3 5	Root is on ⑥ 4 is on ④ 3 is on ③ 5 is on ② **Tensions Nearby:** ♮13 or ♭13 on ② ♭9, ♮9, or #9 on ①

Root ⑤ Drop 3 (Same as Raise 2 and 3)	Dominant 7 Configuration: G7 G7 10fr. ⑤ ③②① R 7 3 5	Root is on ⑤ 7 is on ③ 3 is on ② 5 is on ① **Tensions Nearby:** ♮13, ♭13, ♯11, or ♭5 on ① ♭9, ♮9, or ♯9 on ②
Root ⑥ 7/3 with Tensions	Dominant 7(13) Configuration: D7(13) D7(13) 10fr. ⑥ ④③② R 7 3 13	Root is on ⑥ 7 is on ④ 3 is on ③ 13 is on ② **Tensions Nearby:** ♭13, ♯11, ♯5, or ♭5 on ② ♭9, ♮9, or #9 on ①
Root ⑤ 3/7 with Tensions	Dominant 7(9) Configuration: G7(9) G7(9) 9fr. ⑤④③②① R 3 7 9 5	Root is on ⑤ 3 is on ④ 7 is on ③ 9 is on ② 5 is on ① **Tensions Nearby:** ♮13, ♭13, #11, or ♭5 on ① ♭9, ♮ 9, or #9 on ②

FIG. A.1. Chord Tones and Tensions on the Fretboard

APPENDIX B

Berklee Guitar Department Required Chords

SEMESTER LEVELS 1 AND 3

All students naming guitar as their principal instrument are required to play the following list of chords with randomly requested roots chosen from seven keys. In their first semester, students are required to play one form for each chord and in semester 3, students are required to play two forms.

Chord list: maj7, min7, dom7, min7♭5, dom7sus4, dom7♯5, dim7, maj6, min6, min7(9), 7(9), 7(♭9), 7(♯9), 7(13)

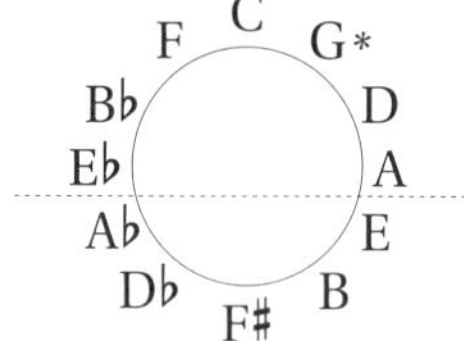

FIG. B.1. Circle of Fourths with Eligible Keys Above the Dotted Line

Here's an exercise that's geared to help anyone prepare the chords. Let's go after two forms for each:

182, 183

Etude: Four-Part Chords

Levels 1 and 3

Rick Peckham

Straight 8ths ♩ = 120

Cmaj7 Fmaj7 Cmin7 Fmin7 F7 F7♯5

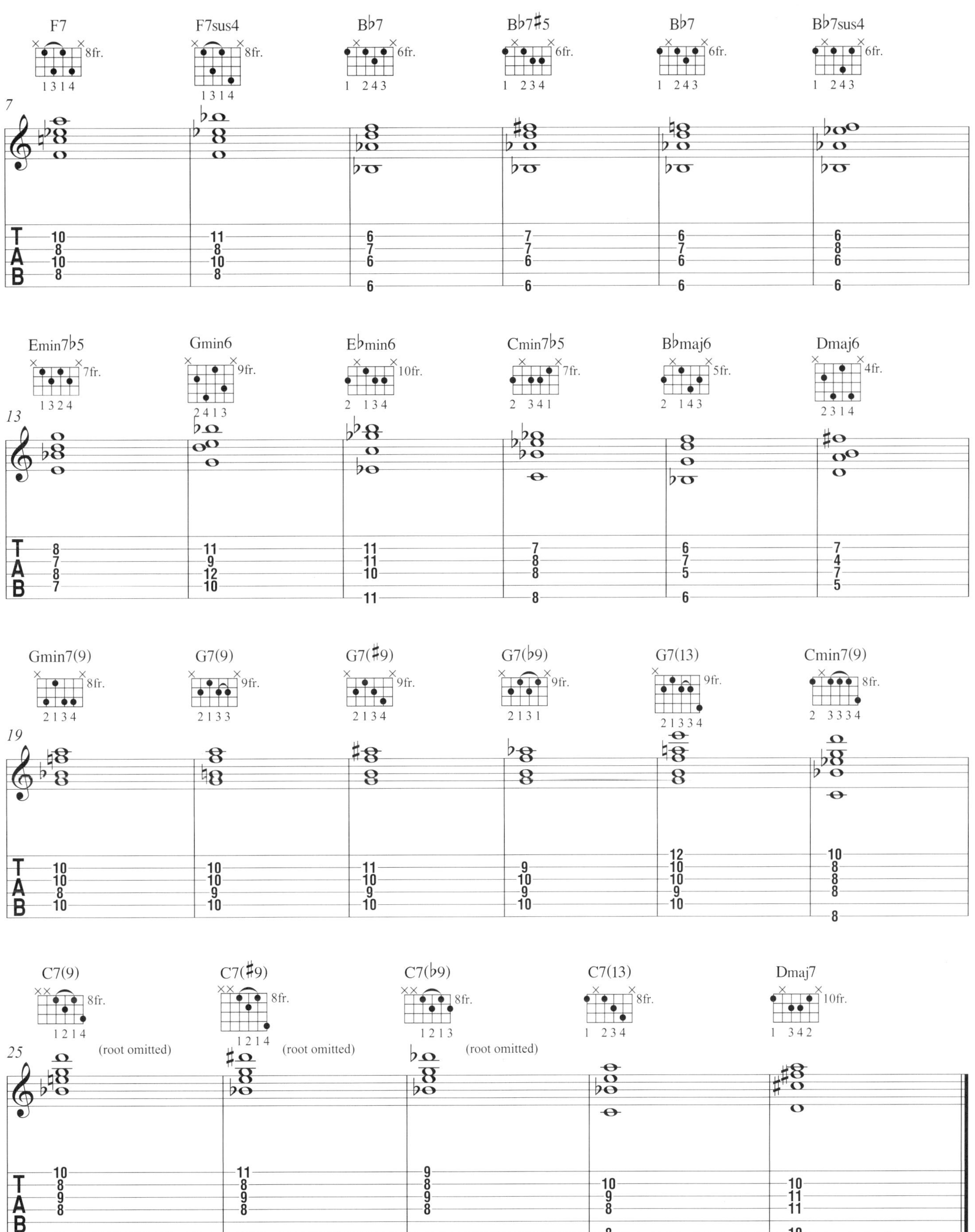

FIG. B.2. Chord Drill for Levels 1 and 3

SEMESTER LEVELS 2 AND 4

All Berklee guitar principal students are required to play the following list of chords with randomly requested roots chosen from seven keys. In their first semester, students are required to play one form for each chord and in semester 4, students are required to play two forms.

Chord list: min(maj7), maj7♯5, maj7♭5, min7♯5, 7♭5, dim(maj7), maj7(9), maj(6/9), min9(maj7), 7(♭9, ♭13), 7(♭9,13), 7(9,♭13)

Etude: Four Part Chords

Level 2 and 4

Rick Peckham

184, 185

Straight 8ths ♩ = 120

Gmin(maj7) | B♭maj7♯5 | C7♭5 | C7♭5 | Dmin(maj7) | Fmaj7♯5

E♭7♭5 | E♭7♭5 | Dmin7♯5 | B♭6/9 | Dmin7♯5 | B♭6/9

Cdim(maj7) | Cmaj7♭5 | Cmaj7(9) (root omitted) | E♭dim(maj7) | E♭maj7♭5 | E♭maj7(9)

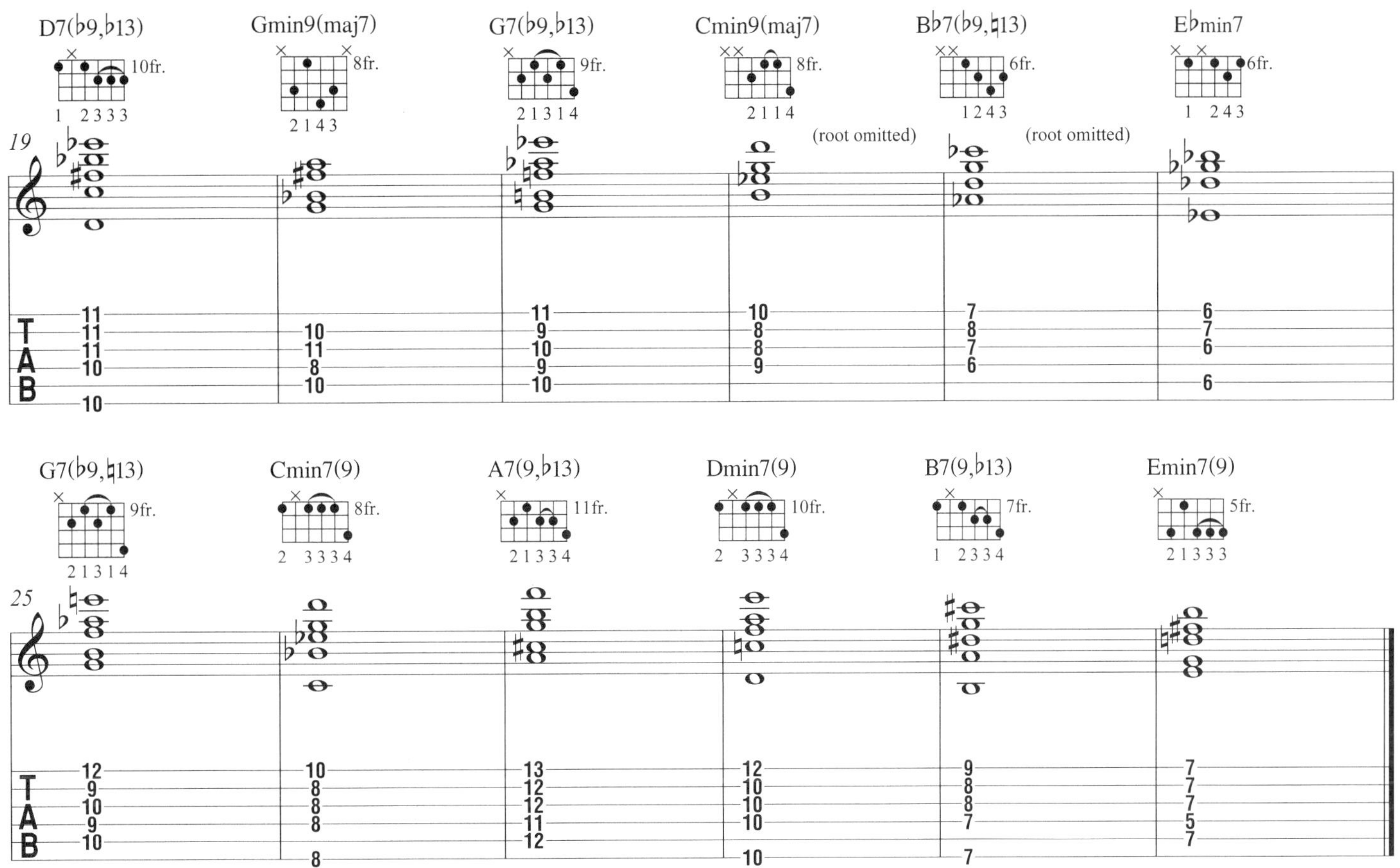

FIG. B.3. Chord Drill Levels 2 and 4

APPENDIX C

Etudes

CARELESS LOVE: CHORD TONE MELODY ETUDE

The highest note in any voicing is often heard as the melody, whether we're thinking of it that way or not. Organizing guitar arrangements with chord voicings emphasizing the melody of songs has fascinated guitarists since the instrument's inception.

Triadic voicings can be selected with focus devoted to the top note.

TRIADIC VOICINGS			
Melody (Lead):	5	R	3
	3	5	R
Bottom Tone:	R	3	5

SPREAD TRIADIC VOICINGS			
Melody (Lead):	3	5	R
	5	R	3
Bottom Tone:	R	3	5

Similarly, drop 2 and drop 3 voicings are available to us too.

DROP 2 VOICINGS				
Melody (Lead):	3	5	7	R
	7	R	3	5
	5	7	R	3
Bottom Tone:	R	3	5	7

DROP 3 VOICINGS				
Melody (Lead):	5	7	R	3
	3	5	7	R
	7	R	3	5
Bottom Tone:	R	3	5	7

Practice this arrangement of "Careless Love," a well-known traditional song, remembering to emphasize the melody while balancing with the other chord tones.

186, 187

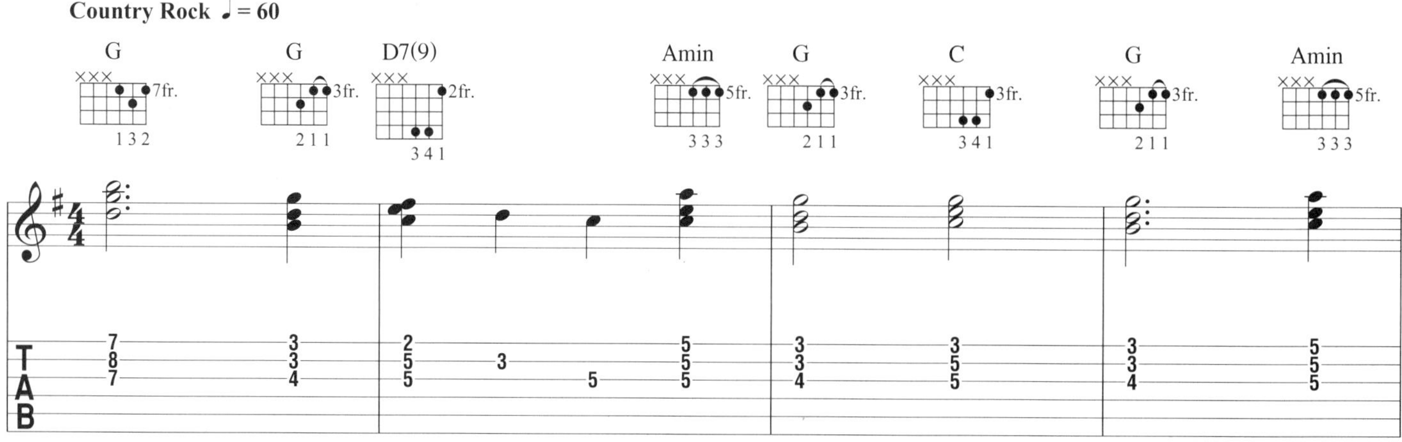

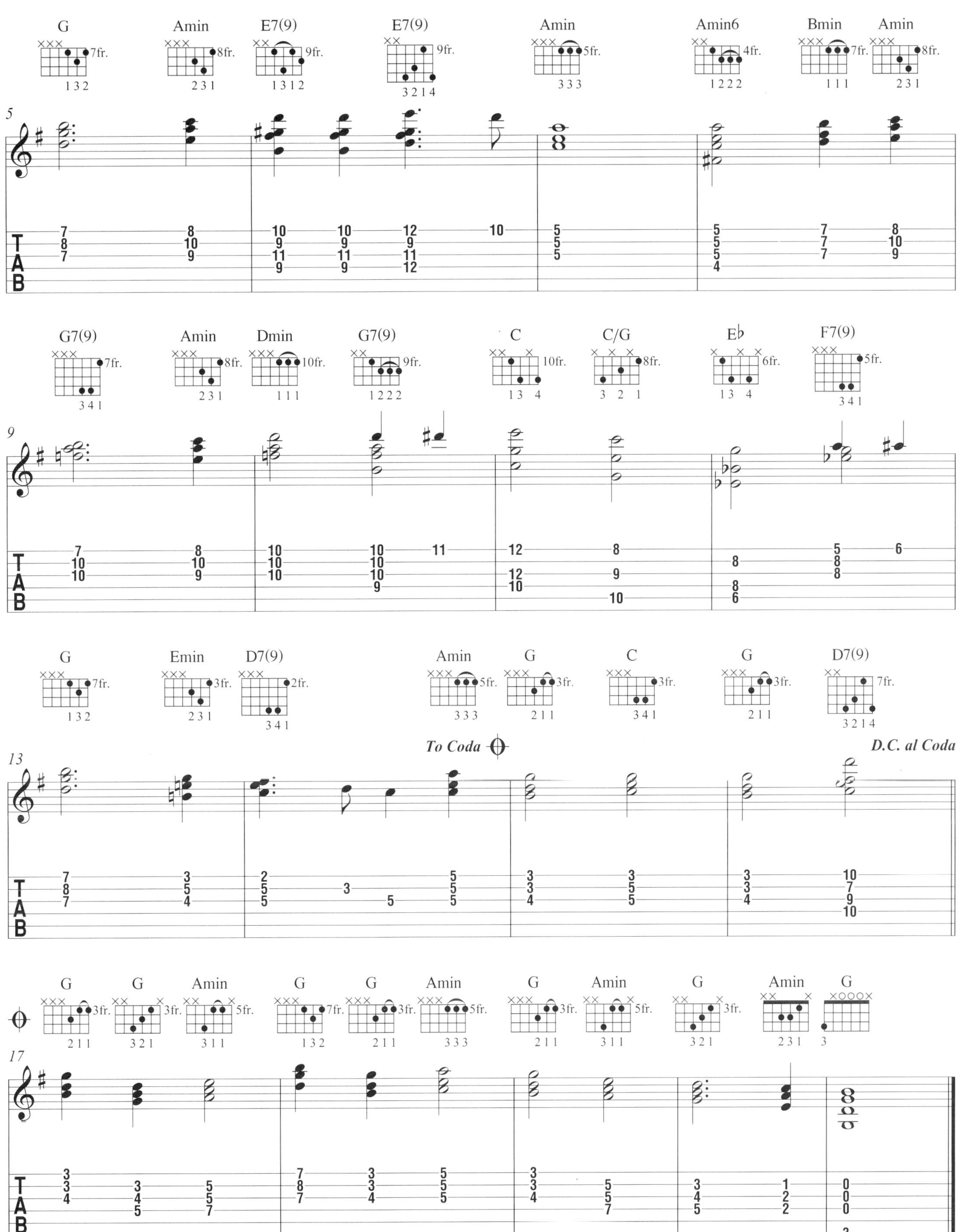

FIG. C.1. "Careless Love" Chord Melody Etude

SOLID TAKE: BASIC STEPS TOWARD CHORD MELODY ARRANGEMENT

Given the correct chord, guitarists analyze the melody note:

1. When using triadic harmony, if the melody note is a chord tone (root, 3, 5), harmonize the voicing with that note on top, using close or spread voicings.
2. If the melody note is a chord tone (root, 3, 5, 7 or 6), harmonize the voicing with that note on top, using drop 2 or drop 3 voicings.
3. If the melody note is a tension (9, 11 or 13), find the nearest melodic chord tone that is found below the given tension. Replace that tone with the tension. This system is frequently used: 9 replaces root, 11 replaces 3, 13 replaces 5.
4. After finding the appropriate voicings, blend melodic and harmonic moments so that the performance has a natural flow.

To summarize the practice of replacing chord tones with tensions, I use this simplified rule:

- 2 replaces 1 (or root)
- 4 replaces 3
- 6 replaces 5

WHISPERING

Root/Guide Tone Voicings Etude

188, 189

Practice using R3/7 and R7/3 voicings on "Whispering" by John Schonberger. Note that the 7 is replaced by the 6 for major 6 and minor 6 voicings.

4-to-the-Bar Swing ♩ = 180

Amaj7 5fr. | Amaj6 4fr. | E♭min7 11fr. | E♭min6 10fr. | Amaj7 5fr. | Amaj6 4fr.

7
C♯min7 9fr. | C♯min6 8fr. | B7 7fr. | B7 7fr. | Bmin7 7fr. | Bmin6 6fr.

1.
13
C♯min7 9fr. | C♯min6 8fr. | Cmin7 8fr. | Cmin6 7fr. | Bmin7 7fr. | Bmin6 6fr.

2.
17
Bmin7 7fr. | Bmin7 7fr. | Bmin7♭5 6fr. | Amaj7 5fr. | Amaj6 4fr.

FIG. C.2. "Whispering" Root/Guide-Tone Voicings Etude

Crossover Transposition Etude

190, 191

Practice the "Whispering" progression using drop 3 voicings in the keys of A and then transposed to D. Pay attention to the literal use of the same voicing structures, moving the shapes across the fretboard. It is an example of the crossover process in action, providing further options for your use.

4-to-the-Bar Swing ♩ = 180

Amaj7 5fr. 1 342 | Amaj6 4fr. 2 143 | E♭min7 11fr. 2 333 | E♭min6 10fr. 2 134 | Amaj7 5fr. 1 342 | Amaj6 4fr. 2 143

7
C♯min7 9fr. 2 333 | C♯min6 8fr. 2 134 | B7 7fr. 1 243 | B7 7fr. 1 243 | Bmin7 7fr. 2 333 | Bmin6 6fr. 2 134

13 (1.)
C♯min7 9fr. 2 333 | C♯min6 8fr. 2 134 | Cmin7 8fr. 2 333 | Cmin6 7fr. 2 134 | Bmin7 7fr. 2 333 | Bmin6 6fr. 2 134

17 (2.)
Bmin7 7fr. 2 333 | Bmin7 7fr. 2 333 | Bmin7♭5 6fr. 2 341 | Amaj7 5fr. 1 342 | Amaj6 4fr. 2 143

FIG. C.3. "Whispering" Crossover Transposition Etude

EXTRA FOR EXPERTS: FOUR-PART CHORDS ETUDE

Use this etude to fully explore four-part chordal vocabulary for guitar principals. Every variation of root position chords is covered here. Go for legato phrasing, balance of voices, and accuracy.

192, 193

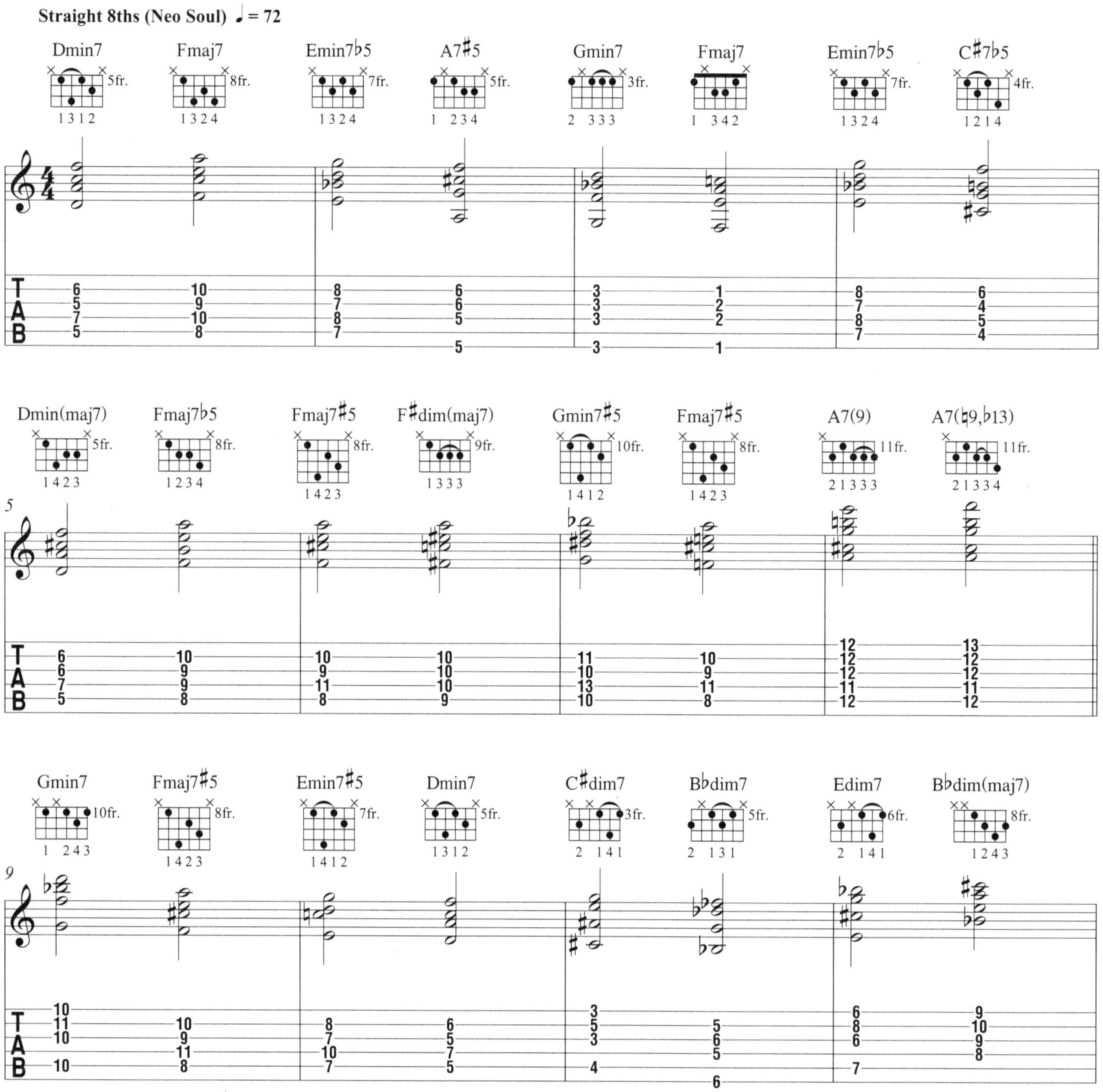

Straight 8ths (Neo Soul) ♩ = 72

Dmin7 Fmaj7 Emin7♭5 A7♯5 Gmin7 Fmaj7 Emin7♭5 C♯7♭5

5
Dmin(maj7) Fmaj7♭5 Fmaj7♯5 F♯dim(maj7) Gmin7♯5 Fmaj7♯5 A7(9) A7(♮9,♭13)

9
Gmin7 Fmaj7♯5 Emin7♯5 Dmin7 C♯dim7 B♭dim7 Edim7 B♭dim(maj7)

FIG. C.4. Four-Part Chords Etude

FINAL THOUGHTS

Thanks for making your way through this book. Intonation, great tone, and time feel are fundamental to any musician who wants to make a connection with any audience or musical group. I've heard from *Berklee Online Chords 101* course participants who've worked their way through this material that they've achieved the ultimate conquest: an unsolicited compliment from a fellow band mate! Hard won praise from an unlikely source, but amazingly satisfying.

If you have found yourself struggling to get new sounds under your fingers, you're not alone! Struggling is part of day-to-day life for musicians who are looking to expand their skills and vocabulary. The struggle is built into the process. I hope that you've found a way to develop a working relationship with the chord voicings that are new to you. You don't have to love the new shapes, you just have to be able to work with them, transforming "today's challenge" into "tomorrow's warm-up." Instead of wondering what's wrong with yourself, remind yourself that you're working to grow. *Everybody* struggles to improve!

If a musical challenge seems too difficult for you, slow down the tempo. "New" and "Fast" don't work well together! Remember, S L O W is fast. If you want to get better fast, practice slowly . . . and then work to build up to your goal tempo.

Start with small segments and build to larger sections. "New, slow, and short" are often more productive than "New, fast, and long!" Use a practical approach when you're adding something new to your skill set. I think this is the best way to develop a working relationship with what you aren't yet able to do.

Whatever you play on the guitar, make it feel and sound good to the listener. If your tastes and experience lead you to more complex harmony, remember to integrate musical polish. Feel, tone, and intonation may seem to be something to add later, but these elements have to be a part of any musical performance. Use the new harmonic shapes to play along with recordings, compose new music, and develop musical connections with other musicians that you encounter. Use your new vocabulary to find your own voice and to help your collaborators realize their musical vision, as well.

ABOUT THE AUTHOR

Photo by Kelly Davidson

Rick Peckham is internationally active as a contemporary guitarist and educator. He has presented performances and clinics on six continents and specializes in a unique blend of styles, including jazz, rock, blues, fusion, and country fingerstyle performance.

Currently a full-time professor in Berklee's Guitar Department, Peckham has been a faculty member since 1986, and served as assistant chair of the Guitar Department—with 1,100 guitar students and 60 guitar faculty—from 1992 to 2013.

His internationally released album *Left End* was named one of *DownBeat Magazine's* best releases of 2005. He organized Berklee's honorary doctoral tributes to Roy Haynes, Joe Zawinul, Jack DeJohnette, and John Scofield, featuring then-Berklee students Kurt Rosenwinkel, Matthew Garrison, Antonio Hart, Abe Laboriel Jr., Melvin Butler, and Seamus Blake. Several Berklee alums he has coached include Lionel Loueke, Lage Lund, Frank Möbus, Jeff Parker, David Rawlings, Brooks Robertson, Matt Stevens, and Nir Felder.

Some of his published works include three online courses: *Berklee Guitar Chords 101* (2007 UCEA award for best online class), *Berklee Guitar Chords 201*, and Coursera's *Guitar Chord Voicings: Playing Up the Neck*. Berklee Press/Hal Leonard books include *Modal Voicings for Guitar*, the *Berklee Jazz Guitar Dictionary* and *Berklee Rock Chord Dictionary*.

More Fine Publications

GUITAR

BERKLEE ESSENTIAL GUITAR SONGBOOK
Kim Perlak, Sheryl Bailey, and Members of the Berklee Guitar Department Faculty
00350814 Book.......$22.99

BERKLEE GUITAR CHORD DICTIONARY
Rick Peckham
50449546 Jazz – Book.......$16.99
50449596 Rock – Book.......$12.99

BERKLEE GUITAR STYLE STUDIES
Jim Kelly
00200377 Book/Online Media.......$24.99

BERKLEE GUITAR THEORY
Kim Perlak and Members of the Berklee Guitar Department Faculty
00276326 Book.......$26.99

BLUES GUITAR TECHNIQUE
Michael Williams
50449623 Book/Online Audio.......$29.99

CLASSICAL TECHNIQUE FOR THE MODERN GUITARIST
Kim Perlak
00148781 Book/Online Audio.......$19.99

COUNTRY GUITAR STYLES
Mike Ihde
00254157 Book/Online Audio.......$24.99

CREATIVE CHORDAL HARMONY FOR GUITAR
Mick Goodrick & Tim Miller
50449613 Book/Online Audio.......$24.99

FUNK/R&B GUITAR
Thaddeus Hogarth
50449569 Book/Online Audio.......$25.99

GUITAR SWEEP PICKING
Joe Stump
00151223 Book/Online Audio.......$24.99

JAZZ GUITAR FRETBOARD NAVIGATION
Mark White
00154107 Book/Online Audio.......$24.99

MODAL VOICINGS FOR GUITAR
Rick Peckham
00151227 Book/Online Media.......$24.99

A MODERN METHOD FOR GUITAR – VOLUMES 1-3 COMPLETE*
William Leavitt
00292990 Book/Online Media.......$54.99
**Individual volumes, media options, and supporting songbooks available.*

A MODERN METHOD FOR GUITAR SCALES
Larry Baione
00199318 Book.......$15.99

TRIADS FOR THE IMPROVISING GUITARIST
Jane Miller
00284857 Book/Online Audio.......$22.99

BASS

BERKLEE JAZZ BASS
Rich Appleman, Whit Browne & Bruce Gertz
50449636 Book/Online Audio.......$25.99

CHORD STUDIES FOR ELECTRIC BASS
Rich Appleman & Joseph Viola
50449750 Book.......$24.99

FUNK BASS FILLS
Anthony Vitti
50449608 Book/Online Audio.......$24.99

INSTANT BASS
Danny Morris
50449502 Book/CD.......$9.99

METAL BASS LINES
David Marvuglio
00122465 Book/Online Audio.......$19.99

READING CONTEMPORARY ELECTRIC BASS
Rich Appleman
50449770 Book.......$24.99

PIANO/KEYBOARD

BERKLEE JAZZ KEYBOARD HARMONY
Suzanna Sifter
00138874 Book/Online Audio.......$29.99

BERKLEE JAZZ PIANO
Ray Santisi
50448047 Book/Online Audio.......$24.99

BERKLEE JAZZ STANDARDS FOR SOLO PIANO
Robert Christopherson, Hey Rim Jeon, Ross Ramsay, Tim Ray
00160482 Book/Online Audio.......$24.99

CHORD-SCALE IMPROVISATION FOR KEYBOARD
Ross Ramsay
50449597 Book/CD.......$19.99

CONTEMPORARY PIANO TECHNIQUE
Stephany Tiernan
50449545 Book/DVD.......$39.99

HAMMOND ORGAN COMPLETE
Dave Limina
00237801 Book/Online Audio.......$27.99

JAZZ PIANO COMPING
Suzanne Davis
50449614 Book/Online Audio.......$26.99

LATIN JAZZ PIANO IMPROVISATION
Rebecca Cline
50449649 Book/Online Audio.......$29.99

PIANO ESSENTIALS
Ross Ramsay
50448046 Book/Online Audio.......$26.99

SOLO JAZZ PIANO
Neil Olmstead
50449641 Book/Online Audio.......$42.99

Berklee Press publications feature material developed at Berklee College of Music.
To browse the complete Berklee Press Catalog, go to **www.berkleepress.com**

DRUMS

BEGINNING DJEMBE
Michael Markus & Joe Galeota
00148210 Book/Online Video.......$16.99

BERKLEE JAZZ DRUMS
Casey Scheuerell
50449612 Book/Online Audio.......$27.99

DRUM SET WARM-UPS
Rod Morgenstein
50449465 Book.......$16.99

A MANUAL FOR THE MODERN DRUMMER
Alan Dawson & Don DeMichael
50449560 Book.......$14.99

MASTERING THE ART OF BRUSHES
Jon Hazilla
50449459 Book/Online Audio.......$19.99

PHRASING
Russ Gold
00120209 Book/Online Media.......$19.99

WORLD JAZZ DRUMMING
Mark Walker
50449568 Book/CD.......$27.99

BERKLEE PRACTICE METHOD

GET YOUR BAND TOGETHER
With additional volumes for other instruments, plus a teacher's guide.

Drum Set
Ron Savage, Casey Scheuerell and the Berklee Faculty
50449429 Book/CD.......$19.99

Guitar
Larry Baione and the Berklee Faculty
50449426 Book/CD.......$29.99

Keyboard
Russell Hoffmann, Paul Schmeling and the Berklee Faculty
50449428 Book/Online Audio.......$22.99

VOICE

BELTING
Jeannie Gagné
00124984 Book/Online Media.......$24.99

THE CONTEMPORARY SINGER
Anne Peckham
50449595 Book/Online Audio.......$29.99

JAZZ VOCAL IMPROVISATION
Mili Bermejo
00159290 Book/Online Audio.......$19.99

TIPS FOR SINGERS
Carolyn Wilkins
50449557 Book/CD.......$19.95

VOCAL WORKOUTS FOR THE CONTEMPORARY SINGER
Anne Peckham
50448044 Book/Online Audio.......$27.99

YOUR SINGING VOICE
Jeannie Gagné
50449619 Book/Online Audio.......$34.99

WOODWINDS & BRASS

TRUMPET SOUND EFFECTS
Craig Pederson & Ueli Dörig
00121626 Book/Online Audio....................$14.99

SAXOPHONE SOUND EFFECTS
Ueli Dörig
50449628 Book/Online Audio................$22.99

THE TECHNIQUE OF THE FLUTE
Joseph Viola
00214012 Book....................$19.99

STRINGS/ROOTS MUSIC

BERKLEE HARP
Felice Pomeranz
00144263 Book/Online Audio..................$26.99

BEYOND BLUEGRASS BANJO
Dave Hollander & Matt Glaser
50449610 Book/CD....................$19.99

BEYOND BLUEGRASS MANDOLIN
John McGann & Matt Glaser
50449609 Book/CD....................$19.99

BLUEGRASS FIDDLE & BEYOND
Matt Glaser
50449602 Book/CD....................$19.99

CONTEMPORARY CELLO ETUDES
Mike Block
00159292 Book/Online Audio..................$24.99

EXPLORING CLASSICAL MANDOLIN
August Watters
00125040 Book/Online Media................$24.99

THE IRISH CELLO BOOK
Liz Davis Maxfield
50449652 Book/Online Audio................$29.99

JAZZ UKULELE
Abe Lagrimas, Jr.
00121624 Book/Online Audio..................$26.99

MUSIC THEORY & EAR TRAINING

BEGINNING EAR TRAINING
Gilson Schachnik
50449548 Book/Online Audio................$22.99

BERKLEE CONTEMPORARY MUSIC NOTATION
Jonathan Feist
00202547 Book....................$27.99

BERKLEE MUSIC THEORY
Paul Schmeling
50449615 Book 1/Online Audio..............$29.99
50449616 Book 2/Online Audio..............$26.99

CONTEMPORARY COUNTERPOINT
Beth Denisch
00147050 Book/Online Audio..................$24.99

MUSIC NOTATION
Mark McGrain
50449399 Book....................$29.99
Matthew Nicholl & Richard Grudzinski
50449540 Book....................$25.99

REHARMONIZATION TECHNIQUES
Randy Felts
50449496 Book....................$29.99

CONDUCTING

CONDUCTING MUSIC TODAY
Bruce Hangen
00237719 Book/Online Media..................$24.99

MUSIC PRODUCTION & ENGINEERING

AUDIO MASTERING
Jonathan Wyner
50449581 Book/CD....................$34.99

AUDIO POST PRODUCTION
Mark Cross
50449627 Book....................$32.99

CREATING COMMERCIAL MUSIC
Peter Bell
00278535 Book/Online Media..................$19.99

HIP-HOP PRODUCTION
Prince Charles Alexander
50449582 Book/Online Audio..................$24.99

THE SINGER-SONGWRITER'S GUIDE TO RECORDING IN THE HOME STUDIO
Shane Adams
00148211 Book....................$24.99

UNDERSTANDING AUDIO
Daniel M. Thompson
00148197 Book....................$49.99

MUSIC BUSINESS

CROWDFUNDING FOR MUSICIANS
Laser Malena-Webber
00285092 Book....................$17.99

ENGAGING THE CONCERT AUDIENCE
David Wallace
00244532 Book/Online Media................$24.99

HOW TO GET A JOB IN THE MUSIC INDUSTRY
Keith Hatschek with Breanne Beseda
00130699 Book....................$39.99

MAKING MUSIC MAKE MONEY
Eric Beall
00355740 Book....................$29.99

MUSIC INDUSTRY FORMS
Jonathan Feist
00121814 Book....................$17.99

MUSIC LAW IN THE DIGITAL AGE
Allen Bargfrede
00366048 Book....................$29.99

MUSIC MARKETING
Mike King
50449588 Book....................$24.99

PROJECT MANAGEMENT FOR MUSICIANS
Jonathan Feist
50449659 Book....................$39.99

ARRANGING & IMPROVISATION

ARRANGING FOR HORNS
Jerry Gates
00121625 Book/Online Audio..................$24.99

BERKLEE BOOK OF JAZZ HARMONY
Joe Mulholland & Tom Hojnacki
00113755 Book/Online Audio..................$34.99

MODERN JAZZ VOICINGS
Ted Pease & Ken Pullig
50449485 Book/Online Audio................$29.99

Prices subject to change without notice. Visit your local music dealer or bookstore, or go to **www.berkleepress.com**

SONGWRITING/COMPOSING

BEGINNING SONGWRITING
Andrea Stolpe with Jan Stolpe
00138503 Book/Online Audio................$22.99

COMPLETE GUIDE TO FILM SCORING
Richard Davis
50449607 Book....................$39.99

THE CRAFT OF SONGWRITING
Scarlet Keys
00159283 Book/Online Audio................$24.99

CREATIVE STRATEGIES IN FILM SCORING
Ben Newhouse
00242911 Book/Online Media..................$27.99

JAZZ COMPOSITION
Ted Pease
50448000 Book/Online Audio..............$49.99

MELODY IN SONGWRITING
Jack Perricone
50449419 Book....................$26.99

MUSIC COMPOSITION FOR FILM AND TELEVISION
Lalo Schifrin
50449604 Book....................$39.99

POPULAR LYRIC WRITING
Andrea Stolpe
50449553 Book....................$17.99

THE SONGWRITER'S WORKSHOP
Jimmy Kachulis
Harmony
50449519 Book/Online Audio................$34.99
Melody
50449518 Book/Online Audio...............$27.99

SONGWRITING: ESSENTIAL GUIDE
Pat Pattison
Lyric Form and Structure
50481582 Book....................$22.99
Rhyming
00124366 Book....................$24.99

SONGWRITING IN PRACTICE
Mark Simos
00244545 Book....................$16.99

SONGWRITING STRATEGIES
Mark Simos
50449621 Book....................$27.99

SONGBOOKS

NEW STANDARDS
Terri Lyne Carrington
00369515 Book....................$29.99

WELLNESS/AUTOBIOGRAPHY

LEARNING TO LISTEN: THE JAZZ JOURNEY OF GARY BURTON
Gary Burton
00117798 Book....................$34.99

MANAGE YOUR STRESS AND PAIN THROUGH MUSIC
Dr. Suzanne B. Hanser & Dr. Susan E. Mandel
50449592 Book/Online Audio..............$34.99

MUSICIAN'S YOGA
Mia Olson
50449587 Book....................$26.99

NEW MUSIC THERAPIST'S HANDBOOK
Dr. Suzanne B. Hanser
00279325 Book....................$34.99